HISTORY OF RELIGION

Chinese Religions

Chinese Religions

D. HOWARD SMITH

Formerly Lecturer in Comparative Religion in the University of Manchester

HISTORY OF RELIGION SERIES

General Editor: E. O. James

Holt, Rinehart and Winston

New York Chicago San Francisco

Library of Congress Catalog Card Number: 68-12215
First Edition

88719254

Printed in Great Britain

CONTENTS

ILLUSTRATIONS

(*between pages* 98 *and* 99)

Acknowledgements

The publishers wish to thank the following for providing illustrations for this volume: British Museum, plates 1, 6 and 7; School of Oriental and African Studies, London, plate 2; Wulf-Diether Graf zu Castell, plate 4.

INTRODUCTION

Religion has played a no less significant role in the life and culture of the Chinese than in other great civilisations. During the course of some 3,500 years of history the Chinese developed their own distinctive ideas concerning man's origin, nature and destiny and his relation to the universe in which he lived. One of their greatest concerns was to find a satisfactory relationship with a transcendental spiritual world. This concern found expression in an elaborate state cult and in a variety of beliefs and religious practices which attracted the allegiance of the common people. As a modern Chinese scholar writes, 'Sacrifice and religious worship are basic to the Chinese philosophy of life, and are responsible to a great extent for the moulding of the Chinese mind.'[1] Professor A. F. Wright has rightly characterised as a baseless myth 'the notion that the Chinese are rationalistic and ethno-centric, and thus somehow immune to religious emotion'. 'We have', writes Professor Wright, 'only to confront this myth with the great surge of religious feeling behind the Yellow Turban uprisings in the second century, or the fanaticism of Chinese converts to Islam, or lately to Communism, and it is apparent that the Chinese capacity for commitment to a saving faith is strong and persisting.'[2]

The history of religion in China is marked by a succession of men distinguished for their learning, piety and devotion; men who preferred martyrdom to the betrayal of conscience, men of outstanding missionary fervour, men who for the sake of religion took the long and perilous pilgrimage to India, men who gave up family and fortune to pursue the religious life. Throughout the centuries the common people sought, and in large measure found, in their religions the answer to their craving for fulness of life, freedom from fear, salvation from ill, and significance beyond the grave. Gripped by intense religious fervour, the simplest Chinese peasant has at times been capable of feats of heroism, endurance and self-sacrifice.

Religion in China has differed from religion in Western societies in that institutionalised religion has been relatively weak. 'There was in

China no independent religious heritage comparable to that of the Hebrew tradition, and no such solid organisation of priests as that of Christendom. Therefore no such religious system is found in China as in the West.'[3] Religion, however, permeated the wider cultural setting. Every traditional Chinese home was a religious shrine, whilst the concept and structure of all major Chinese institutions contained religious elements. As Professor C. K. Yang writes, 'In China the beliefs and rituals of diffused religion develop their organisational system as an integral part of the organised social pattern, and perform a pervasive function in every major aspect of Chinese social life.'[4]

Another feature of Chinese religion has been the close control of religious expression by centralised government. From at least the T'ang dynasty (AD 618–907) onwards successive governments in China, though on the whole tolerant of personal belief, have ruthlessly persecuted religious societies which in any way seemed to challenge the absolute control of government over the lives and destinies of the people. Not only over the state cult, but over Taoism and Buddhism, and later over Islam and Christianity, successive dynasties have exercised the strictest control whenever the centralised authority has felt itself strong enough to do so. It was a strongly held belief in China that without such rigorous control pernicious heresies would arise to undermine the foundations of the state and lead to anarchy and immorality. All men owed a supreme loyalty to the ruler, conceived of as the vice-regent of heaven on earth, and no personally held religious convictions could be allowed to take precedence over such loyalty.

Broadly speaking the history of Chinese religion may be divided into three periods:

1. From the middle of the second millennium BC up to the close of the Western Han dynasty (AD 9). In this period we follow the development of indigenous religious concepts, the belief in the overruling providence of heaven, the cult of ancestors, the development of an elaborate sacrificial system, and the philosophies of Confucianism and Taoism which provided an intellectual basis for the state cult and religious Taoism.

2. From the beginning of the Christian era up to the eleventh century AD, when religious Taoism and Buddhism arose, grew strong and flourished to compete with the traditional religion. 'With the rise of religious Taoism and the entrance of Buddhism into China for the first time membership in a consciously organised religion was based not on

inherited affiliations with a community but upon conversion and voluntary choice by individual believers.'[5]

3. From the eleventh century to present times, when religion had become more and more eclectic by the interpenetration of Confucianism, Taoism and Buddhism. In this period the educated classes were more or less rationalistic and humanistic, whilst the religion of the people was a strange mixture of crude animistic beliefs, the cult of ancestors and ideas incorporated from Confucianism, Taoism and Buddhism.

In the early decades of this century, apart from some two or three million Christians, and a Muslim community variously estimated between ten and fifty millions, China witnesses to a bewildering variety of religious beliefs and practices. Educated people, tending to agnosticism, accepted the ethical standards of Confucianism, but were often deeply influenced by Taoist and Buddhist concepts. Devout people in all grades of society became ardent Buddhists or Taoists, and joined themselves to one or other of the numerous religious or lay sects, yet remaining extremely tolerant of other forms of religious expression. Religion in China was seldom dogmatic or credal.

Every large city in China had a variety of buildings designed to cater for the religious needs of the community; temples connected with the state cult, Buddhist temples, monasteries and pagodas, Taoist shrines, Muslim mosques and Christian churches. Each city had its Ch'êng Wang Miao dedicated to the guardian god of the city. Each village had its T'u Ti Miao erected for the worship of the local tutelary deity. Most wealthy families had their own ancestral temple in which were stored the spirit-tablets of the ancestors. Each trade guild had its patron god with his appropriate festival. Innumerable wayside shrines testified to the religious instincts of the people, whilst frequent pilgrimages were organised to visit famous temples on sacred mountains.

In most homes simple religious ceremonies were performed at which the protection and goodwill of the gods and ancestor spirits were invoked. The great festivals throughout the year, and particularly the New Year festival, were semi-religious in character. The services of Buddhist or Taoist priests were sought at the great events of family life, and particularly during the rites of death and mourning.

Much of the popular peasant religion was a crude animism with a veneer of more sophisticated Buddhist or Taoist thought. It was dominated by a strong belief in gods and spirits, both good and evil, who were ubiquitous and pervasive in their influence. Hence the almost universal belief in and practice of geomancy or 'fêng shui', the keen interest in fortune-telling, spiritism, necromancy and the like.

If we ask how this amalgam of religious beliefs and practices grew up, we find that there are four main streams which make up Chinese religion.

1. A primitive animism which goes back to the dawn of history, in which a cult of ancestors forms a prominent part.

2. Confucianism, which did not become a dominant philosophy of life and a state cult until about the second century BC, some three hundred years after the death of Confucius. By that time it had been powerfully influenced by many and varied schools of thought which flourished in what is known as the Classical period, though the life and work of Confucius remained a dominating influence.

3. Taoism, which arose as a philosophy and way of life in some ways diametrically opposed to Confucianism. Its most formative teachings are contained in two great works, the *Tao Tê Ching*, attributed to Lao Tzŭ, and the *Book of Chuang Tzŭ*. But as a popular religion Taoism did not come into prominence until the early centuries of the Christian era, and as such took up into itself many of the beliefs and practices which appertained to the earlier popular religion.

4. Buddhism, which was introduced into China by way of central Asia either during or before the first century AD. Throughout subsequent centuries it developed in China with amazing rapidity. Direct contact with India was established, both by missionaries from India and by Chinese pilgrims to India. The great works of Indian Buddhism, particularly the Mahāyāna, were translated into Chinese, and to these works were added the commentaries of distinguished Chinese Buddhist saints and scholars to add a permanent contribution to Chinese religious thought. Great monastic foundations were established, often with royal patronage, and from these there flowed out an indigenous Buddhist literature and a distinctively Chinese expression of Buddhism which was to have a profound influence, not only on the religious life of China, but on Korea and Japan.

In later centuries the impact of Islam and Christianity on Chinese religious thought has been far from negligible. In fact the witness of these two religions to belief in One True God has greatly strengthened the theistic strain in indigenous religion.

It is our purpose to study the development of these four main streams which go to make up Chinese religion, not forgetting the minor role played by Islam and Christianity, which began to make their impact on China in the period of Chinese expansionism during the great T'ang dynasty. Even Manichaeism, Zoroastrianism and Judaism made some slight impact, though it is difficult to trace any substantial contribution of these religions to Chinese religious development.

As far as possible, by the use of extensive quotations, we shall allow the Chinese texts to speak for themselves. In the selection of these texts we are not so much concerned with Chinese philosophical and ethico-political thought as with illustrating distinctively religious ideas and practices. All too often books on Chinese religion have placed their main emphasis on the more philosophical and ethical teachings of Confucianism. In all cases when we have made quotations from the Chinese classics we have consulted the original texts; but we have made extensive use of translations already available, and acknowledge a special debt in this connection to the excellent translations of J. Legge, Arthur Waley, E. R. Hughes, Fêng Yu-lan and W. T. Ch'an, and to the English translations of the *Ethical and Political Works of Mo-tzŭ* by Y. P. Mei, and of *Hsün-tzû's Works* by H. H. Dubs.

The substance of the first three chapters has appeared in articles published in *Numen, The History of Religions* and *The Bulletin of John Ryland's Library*. The author desires to thank the editors of these journals for permission to republish this material in book form. He also expresses his sincere thanks to the Rev. M. W. Earl who read through the chapters on 'The Rise and Development of Religious Taoism' and 'Buddhism in China', and made many valuable suggestions. To Professor S. G. F. Brandon, head of the Department of Comparative Religion in the University of Manchester, the author is especially indebted for constant encouragement and advice.

CHAPTER ONE

CHINESE RELIGION IN THE SHANG DYNASTY

Chinese tradition assigns the beginnings of Chinese civilisation to the latter part of the third millennium BC, but though there are *a priori* reasons for assuming that the first Chinese dynasty, the Hsia, was established about that time, no direct archaeological evidence in respect of the Hsia has, as yet, been forthcoming.

Hundreds of neolithic sites have been recorded in China, revealing several distinct neolithic cultures. Though early foreign influences on the development of Chinese civilisation may have been considerable, there was a cultural development continuous in China from neolithic times onwards, and the theory that the proto-Chinese were a conquering race which invaded China from the west is no longer acceptable. The neolithic ancestors of the Chinese lived in villages and practised agriculture and the domestication of animals as their main source of livelihood, regarding hunting and fishing as important but subsidiary occupations. They already possessed highly developed techniques for the production of pottery and implements of stone, bone and ivory.[1] Though very little can be deduced from archaeological evidence concerning neolithic religious ideas and practices, the highly developed religion of the Shang dynasty, which traditionally began in 1766 BC, with its cult of ancestor spirits, its elaborate mortuary rituals and its highly developed sacrificial system, must have had a long development in prehistoric times. One might reasonably infer that the earliest religion in China, as for other agricultural peoples, centred in a cult of ancestors, a concern for fertility, and the worship of numerous nature spirits which included the powerful gods of wind and rain.

To these early ancestors of the Chinese the world seemed full of powers, manifesting themselves in animal and vegetable life, in the heavens above and in the waters below, in the mysterious processes of birth, growth and decay, and in the incidence of disease and death.

The community consisted not only of the living but of the dead ancestors, who were custodians of the source of life, and watched over fertility, sustenance and growth. They were conceived of as still active. They showed their approval by giving abundant fertility in plants and animals, and success in hunting and war. The places set aside for their worship became 'holy places' from which flowed the prosperity and well-being of the various clans.

It is with the Shang dynasty that we enter upon historical times, and especially with the establishment of Yin as the capital city of their confederacy in the time of the ruler P'an Kêng. This event is attributed to the fifteenth year of P'an Kêng's reign (*c.* 1384 BC). Yin remained the capital of the Shang dynasty for some two hundred and seventy years until its final overthrow and complete destruction by the Chou. Intense archaeological activity on the site of this capital city, at Hsiao T'un and Hou Chia Chuang, near the modern city of Anyang in Honan province, has recovered sufficient evidence on which to construct a fairly reliable picture of the cultural and religious life of the Shang people. It was from Hsiao T'un that nearly all the written records on 'oracle bones' have been excavated, as well as the remains of an extensive city.[2] From the tombs of the Shang cemeteries, situated near Hou Chia Chuang, a significant collection of funerary bronzes and tomb furnishings witnesses not only to an advanced bronze-age culture but to an intense concern on the part of the Shang aristocracy for life after death.[3]

Most of the oracle bones can be dated as belonging to a period roughly extending from the reign of Wu-ting (*c.* 1324 BC) to the beginning of the reign of Ti-hsin (*c.* 1225 BC). As the bones were used in divination, and questions and answers were often inscribed thereon, they give us considerable insight into the concerns which dominated the thought of the Shang. Some three thousand characters have been identified, and these include most of the names of the kings of the Shang dynasty.

Throughout this period there existed in the basin of the Yellow River and its tributaries a highly developed civilisation which seems to have had considerable contact with peoples dwelling in far distant regions of present-day China, and probably receiving cultural influences from the west.[4]

A slave-owning aristocracy, dwelling in cities, was super-imposed upon a rural peasantry mainly devoted to agriculture and the domestication of animals. Professor Li Chi writes that theirs was 'a theocratic religion dominated by excessive devotion to ancestor worship'.[5] The hunting of wild animals seems to have been a favourite pastime of the Shang nobility, and they were engaged in almost incessant warfare with barbarian tribes. 'The royal passion for sport may be testified to by the fact that, underneath the wooden chambers where the royal coffins were placed, there were always sacrificial pits in which large dogs accompanied by big adult males were sacrificed. These men and dogs were the king's company in his lifetime; as they followed him in his moments of pleasure, so they accompanied him to another world.'[6]

The clans of the noble families were held together by an elaborate system of rights, privileges and relationships which were already sacrosanct by tradition and made obligatory by a fixed obedience to the will of a tribal ancestor. Thus what we know as the *li,* that is, the rites and ceremonies governing the various relationships of human life and society, together with the ceremonies by which the gods and ancestors were worshipped, were already a binding cement which held together the Chinese clans in a unified system.[7] But those ritual rules, so binding upon the great clans which formed the Chinese hegemony in their mutual relationships, did not apply either to their relations with the numerous barbarian tribes on their borders, or to the common people by which the aristocracy was served.

In seeking to appraise the ethical and religious thought of the Shang great care is needed lest we read back into the characters inscribed on oracle bones meanings which only developed later. There is little evidence that the rulers showed moral responsibility either to the ancestor spirits whom they worshipped or to the people over whom they ruled. There is little or no trace of ethical thinking to be found in oracle bone inscriptions. Even such characters as 'good' and 'bad' are related to ideas of prosperity and calamity, good fortune and evil fortune occasioned by wind and rain, crop failure, or success in hunting and war.

The oracle bone inscriptions and the bronze sacrificial vessels deposited in the tombs of kings and nobles witness alike to the fact that the world view of the Shang was determined by the thought of a primeval ancestor-god. The frequently used character *pu,* meaning to divine or foretell, suggests the idea of asking the spirit of the departed ancestor to send down his advice or commands. The worship of the great ancestor spirit and with him the spirits of all the deceased kings was the main feature of Shang religion.

In earlier times the earth had been thought of as the home of the dead. The vital spirit was believed to linger with or near the corpse which had been for a long time its home. But as the corpse disintegrated this vital spirit was inevitably forced to leave it, to merge again into that mysterious source of creative energy down in the earth which is referred to in later literature as the 'yellow springs'. It was therefore a kindness both to the living and to the dead to do everything possible to preserve the corpse from dissolution: to the dead, because only so could the vital spirit continue to live on and retain its identity; to the living, because only thus could the ancestor spirits continue to interest themselves in the affairs of their descendants. In the funeral customs of the Shang we find abundant evidence of a desire to preserve the corpse from decay. The elaborate tombs suggest this underlying motive, together with the thick wooden coffins which were deposited therein. Though there is no evidence of the art of embalming, as practised by the Egyptians, the elaborate preparation of the corpse, the use of what were believed to be life-preserving agencies such as jade, the stopping up of all the orifices of the body, all witness to the attempt to provide the soul of the deceased with as permanent a home as possible. It seems also that there was the fear that if the corpse, because of mishap or unnatural death, was not ritually laid to rest within the tomb, its vital spirit, still retaining some of its energies, would become a ghost or prêta,[8] preying on the living or seeking entrance into some other body. The customary offerings to the dead of food and drink seem to have had two main objects: to give sustenance to the spirit in its subterranean home, and to appease it lest it disturb the living by acts of malevolence. Chinese folklore from the time of the Ch'un Ch'iu period onwards bears witness to these primitive but persistent beliefs.

Though this concept of the soul as a *kuei* which after death was associated for a while with the tomb, and finally was absorbed into the earth from which it had issued forth, was the most primitive, by the time of the Shang dynasty, at least among the aristocracy, there had grown up a belief that the ancestor spirits became powerful divine beings dwelling on high, probably in a region of the heavens centred in the pole star. Thus a certain ambivalence in the concept of post-mortem existence is already in evidence. The spirits of deceased kings and nobles, though thought of as living on in the elaborate tombs in which they have been ceremonially buried, are also conceived of as dwelling above in heaven. This was undoubtedly an important factor in the development later of the peculiar Chinese belief that man produced two soul elements, the *hun* which on death became a *shen* and partook of the nature of heaven, and the *p'o* which turned into a *kuei* and was earthy by nature.

The founder-spirit of the Shang dynasty, from which the members of all the noble families sought to trace their descent, was worshipped as a supreme god, exercising control over people and land, so that in all matters of grave import his help and guidance had to be sought by divination, and his goodwill maintained by the regular and meticulous offering of appropriate sacrifices. He sent down both blessings and calamities. He rewarded loyalty to his mandate, and punished all acts of disobedience.

The significance of the great ancestor seems to have been derived from his procreative power, his ability as a ruler and his success as a leader in war. The character *tsu* by which the ancestor spirits of the clans were designated seems originally to have represented a phallus. The spirits who were worshipped in the ancestral shrines within the homes, and the protective spirits of the soil and grain which were worshipped at the earth-altars built under the open sky were both represented by characters which some modern Chinese scholars derive from the same phallic symbol (A). Thus the twin foci of early Chinese religion, the ancestral temple and the earth altar, both derived their significance from the same primeval ancestor spirit.[9]

It has been suggested that there are slight indications that in very early times Chinese society was totemistic. In the names of early Shang dynasty kings there are characters for walrus, scorpion, tiger, bear, etc., whilst surrounding tribal areas were designated as horse-district, sheep-district, tiger-district, etc.[10] It is probable that, while surrounding barbarian tribes continued to be totemistic, the Shang learned to put their faith in the great ancestor-spirit who had led them forth to battle against the animal totem gods and had given them victory. Yet as we shall see later in this chapter, the gods worshipped by the Shang were often represented in animal form.

The deified ancestors of the Shang were known as *Ti*. When a ruler died he became a *Ti,* associated on high with the first ancestor-spirit who was regarded as the supreme *Ti*. A study of this character as it is used in the oracle bone inscriptions suggests that this founder ancestor of the Shang dynasty was thought of as a supreme god, dwelling on high. The character is used in three different, yet related, senses. Fu Ssŭ-nien has made an exhaustive study of this character on all the oracle bone inscriptions recorded by Sun Hai-po in his *Chia Ku Wên Pien*. Sixty-four instances of the use of the character are recorded of which one is a duplicate. In seventeen instances the character is used as equivalent to the verb 'to sacrifice', probably its original meaning. In six instances the character is used coupled with the name of a previous king and indicates that a particular apotheosised ancestor is referred to. In fourteen cases the sense of the character is uncertain. But in no less than twenty-six instances the use of the character without any title suggests that a supreme deity is referred to, who is invoked and worshipped simply as *Ti*. This deity is conceived of as dwelling above, the lord over other gods, spirits and deified ancestors. He is called upon for rain and good harvests. He grants his approval and bestows many blessings.[11] When a ruler dies his spirit will no longer simply go down into the earth, but will mount on high to be associated with the supreme *Ti*. There may be some similarity here with the cult of Osiris in Egypt, but as far as is known the Shang kings were not thought of as 'gods' while they ruled on earth.

Associated with the court of the Shang dynasty kings were the *chên jên* or *wu jên*, priests or shaman-diviners who were important members of the community because kings and nobles turned to them for advice and guidance in everything that appertained to the spiritual world. Religious functions were also exercised by the *chu,* who seem to have officiated at the sacrifices in the capacity of 'master of ceremonies'. They were responsible for the compilation of the prayers which were ceremonially offered, and for the arrangements of the meticulous details of the sacrificial rituals. They ceremonially welcomed the gods and the participants in the worship, and escorted them, according to rank and precedence, to their seats, probably to the accompaniment of music. There was also a class of men associated with the court whose task was to chronicle every important event. On the oracle bones is a character which depicts a hand holding a stylus or brush, and from this character were derived characters which in later times signified 'historian', 'government official' and 'affairs'. Thus from the earliest times, the government of the country was closely linked with religious observance, and all down through the history of China government officials assisted the supreme ruler in performing the various functions of an elaborate state cult.

Prodigies, strange natural phenomena and all disturbances in the natural order were regarded as intimations from the spirit world that all was not well, and it was the duty of 'wise men' to interpret these events. The most important government officials were those who were gifted with the power of communicating with the spirits and recording their commands and wishes for the guidance of the king. Divination played a very important part in the life of the Shang people. Anything that affected the welfare of king and state demanded the services of an expert diviner. Divination was a necessary prelude to making a journey, engaging in hunting or war, or in respect of sickness, the weather or the harvest. It was the chief means by which communications were made with the ancestor spirits.

The ancestral temple was the centre of governmental activities. It was the place where weapons of war were stored, where vassals were enfeoffed, where the great royal feasts were held. It was the symbol of the state itself. No great feasts were held there without inviting the gods and ancestor spirits as honoured guests, and this demanded an elaborate ritual pattern. Though we have scarcely any literary records from the Shang dynasty of this elaborate ritual, there is ample evidence in the early poems of the Chou dynasty which took over, in its main particulars, the religion of its predecessor. The oracle bone inscriptions, however, reveal the vast variety of utensils and offerings used in Shang sacrifices, and indicate that sometimes even hundreds of animals were sacrificed to the *Ti* at one time.[12]

The excavation of numerous tombs reveals that the religion of the Shang was dominated by a deep concern for life and significance beyond the grave. In the case of persons of royal or noble blood the most costly and elaborate tombs were constructed. These were provided with rich furnishings, and all the objects deemed necessary for an existence after life on earth. Carriages, utensils, sacrificial vessels and weapons were deposited with the corpse. Weapons and sacrificial vessels were the most numerous because war and sacrifice were the two most important enterprises of Shang times. There is evidence that a large retinue of servants, wives and slaves and numerous horses were buried alive with the king. About four hundred victims were discovered in each of the larger tombs at Anyang.[13] Certain objects, particularly those made of jade, were buried along with the corpse because they were deemed to possess preservative powers against corruption and decay, or because they symbolised immortality.

Besides the cult of ancestors in which the supreme ancestor was worshipped as a 'high god', the Shang dynasty religion was characterised by a strong belief in the influence of natural phenomena on man's life, both for good and evil. The gods of the soil and grain seem to have held paramount importance. As the hierarchical structure of society developed each territorial unit had its own god of the soil whose importance varied according to the size and importance of the territory over which he exercised spiritual control. As Chavannes wrote, 'The earth god is the personification of the power inherent in the earth. Each plot of earth possesses a god of its own, but the earth is split up according to the human groupings which occupy it. A complete hierarchy of earth gods corresponds to these various territorial divisions.'[14] Though all the earth was considered to be sacred, a special spot was chosen on which a mound was erected, but not only a mound but a tree was required to represent the god. Thus, 'In antiquity, the tree was essential to the altar of the earth god; indeed it is indistinguishable from the earth god itself: it is the earth god. After all, would not all the creative and nutritious qualities of the earth be concentrated where a fine tree grows? Does not this tree sprout from the very bosom of the earth as the living expression of its fertility?'[15]

The philosopher Mo-tzŭ (fifth century BC) wrote, 'formerly in the times of the sacred kings of the Three Dynasties, when they first founded their kingdoms and established their capitals, they selected a site for the principal earth altar of the kingdom, erected the ancestral temple, and chose luxuriant trees to make a sacred grove.'[16] There is no need, I believe, to accept the suggestion of Quaritch Wales that there was the possibility of Mesopotamian influence in this connection. He writes that 'the representation of the Chinese god of the soil by mound and tree corresponds quite closely to Mesopotamian representations of Enlil and Tammuz.'[17]

The gods of the soil were numerous. Each homestead had its own 'god of the soil' who presided over the family acres. Each group of families, each feudal fief, and the country as a whole had its god of the soil, and these gods formed a divine hierarchy corresponding to the hierarchical structure of the society on which it was super-imposed. The sign of the complete extirpation of a rebellious house was that its ancestral temple was destroyed, the tree by the earth altar cut down, and the altar itself roofed over so that it no longer enjoyed the beneficent influences of sun, wind and rain.

Besides the gods of soil and grain, of mountains and rivers, of wind and rain, many animals were regarded as possessing a spiritual potency, and the mysterious powers of nature were symbolised and worshipped in animal form. This was perhaps natural in a country where hunting was a major occupation of the nobility. The ferocious beasts which man hunted symbolised for him both the mysterious and terrifying experience of death, and the violent and awe-inspiring storms which preluded the fructifying rains of summer.

Two semi-mythical animal figures, both composite in form, were especially important and have become a recurrent theme in Chinese art motifs throughout history. They were the dragon and the *t'ao t'ieh*. The dragon was early associated with storm and cloud, rain and fertility, rivers and marshes, and with awe-inspiring and kingly power. A certain ambivalence is to be found in the concept of the dragon. On the one hand he inspired awe and terror, but on the other hand he was worshipped as a beneficent being who sent down the fructifying rains. The same ambivalence is seen in the concept of kingly majesty, sitting aloft on his dragon throne and inspiring such terror that he can only be approached with abject mien and downcast eyes, but at the same time the 'father and mother' of his people. That the dragon was significant for Shang dynasty religion is proved conclusively by the fact that in the *Chia Pien* list of oracle bone inscriptions no less than forty-one characters are considered to be forms of *lung,* the dragon.[18] Andersson affirms that the dragon motif appears in the earliest Chinese art, and says that in Kansu in the early part of the second millennium BC a snake-like form with forelegs and horns is represented.[19]

The *T'ao t'ieh* or ogre mask, which appears, highly stylised, as a constant motif in the designs on Shang dynasty sacrificial bronzes, is a compound of more than one kind of animal, yet the feline characteristics predominate. It should be remembered that throughout historical times the tiger was thought of as the guardian of graves, frightening away evil spirits, and was also depicted on the shields of soldiers to inspire terror in the enemy. To some scholars the *t'ao t'ieh,* with wide-open jaws and fearsome aspect, has suggested death which swallows up all living things without exception in its gluttonous jaws. Carl Hentze sees in the *t'ao t'ieh* evidence of a magico-religious concept of birth and death, light and darkness, indicative of a dualistic world-view.[20] His opinion must be considered as no more than highly speculative. It seems more likely that this terrifying creature represented a powerful divinity which protected the grave and the corpse from evil spirits, and guarded the tasty sacrifices which the pious descendants offered to their ancestor spirits. The Chinese have always been deeply concerned to protect themselves from evil spirits. Associated with graves from the fourth century BC onwards guardian spirits in the form of grotesque animals have been discovered, whilst the ubiquitous door-gods in the form of fearsome warriors which protect the Chinese home seem to have the same underlying purpose.

Of all animals the tortoise was thought to possess mysterious and oracular powers, and consequently its shell was used in divination. The cicada was also a common motif in Shang mortuary art. It seems to have been recognised as a symbol of immortality. Pieces of jade in the shape of a cicada were placed on the tongues of the dead before burial.[21]

The kings of the Shang dynasty were not thought of as divine during their lifetime, but were considered to possess sacral powers. Their title *wang* was in later times explained as depicting one who united in his person heaven, earth and man. The Shang dynasty king owed his position as supreme ruler to the military prowess of his divine ancestor. He maintained that position by means of alliances with the virtually autonomous clans which formed the Chinese hegemony.[22] In later times Chinese historians conceived of these kings as 'emperors' and great masters of a national religion, an idea which is entirely false. Yet the contemporary evidence from oracle bone inscriptions, and the archaeological discoveries which date from the Shang dynasty reveal that the king exercised important religious functions which were considered to be essential for the well-being of the state. In fact the primary duty of the king, and indeed of every territorial magnate, was that of preserving the prosperity of the land by means of rituals of a magico-religious nature. By the correct performance of the prescribed rituals he ensured the regularity of the seasons, the fertility of the crops, the natural and timely reproduction of domestic animals, and he maintained a harmonious relationship between heaven, earth and man. By the same rituals he ensured to the people the protection and blessing of the supreme ancestor spirit above. It was these ritual functions which gave to the king his unique religious status. Under his direction the movements of the heavenly bodies were observed and recorded, and to him alone appertained the promulgation of a yearly calendar for the guidance and control of the seasonal activities of the people. Thus an early Chou dynasty text informs us that the mythical emperor Yao commanded two of his ministers, Hsi and Ho 'reverently in accord with the Will of Heaven, to calculate and represent the progress of the sun, moon and stars, so as to promulgate with care and reverence the appropriate times for men's work.'[23]

From this short survey of Shang dynasty religion we see that the most distinctive ideas of a peculiarly Chinese world-view were already in evidence: a cult of ancestors which resulted in a highly organised sacrificial and mortuary ritual, the belief in a supreme being who presides over a hierarchical structure in the spiritual world which was intimately related to man's life and destiny; the idea that only those designated by superior authority were fitted to perform religious functions, the people being merely spectators, which led to the intimate connection of religion with the state; the intense concern for the correct and meticulous observance of ceremonial; and the belief that the main purpose of religion was to maintain a harmonious relationship between heaven, earth and man.

CHAPTER TWO

RELIGIOUS DEVELOPMENTS FROM THE ESTABLISHMENT OF THE CHOU DYNASTY TO THE BIRTH OF CONFUCIUS

The extant literature which can be confidently ascribed to the period prior to Confucius is limited in extent. The inscriptions found on bronze sacrificial vessels, though trustworthy, seldom contain more than a few scores of characters. The same standard phrases occur again and again, and they reveal very little of the religious ideas of the early Chou period.[1] Seven sections of the *Book of Documents* (*Shu Ching*) are accepted by most scholars as reliable contemporary evidence.[2] The poems of the *Book of Odes* (*Shih Ching*) are extremely valuable for the light which they shed on the religious beliefs and practices of the early centuries of the first millennium BC. Though the date of many of these poems can be determined with considerable accuracy from internal evidence, the majority of them are undateable and all that can be said of them with certainty is that they are prior in time to Confucius.[3] The remaining Confucian classics, though undoubtedly containing much material which originated in the early centuries of the Chou dynasty, are the product of post-Confucian times, and are, in their present form, the compilations of Han dynasty scholars.[4]

Using only such passages from the literature as bear the stamp of Western Chou origin, we find that a remarkable and even revolutionary change took place about 1000 BC in religious and ethical thinking. As has so often happened in history, this change was to a large extent occasioned by political necessity.

In the middle of the eleventh century BC the strong and virile Chou clans, who occupied the north-western territories of the Chinese hegemony, led by an able chieftain called Fa, and known subsequently as King Wu, successfully rebelled against their Shang overlords. About the year 1027 BC the great capital city called Yin was captured and looted. The last king of the Shang dynasty was killed, and King Wu established himself as head over the Chinese states. He seems to have treated those who capitulated with remarkable clemency. The son of the late Shang king was allowed to rule over the ancient Yin capital and its surrounding territories, but two of King Wu's brothers were assigned neighbouring fiefs to act as watch-dogs. Whilst King Wu continued to exercise personal rule over the ancient Chou patrimony in the west, he placed a trustworthy cousin, the duke of Shao, as suzerain over the newly conquered territories in the east, and granted fiefs to his own eight younger brothers and to those who had assisted in his campaigns. For a while all went well, but on the death of King Wu dissensions arose among the brothers. King Wu had followed the Chou custom of appointing his young son, Ch'êng, to succeed him. The Shang dynasty had followed a system of fraternal inheritance, and of the king's younger brothers, the next in seniority, Duke Hsien, considered that he had every right to succeed to the royal title, especially as King Wu's son was young and inexperienced. Winning over to his side another brother, and allying himself with the son of the deposed Shang king and certain barbarian tribes in the east, Hsien raised the standard of revolt. A period of bitter strife followed which finally ended in the defeat of Hsien and his associates. This led to the complete and utter destruction of the Shang capital Yin, and the pacification of the country under the able regency of the duke of Chou, the young king's uncle. This was the famous Tan, duke of Chou, who in later times was regarded as a paragon of royal virtue, and in the eyes of Confucius a great hero and wise statesman.[5]

The overthrow of the Shang dynasty and the pacification of the country had been achieved only with the greatest difficulty. But even more difficult were the problems of government which faced the new rulers. They could hope to retain power in their hands only if they could persuade the nobles and the numerous officials and administrators, who had formerly given their allegiance to the Shang, that their title to kingship was just and reasonable. This they did by enunciating a doctrine of kingship and a philosophy of history which have generally been attributed to the duke of Chou.[6] This doctrine, which is clearly stated in the seven authentic chapters of the *Shu Ching,* was firmly based in morality and religion. It was this doctrine, which came to be generally accepted in China, which led to a remarkable revolution in religious thinking, and proved to be a significant step towards an ethical monotheism. The Chou, less cultured than the Shang whom they had overthrown, took over the Shang institutions. They conserved the ancient clan structure, and the religious ideas and ceremonial system of the conquered, but they infused a new outlook and a new morality.

From the first, the ruling principle of Chou administration was that government is founded in religion. All great matters of state, even the founding of a state itself, were related, not only as with the Shang to the deified spirits of deceased ancestors, but to a supreme God, whom they called *T'ien* or *Shang Ti*. This God, who became the supreme object of worship, was no longer a primeval ancestor-spirit but a high God, independent and supreme, who graciously associated the ancestor spirits with himself in heaven above.

How did this momentous change come about? The God, who had been the original ancestor spirit of the Shang dynasty for some five hundred years, could not lightly be thrust aside. Generation after generation had worshipped *Ti* as the most powerful of all the gods and supreme over all other deities. The Chou kings could not hope to displace him from that supreme position by substituting for him the but recently apotheosised founders of their own dynasty, the kings Wen and Wu. Nor could they allow his worship to continue unchanged, for he was the founder-ancestor of the Shang dynasty, and their rebellion was tantamount to rebellion against the supreme god. They could neither reject *Ti* altogether, nor could they allow the concept of *Ti* and his worship to remain as it had been. Political necessity made a change imperative. They therefore transformed the concept of *Ti* from that of a primeval ancestor-spirit, having blood relationship with his royal descendants, to that of a supreme high God, whose concern was for the prosperity and well-being of the whole Chinese race. They emphasised the title *Shang Ti* that is, the *Ti* above, or the 'supreme *Ti*', and equated it with *T'ien*,[7] a deity who seems to have been, together with Earth, a supreme object of worship in a primitive nature cult. They insisted, furthermore, that this supreme God demanded righteousness and good government. It was for that reason that the Shang dynasty had been overthrown. This God chose whom he would to be ruler, and deposed those who, like the last king of the Shang dynasty, had rebelled against him by misrule and licentiousness.

The importance of this change cannot be over-emphasised. According to this new Chou theology, it was the supreme God who had appointed the Shang dynasty kings to rule in the first place, and so long as they had ruled well he had approved of them. In fact it was he who, five hundred years before, had raised up the first Shang king, T'ang the Conqueror, to overthrow the previous Hsia dynasty when it too had become abhorrent to him through misrule and evil conduct. Whenever a king failed, by persistent misrule, in his duties to God, then God rejected him and sought for a suitable substitute. After many warnings, and by diligent search over the whole country, God had found in King Wu a man after his own heart and had transferred the mandate to him. This reading of history provided a theological justification for the usurpation of power by the Chou kings, but it also had within it the implication that if they, in their turn, ceased to rule justly and wisely, *T'ien* would likewise dispose of them. Thus the belief in a supreme deity carried with it strong ethical implications.

A few quotations from the authentic chapters of the *Shu Ching* will make this point abundantly clear:

I constantly say to myself, *T'ien* purposed to destroy Yin, as a husbandman [destroys weeds]. How dare I neglect to complete the work of my fields! *T'ien* seeks in this way to bless me [by bringing to completion the work of the former pacificators of the country]. (*Shu*: Ta Kao 14)

His [King Wên] fame reached up to *Shang Ti* who blessed him. *T'ien* therefore bestowed its great command on King Wên to extirpate the dynasty of Yin, to receive the mandate, and take over its territories and people, that they might be well-governed. (K'ang Kao 4)

The capital of Shang was full of crime. [The king] was not distressed that the kingdom of Yin was ruined. Nor did he care that the fragrance of virtue should rise up from the sacrifices to plead with *T'ien*. Instead the complaints of the people and the rank odour of drunken orgies were felt on high. Therefore *T'ien* determined to destroy Yin. It loved Yin no more, because of Yin's excesses. It is not *T'ien* that is cruel. It is people who bring evil on themselves. (Chiu Kao 11)

The king said, 'Ye numerous officers who survive from the dynasty of Yin, lament not that compassionate *T'ien* has sent down great destruction on Yin, and we, the princes of Chou, protected by the mandate and endowed with *T'ien's* bright terrors, have carried out the kingly task of punishment, and received [at *T'ien's* hand] Yin's mandate and accomplished the work of *Ti*.' (To Shih 2)

Our little country would not have dared to seize the mandate of Yin. It was *T'ien* who would not let it remain with them. Indeed it would not tolerate their misrule. It assisted us. How could we ourselves dare to aspire to the throne? (To Shih 3)

I have heard it said, '*Shang Ti* leads men to tranquillity'. But the sovereign of Hsia [Chieh] would not seek tranquillity, and so *Ti* sent down corrections to show his will to the Hsia by timely warnings. He would not be warned by *Ti*. He plunged into greater excesses and excused his conduct. Then *T'ien* refused to hear him, took away his appointment and inflicted extreme punishment. (To Shih, 5)

Then it [*T'ien*] charged your first ancestor, T'ang the victorious, to remove Hsia, and able men ruled the land. You yourselves know that your Yin forerunners had their annals and archives which related how Yin took the mandate from Hsia. (To Shih, 6, 19)

Without pity *T'ien* has brought destruction on Yin, since Yin has lost its mandate to rule, which we of the house of Chou have received. I do not dare to affirm that what we have established will continue for ever in prosperity. Yet, if *T'ien* assists those who are sincere, I would not dare to affirm that it will end in misfortune. (Chün Shih 2)

The mandate of *T'ien* was not easy to keep. It is difficult to trust in *T'ien's* constancy. He who loses the mandate does so because he is not able to continue in the illustrious virtue which characterised the men of old. (Chün Shih 4)

Even the wise by thoughtlessness become reckless, and the reckless by taking thought become wise. *T'ien* for five years left the descendant [of Yin] in peace to see if he would be a [true] ruler of the people. But he would not reflect or listen. Then *T'ien* sought throughout the numerous regions, rousing by its terrors to move someone who would look up to *T'ien*. But in all the numerous regions none was found. Only our king of Chou treated his people well and was able to bear the burden of practising virtue. He presided over [the sacrifices to] the spirits and to *T'ien*. *T'ien* therefore taught us, blessed us, and chose us to take over the mandate of Yin and govern the numerous regions. (To Fang 17–19)

In the above quotations we see clearly enunciated the idea that the government of the people was God's concern, for had not God given birth to all the people? (*Shih*: 3: 3, 6). It was because of his loving concern and care for the people that God chose and appointed a man who was qualified to rule over them justly and wisely. When the early literature speaks of the king 'receiving' (*shou*) the people and the land, it means receiving them from the hand of God, by God's decree or mandate. This word 'mandate' (*ming*), which signifies an important concept in Chou religion, was derived from a pictogram which represents the feudal vassal receiving the patents of office in the ancestral temple of his lord. Thus God was thought of as handing over to a ruler his authority to rule. He was, therefore, God's vassal, God's vice-regent, and the authority could be recalled if necessary.

No longer, as with the Shang, is the primeval ancestor-spirit a supreme deity. When contemporary literature speaks of the ancestors of the Chou dynasty, the kings Wên and Wu, or even of the original founder of the Chou clans, the mythical Hou Chi, god of millet, it speaks of them as 'associated with' the supreme God on high, as descending *with him* to partake of the sacrifices, and as having powers delegated by him to bestow tranquillity and prosperity upon their filial descendants. The evidence from the *Shih Ching* (Book of Odes) is quite clear.

> Sovereign *T'ien* conferred its mandate. The two rulers [Wên and Wu] received it. King Chêng [their successor] dared not remain idle, but day and night laboured to establish his charge. (*Shih*: 4: 1, 6)

> At the appropriate time King Wu toured the states. Sovereign *T'ien* regarded him as its son. *T'ien* raised the house of Chou above all princely families . . . King Wu drew to himself a host of spiritual beings, the gods of rivers and mountains, and thus was sovereign ruler over all the land. (4: 1; 8, 1-2)

> Accomplished art thou, Hou Chi [the primeval ancestor of the Chou clans], worthy to associate with *T'ien*. Owing to thy great bounty our people possess the grain. Thou hast bestowed the wheat and the barley which *T'ien* destined for all. Without considering territorial boundaries, thou hast taught and caused to be observed man's social duties. (4: 1, 10)

> Throughout the states there is peace. Year by year the harvest is plentiful. *T'ien's* mandate does not cease. The valorous King Wu keeps the confidence of all his officers, who, dispersed throughout the realm, give security to his house. How bright he shines in heaven, made king to end the rule of Shang. (4: 3, 9)

> I bring and present my offering, a bullock and a ram. May *T'ien* descend and accept them. I faithfully observe the statutes of King Wên, maintaining tranquillity throughout the realm. From King Wên come great blessings. He descends and partakes of my sacrifice. Day and night I reverence *T'ien's* majesty, thus constantly preserving the favour bestowed upon Chou. (4: 1, 7)

In the third section of the *Book of Odes,* the *Ta Ya,* the poems relating to King Wên are sacrificial odes in which the distinction is always made between God (*T'ien* or *Shang Ti*), and the apotheosised ancestor, King Wên, although the latter is conceived of as living on high with God, and descending with him to partake of the sacrifices.

King Wên is on high, brilliant in heaven. Though Chou is an ancient state, its mandate to rule is new. Are not the kings of Chou illustrious? Was not *Ti's* mandate timely? King Wên ascends and descends, accompanying *Ti* to the sacrifices. (*Shih*: 3: 1, 1)

This close association of the deceased ancestors with the supreme God, together with a refusal to identify them with God, is a mark of early Chou religion.

It is probable that originally *Shang Ti* and *T'ien* were two quite different deities, but by the time of the Western Chou the concepts of *Shang Ti* and *T'ien* were fused to form one supreme God. In process of time the term *Shang Ti* was used less frequently to designate this supreme being, and when we come to the *Analects of Confucius* we find that the character *T'ien* is invariably used. Right down to the time of Confucius and Mo-tzŭ this God is thought of anthropomorphically as a personal God who stood at the head of a hierarchical structure in the spiritual world, omniscient and omnipotent. As such he demands implicit obedience and was swift to punish and to bless. He delighted in the sacrifices which were offered to him in costly and elaborate rites. Yet it was recognised that the most sumptuous sacrifices and the loudest protestations of innocence could not divert him from the chastisement of the wicked. Above all he loved virtue, so that the virtue of the ruler became in large measure the guarantee of the peace and prosperity of the land. The following texts illustrate the character and attributes of God as he was worshipped in pre-Confucian China.

1 *T'ien sees and hears; is clear-sighted and cannot be deceived.*

T'ien sees as my people see,
T'ien hears as my people hear. (*Shu*: T'ai Shih Chung 7)

T'ien sees and hears as our people see and hear.
T'ien displays His majesty as our people display their reverence.
(Kao Yao Mu 7)

T'ien sees and hears everything. The sage-king takes it as his pattern. His ministers respectfully follow his example, and the people are well-governed. (Shuo Ming Chung 3)

August *T'ien* is most clear-sighted. (*Shih*: 3: 3; 2, 11)

How bright is *T'ien* above, looking down with care and concern upon the earth below! (2: 6, 3)

T'ien inspects the people below, keeping account of their righteousness, and regulating accordingly their span of life. It is not *T'ien* who destroys men. They, by their evil doing, cut short their own lives. (*Shu*: Kao Tsung 3)

2 *T'ien is omniscient and omnipresent.*

Fear the anger of *T'ien* and do not give way to dissipation. Fear lest *T'ien* changes towards you, and do not dare to rush into evil ways. Majestic *T'ien* is clear-sighted, and extends to wheresoever you go. Majestic *T'ien* is all-seeing as the rising sun, and reaches you in all your licentious wanderings. (*Shih*: 3: 2; 10, 8)

Be reverent! Be reverent! *T'ien* has revealed its will. Its mandate is not easy to preserve. Do not say that *T'ien* is far distant above. It ascends and descends, concerning itself with our affairs, and daily examines all our doings. (4: 3; 3, 1)

3 *T'ien blesses, protects and sends happiness.*

May *T'ien* protect and settle you, making you perfectly secure. That you may be truly virtuous what happiness does it withhold? It causes you to receive many blessings. They are indeed numerous. (2: 1; 6, 1)

4 *T'ien punishes the wicked.*

How all-embracing is *T'ien* above, sovereign over all the people below! How arrayed in terrors is *T'ien* above! It decrees many punishments. (3: 3, 1)

5 *T'ien created the people and gave them their dispositions.*

In giving birth to all the people, *T'ien* ordained that their natures should be undependable. There are some who begin well, but few remain good till death. (3: 3, 1)

When *T'ien* gave birth to all the people, to every constitutive faculty it annexed its law. It was their natural disposition to love admirable virtue. (3: 3, 6)

Towards the end of the Western Chou period, in the eighth century

BC, the misgovernment and licentiousness of the Chou rulers plunged the country into anarchy and ruin. Poems written about this time reflect the sense of bewilderment over the fact that *T'ien* seemed to be unconcerned for the welfare of the people. Was *T'ien* indifferent to the sufferings of the people? Or was it possible that *T'ien* was impotent? Why did *T'ien* allow calamities and sufferings to fall upon the innocent? Why did the frequent and costly sacrifices made to *T'ien* and the ancestor spirits prove of no avail? It is questions of this nature which occur over and over again in the writings of the Ch'un Ch'iu period prior to Confucius, and which led many thoughtful minds towards agnosticism and finally to a belief that *T'ien* was a purely naturalistic principle, indifferent alike to good and evil. It was the rise of a naturalistic philosophy which profoundly influenced Confucian and Taoist writers alike, and this together with the Confucian ethical emphasis has led many scholars to affirm that the Chinese are not fundamentally religious. Yet, however much individual thinkers from the time of the Ch'un Ch'iu period onwards accepted a purely naturalistic or humanistic interpretation, the majority of the Chinese people have conceived of *T'ien* as a supreme God, who should be reverenced and worshipped, to whom prayer should be offered and sacrifices made, a transcendental being deeply concerned for the welfare of the people whom he created.

The following quotations reveal the acute distress of mind caused when faith in the providence of a supreme deity is challenged by the problems of suffering and evil:

Oh, vast far-spreading *T'ien,* whom we all call parent! I am innocent and blameless, yet I suffer from such great disorders. Majestic *T'ien,* you are too stern; for truly I am innocent. Majestic *T'ien,* you are too cruel, for truly I am blameless. (*Shih*: 2: 5, 4)

The proud rejoice. The troubled are in great distress. Oh, azure, *T'ien*! Oh, azure *T'ien!* Look upon these proud men and have pity on the troubled. Those slanderous men, who was it who devised their plans? I would take those slanderous men and throw them to the wolves and tigers. If wolves and tigers refuse to devour them, I would throw them into the northlands. If the northlands refused to receive them, I would throw them into the hands of August *T'ien.* (2: 5; 6, 5–6)

I gaze up to August *T'ien,* but it does not favour us. For long these cruel afflictions which it has sent down greatly distressed us. The state is unsettled. Officers and people suffer. (3: 3, 10)

Now the people in their peril look to *T'ien*, but find no clear guidance. But let *T'ien* once decide, and there is none that it cannot overcome. This August *Shang Ti* above, can he hate anyone? (2; 4, 8)

The net which *T'ien* lets down is full of calamities. Good men are perishing, and my heart is grieved. (3: 3; 10, 6)

Overshadowing *T'ien* is angered. *T'ien* is indeed sending down destruction, distressing us with famine. The people are all perishing. Settled lands and border fields are all lying waste. (3: 3; 11, 1)

A characteristic of Western Chou religion was the elaborate sacrificial and ceremonial cult, which was closely bound up with all that appertained to the government of the country, and the well-being and prosperity of each individual clan. This cult had been in large measure inherited from the previous Shang dynasty and it was to remain as one of the main features of Chinese religion, with appropriate modifications, right down to the abolition of the monarchy in 1912.[8] The chief ministrant at the great sacrifices was the ruler himself; but as the relationship between the spiritual world and the world of men was so important, the great sacrifices also demanded the participation of all the feudal lords or their representatives. The ritual required the services of specialists, similar to those who had functioned at the court of Shang kings.[9] From them derived the scholar-class which played such an important role throughout Chinese history.

The sacrificial feasts at which the clan ancestors were honoured followed a prescribed pattern. First, an auspicious day was chosen with the help of expert diviners. The participants underwent a previous purification and fast. All the oblations were carefully selected and prepared, the sacrificial victims having to be of one colour and without blemish. The prayers, the rituals and the music followed a prescribed pattern. Finally the ancestors were represented by living personators. These were chosen, if possible, from the sons of the head of the clan, who himself acted as chief petitioner and sacrificer. These 'personators' were conducted with great ceremony to the seats of honour reserved for the ancestral spirits and they were treated *as if*, for the time being, the ancestral spirits had taken up their abode in them. Thus the clan feast was a feast at which the living and the dead all shared in a common meal.

You choose an auspicious day, and having made the prescribed purifications you prepare the sacrifices to be made to your ancestors. In spring, summer, autumn and winter you make the appropriate offerings to the former rulers of your family. Your ancestors [through their representatives] promise you long life, life without end. The spirits of your ancestors are present, and obtain for you many blessings. (*Shih*: 2: 1; 6)

The following texts, chosen from a large number of poems which have as their theme the great sacrificial feasts, illustrate the central position of the cult of ancestors in the religion of Western Chou.

Within the temple, solemn and serene, in full accord and reverently, the assisting nobles and numerous officers uphold the virtue of King Wên, and make their response to him in heaven. Attentively they hasten [to perform their service] in the temple. (*Shih*: 4: 1, 1)

I bring my offering, a ram and a bullock. May *T'ien* receive them! I take the statutes of King Wên as my rule, and maintain constant tranquillity throughout my realm. King Wên bestows on us prosperity, and descends upon the right hand to partake of our sacrifices. (4: 1, 7)

A bountiful harvest, millet and rice in abundance! The granaries are piled high with measureless stacks of grain. We make fermented liquor to offer to our ancestors, both male and female. We carry out all our ceremonies so that they will send down blessings upon us. (4: 2, 4)

The feudal lords gather in full concord, assembled reverently to assist the son of *T'ien,* solemn and majestic. He offers a noble bullock, and they assist in setting forth the sacrifice. Oh, thou great kingly ancestor, give thine aid to thy filial son! [The ancestor King Wên] was a man of comprehensive wisdom, a prince in peace and war. The tranquillity which he gives reaches even to August *T'ien,* and ensures prosperity to his descendants. He [the present king] gains for us long life and many blessings, since thus he honours his august father and his accomplished mother. (4: 2, 7)

We proceed to make fermented liquor and to prepare viands for the offerings and for sacrifice. We seat the representatives of the dead and urge them to eat. Thus we seek to increase our bright happiness. We with grave looks and reverent attitude choose our sacrificial victims without blemish, oxen and sheep, to serve in the autumn and winter sacrifices. Some slay the animals; others attend to the cooking; some put the meat on stands; some arrange it for sacrifice. The master of ceremonies (*chu*), stands at the temple gate to await the arrival of the ancestor spirits. The sacrifices all ready in brilliant array. The ancestor spirits arrive and accept of our offerings. Their filial descendant receives their blessing. The spirits reward him with happiness and long life. Some reverently tend the fires, whilst others place in position the great stands [for the meat]. The queen reverently sets out a large number of smaller dishes. The guests and visitors draw near and a toast is drunk. All the ceremonies are meticulously observed; each smile, each word in perfect decorum. The personators of the ancestor spirits arrive and promise every blessing and ten thousand years of happiness.

We have done all within our power and performed the rites without error. The master of ceremonies conveys the message of the ancestors to their filial descendant.

'Your sacrifice has filled the air with fragrance. The spirits have enjoyed your pious offerings. They reward you with many blessings suited to your desires. You have been respectful, prompt, meticulous and obedient. The spirits will bestow on you signal favours throughout a myriad years.'

The ceremonies are ended. Drums and bells proclaim the fact. The filial descendant returns to his seat. The master of ceremonies informs him that the spirits have all drunk to satisfaction. The personators of the spirits arise and leave, to the accompaniment of bells and drums. The queen and all the servitors hasten to remove the sacrificial offerings. Then all the male relatives take part in a special feast. (2: 6; 5, 1–5)

A pure libation is poured out, and then a red bullock is taken to offer to my ancestors. With a knife, adorned round the haft with little bells, I make a cut through the hair, and take away the blood and the intestines. Then I present the offerings which exhale a fragrant odour. How brilliant is the sacrifice! The ancestors come and recompense me with great blessings and long life. (2: 6; 6, 5–6)

From the above passages we see how the cult of ancestors and the worship of the supreme God and the host of spiritual beings found expression in a highly developed ritual in which meticulous observance of appropriate actions was of paramount importance. The gods and ancestors demanded service and sacrifice, and so long as these were offered reverently and respectfully and with careful observance of the prescribed etiquette, the spirits were obligated to perform their side of the bargain and bestow long life and happiness on the worshippers. Furthermore, these great ceremonies provided a binding cement in a society where rank and precedence needed to be carefully preserved.

Nevertheless, the ethical demands of *T'ien* and of the ancestors were never lost sight of. The king stood in relation to *T'ien* in much the same way as the eldest living son stood to the deceased ancestors of the clan. The title given to him was *T'ien tzŭ*, that is, 'son of heaven'. His attitude to *T'ien* must be one of filial obedience. It is significant that from the beginning of the Chou dynasty the reign titles by which the kings became known were titles with an ethical connotation.

From a study of many passages in the *Shu Ching* and the *Shih Ching* we see that the quality which made it possible for the early kings to receive and hold *T'ien's* mandate, by which they were deemed worthy to take their place on high with God, the quality which was in fact the basis of *T'ien's* majesty was *Tê*. This character in its earliest usages signifies 'power', the power of personality which the gods invariably possess, and with which some persons were endowed to an extraordinary degree. It was a quality somewhat like 'mana' or 'baraka', which all gods and spirits possess in some measure, and which in a great man causes him to subdue his enemies, gain a following, impose his authority and influence over his fellows. This 'power' or 'force' might work alike for good or evil; it might manifest itself in benevolence or wrath. Undoubtedly this older concept of *Tê* was not entirely superseded, but during this period it was charged with a new ethical meaning. *Tê* was 'virtue'. It was divine or kingly power used for the good of people and land. It was, above all, what made the king acceptable and worthy in the sight of *T'ien*. It flowed out from the king into all his territories, bringing peace, prosperity and blessing. Only by maintaining his 'virtue' could a king hope to retain his mandate to rule.

Your illustrious and distinguished father, King Wên, in displaying his *Tê*, was careful in the use of punishments . . . His fame reached *Shang Ti* and *Shang Ti* approved of him. *T'ien* gave him the mandate to exterminate the Yin and to receive the appointment. (*Shu*: K'ang Kao 3–4)

The king said, 'O Feng, be reverent! Do nothing to excite grievances. Do not follow evil counsels or iniquitous ways. With constant care imitate the *Tê* of the ancestors, that your heart may be at peace. Set your heart on *Tê*, plan well ahead, let your benevolence bring repose to the people. Do nothing to merit blame or degradation.' (K'ang Kao 22)

Let the young listen with attention to the instruction of their fathers and ancestors, and let them practise *Tê* in things both great and small (Chiu Kao 5)

T'ien itself will approve of your great *Tê*, and you will never be forgotten in the royal house. (Chiu Kao 7)

Do you, O king, by the sole exercise of your *Tê* bring harmony to the deluded people, and thus please the former kings who received the mandate to rule. (Tzŭ Ts'ai 7)

Since your occupation of this new city, your majesty has sedulously practised *Tê*. Let your majesty continue in the cultivation of *Tê,* thus seeking the abiding mandate of *T'ien*. (Chao Kao 20)

Another concept of great ethical significance came into frequent use; the concept of filial piety or *hsiao*. This character, as far as we know, is not found on the oracle bones of the Shang dynasty, but it is found on the early bronzes of the Chou dynasty, and also in the *Shu Ching* and the *Shih Ching,* to designate that attitude of respectful obedience which a son owes to his parents and to his ancestors. Kings Wên and Wu, the founders of the dynasty, were held up as models of filial piety.

The king said: 'Great criminals should be detested, but how much more those who lack filial piety and brotherly love; the son who does not reverently attend to his father's needs, and wounds the heart of his ancestors.' (*Shu*: K'ang Kao 16)

The king said: 'Uncle Yi Ho, you have brought added glory to your ancestors. You are first in following the example of Wên and Wu, renewing again the well-nigh broken traditions of our line. You have revived again the filial piety of our accomplished ancestors.' (Wên Hou 3)

I offer this noble bull, assisted by the nobles in setting out the sacrifices. Oh, august father, bless your filial son. (*Shih*: 4: 2; 7, 2)

Oh, my august father, throughout all your life you practised filial piety. (4: 3; 1, 1)

He gained the people's confidence and was an example to all below. Ever pondering how to be filial, his filial piety was a pattern. (3: 1; 9, 3)

The two concepts *Tê* and *Hsiao* were brought into close relationship, and formed the moral principles for the control of society. *Tê* was more frequently thought of in relation to *T'ien*; *Hsiao* in relation to the ancestors. Two short extracts, taken from poems written when the power of the Chou kings had declined and the country was disrupted by political and economic disorder, reveal the strength of filial piety and family affection. They speak for themselves.

Oh my father, who begat me!
Oh, my mother, who nourished me!
You petted me, you fed me,
You developed me, you nourished me.
You cared for me. You could not leave me,
But everywhere bore me in your arms.
Oh, that I could requite such kindness!
It is like Great *T'ien,* illimitable. (*Shih*: 2: 5, 8)

Of all men in the world there is none equal to brothers. On the dreaded occasions of death and burial, it is brothers who most sympathise. When the fugitives gather together on the heights, or on the low grounds, it is brothers who will seek one another out. (2: 1; 4, 1–2)

The belief in divination, auspicious days, the influence on human affairs of eclipses of the sun and strange prodigies of nature, inherited from the distant past, were still important features of Chou religion, and were to continue to exercise a strong hold over the people right down to modern times, in spite of the scorn and ridicule poured upon these magico-religious ideas by sceptical and rationalistic philosophers. For the purposes of divination the stalks of the milfoil, which were regarded as specially suited for divining, came into common use in place of the scapula bones of sheep and oxen. On great and important occasions, and for those who could afford the cost, the shell of the tortoise continued to be used. The following extracts illustrate how varied were the occasions on which men turned to divination.

The transport waggons did not come. Great was the distress of my sorrowing heart. For he did not arrive when the time was due, so that I am full of grief. Yet I have divined by tortoise shell and by the stalks; and they agree in saying that he is near. My soldier [husband] is at hand. (*Shih*: 2: 1; 9, 4)

A lucky day was *Mao,* and we sacrificed to the ancestor of horses and prayed. (2: 3, 6)

Divine for me my dreams. What dreams are lucky? I dreamt of bears and snakes. The chief diviner divines thereon. The bears are omens of male children. The snakes are omens of female children. (2: 4; 5, 6–7)

The king deliberated and divined as to whether he dwell in the capital of *Hao*. [The site] was determined by the tortoise shell. So the king completed the city. (3: 1; 10, 7)

In the tenth month, at the conjunction [of sun and moon] on the day of *Hsin Mao,* the first of the month, the sun was eclipsed. It was an event of great evil. On former occasions the moon has been eclipsed. But now the sun is eclipsed, and great will be the suffering of the people. (2: 4; 9, 1)

The sun and moon announce evil tidings. They do not follow their ordained paths. Throughout all the kingdom government fails, because worthy men are not employed. For yon moon to be eclipsed is but an ordinary affair; but for the sun to be eclipsed, how lamentable it is! (2: 4; 9, 2)

We have seen that during the prosperous period of the Western Chou religion was centred in the concept of an over-ruling, all-powerful God, called *T'ien* or *Shang Ti,* whose care and solicitude for the people and the land was evidenced in the 'mandate of *T'ien*', bestowed upon wise and powerful rulers. Associated with *T'ien* were the powerful and beneficent ancestor spirits who presided over the life and destiny of their own clans. Religion was thus closely linked to government and to clan organisation. How was religion to be affected when the king lost his power and authority and became a mere puppet in the hands of unscrupulous usurpers? What was to be the effect on religious thinking of almost continuous civil strife, when ancient families crashed to ruin, and upstarts with no pretensions to nobility seized power by force of arms, and the land was filled with violence? In early Chou religion there were the seeds of an ethical monotheism which might possibly have developed along lines similar in some respects to those followed by the prophetic religion of the Old Testament. Such development in China was not to be. There arose no priestly or prophetic tradition in China which owed sole allegiance to the supreme God and which was prepared in his name to challenge political authority. The functions of priest, diviner and chronicler were, from first to last, under the strictest supervision of the rulers. Religion was an adjunct of the state. Whenever a state declined, the sacrificial cult by which its gods and ancestors were honoured declined with it. Throughout the whole period of the Ch'un Ch'iu (*c.* 720–481 BC) and immediately prior to the advent of Confucius, the tendency of Chinese thought was more and more towards those naturalistic and materialistic philosophies which were to find fuller expression in later times in the writings of both Confucians and Taoists.

The early signs of this changed attitude to religion are to be observed in many of the *Ya* poems of the *Shih Ching,* the products of an age of social anarchy and despair. God is not only blamed for the troubles which fell on rich and poor alike, but doubts concerning him almost approach to a denial of him. This God who sent down evil was an opponent to be cursed. The most passionate appeals to him seemed to fall on deaf ears. The most meticulous observance of the rituals failed to bring any relief. In the midst of a distressful situation no help was forthcoming from the spirit-world. Man must therefore help himself, and in doing so it was brute force which seemed to be all-powerful.

I raise my eyes to August *T'ien,* but it does not pity us. It sends down great afflictions without respite. There is no stability in the land. Officers and people alike suffer. (*Shih*: 3: 3; 10, 1)

Compassionate *T'ien* rages in fury, sending down death and afflicting with famine. The people wander about and perish. Everywhere destruction reigns. (3: 3; 11, 1)

Oh, great far-spreading *T'ien*, whom we call father and mother! Though guiltless, on me these troubles fall. Great *T'ien*, you are too stern. I have examined myself and am without fault. Great *T'ien*, you send down afflictions, but I am blameless. (2: 5; 4, 1)

T'ien is sending down calamities to put an end to the country. (3: 3; 2, 12)

Vast, far-spreading *T'ien* does not extend its virtue [*Tê*] but sends down death and famine to destroy the land. Pitiful *T'ien* now strikes terror without rhyme or reason. It is right that sinners should be punished for their crimes, but why should innocent people be overwhelmed with ruin? (2: 4; 10, 1)

August *T'ien* is not just sending down these troubles.
August *T'ien* has no pity in sending down these evils . . .
August *T'ien* is unpitying. Disorders have no end.
Month by month they grow, and men have no repose. (2: 4; 7, 5–6)

The period known as the Ch'un Ch'iu witnessed the decline of centralised authority. The lineal descendants of the kingly house of Chou became mere figureheads, retaining their titles, a semblance of authority and their religious functions. Even these latter were often usurped by powerful feudal lords who 'did what was right in their own eyes', and who regarded the splendour of their own sacrifices and ceremonial worship as indications of their strength. The destruction of the weaker states by the stronger was signalised by the desecration of ancestral temples and the covering over of earth altars.

The forms of the ancient religion were meticulously observed as of political necessity, but they were in large measure shorn of ethical or spiritual content. On the surface religion seemed to play a large part in the life of the nobility. Military engagements began with a solemn sacrifice and the services of an expert diviner. Alliances were ratified by animal sacrifice to the gods and spirits over which the most solemn oaths were sworn. The contracting parties appealed to the gods and spirits to cause anyone violating the terms of an agreement to suffer the same fate as the sacrificial victim. Besides the regular sacrifices at the ancestral temples and the earth altars, every eclipse, every unusual natural event, every sign of calamity was an occasion for sacrifices to be made. The belief was universally held that an intimate relationship existed between the natural world and the world of human affairs, and every feudal court had its specialists to observe celestial and terrestrial phenomena, and to discern by means of magical arts and divination the will of the spirits. The following quotations illustrate the beliefs and religious practices in the century prior to the birth of Confucius.

In the sixth month, on the day *Hsin Wei,* the first day of the moon, the sun was eclipsed. We beat drums and offered sacrifices on the altars of the land.[10]

In the third year of Duke Hsüan, in the spring, in the king's first month, the mouth of the ox to be used at the border sacrifice received injury. It was changed and the oracle consulted. The ox died and so the border sacrifice was cancelled.[11]

[The minister Chi Liang] said, 'What I call the Way [for a prince to follow] is to be faithful to the people and devoted to the spirits. The ruler is faithful when he thinks how best to benefit the people. The invoker at the sacrifices is devoted when his words are sincere. At the present time the people starve, whilst princes indulge themselves, and the ministrants at the sacrifices dissemble. Your servant does not know how such a state of affairs will bring success.' The Duke said, 'My sacrificial victims are sleek and fat, and the grain is piled up abundantly in the vessels. How then can there be a lack of devotion?' Chi Liang replied, 'It is the people who are of greater concern than the spirits. That is why the sage-kings first satisfied the people, and only then exerted themselves in service of the spirits.'[12]

Towards the end of the sixth century BC, Tzŭ Ch'an, prime minister of the small state of Chêng, had laws inscribed on newly cast bronzes. This was perhaps the first attempt to codify the laws and at the time it roused fierce opposition. Here was something which struck at the basis of feudal society. No longer would the people be content to accept the arbitrary rule of those above them. They would appeal to the laws, and seek to find justification for their point of view in the written code. This, it was argued, would lead to weaker government and the further decline of society.

In the third month [Tzŭ Ch'an for] the people of Chêng had a penal code cast in bronze. Shu Liang sent a message to Tzŭ Ch'an saying, 'At first I esteemed you greatly, but now I can do so no longer. Formerly the ancient kings judged each case on its merits, and had no penal code because they feared that such would lead to strife among the people. Yet, as they could not hinder [crime] altogether, they controlled the people by righteousness, corrected them by administration, led them by propriety [*li*], held them by good faith, and served them with benevolence. They instituted rewards to encourage them to follow, and severe penalties to intimidate them from committing excesses. Fearing that their methods were still not sufficient they instructed them in loyalty, incited them by good character, taught them their obligations, used them peacefully, approached them respectfully, governed them with strength, and made decisions with firmness. Moreover, they sought to have the good and wise in the highest positions, gave office to men of discrimination, made the loyal and true into elders, and the kind and gentle into teachers. In this manner the people performed their duties without any disaster or disorder arising.

But when the people come to know these laws, they will have no fear of those above them. Contention will arise as they seek justification from the written code, airing their grievances as they find proof for their point of view. This is not the way to act.'[13]

In Tzŭ Ch'an, who was prime minister of the state of Chêng when Confucius was growing to manhood in the nearby state of Lu, we see evidence of the growing tendency towards humanism and a more rationalistic interpretation. In the year 524 BC the central plain of China was struck by a typhoon of exceptional violence, and this was followed by destructive fires which raged in four of the states. The master of divination in the state of Chêng, who claimed to have predicted the fires in the previous year from astronomical indications, urged Tzŭ Ch'an to seek to avert calamity by means of sacrifices. Tzŭ Ch'an ignored his advice. 'Heaven's way', he said, 'is far removed; it is man's way that is near to us. We cannot reach the former; what means have we of knowing it?'[14] Here, in Tzŭ Ch'an's attitude we do not have a denial of the existence of a 'Way of heaven', but rather the belief that an understanding of *T'ien* is beyond man's competence. The influences which come from the spiritual world are unpredictable. Man will be best employed in controlling and regulating those matters which directly affect the people's happiness and well-being. This same attitude is revealed in Confucius, where he says, 'Respect the spirits, but keep them at a distance' (*Ana.* 6:20). Again, when asked by a disciple questions regarding the spirits and the state of the dead, Confucius replied, 'Till you have learned to serve men, how can you serve the spirits? Till you know about the living, how can you know about the dead?' (*Ana.* 11:11).

Nevertheless, in spite of the growing tendency towards a humanistic and rationalistic interpretation of man's place in the universe, both Confucius and Mo-tzŭ, as we shall see, accepted the deeper insights of Chou religion which they had inherited. In particular, they both had a profound belief in and reverence for *T'ien*, as the omnipotent and omniscient ruler of the universe, and the author of the moral order. Only in obedience to the will of *T'ien* and the decrees of *T'ien* could man hope to find his own true way of life.

CHAPTER THREE

THE SIGNIFICANCE OF CONFUCIUS FOR RELIGION

What is known in the West as Confucianism has its roots in pre-Confucian times in the teachings of the Ju, a scholar class, the origin of which has been hotly debated by Chinese scholars in recent years.[1] These Ju seem to have been experts in the performance and interpretation of religious rites, and were the holders and transmitters of traditional learning. Confucius acknowledged his indebtedness to these teachers of the past. 'I transmit but do not create,' he said.[2] The Ju Chiao or Confucianism exercised a dominant role in the development of Chinese civilisation throughout more than two millennia.

Several centuries after his death Confucius came to be recognised throughout China as 'China's greatest sage'. At times extravagant titles were accorded to him, such as 'king', 'perfect sage', 'co-equal with heaven and earth'. Some scholars of the Western Han period (202 BC–AD 9) regarded him virtually as a deity. Temples were erected to his honour, and even in the early years of the present century a serious but abortive attempt was made to make Confucianism into a state religion.[3] Yet Confucius did not found a religion, and many distinguished students of Chinese culture, both in the East and in the West, have refused to call Confucianism a religion at all. Confucius, they maintain, was primarily a great ethical teacher, concerned in the main with social and political problems. The question arises, however, as to whether his ethical and socio-political teachings were grounded in a rationalistic humanism or based on a deep religious faith which manifested itself in a devout acceptance of traditional religious practices and in a humble reliance on a supreme divine power. It is the answer to that question which will determine whether or not Confucianism may be ranked among the world's great religious systems.

It has been argued, and not without reason, that Confucianism lacks many of the important characteristics which are to be found in most of the great historical religions of mankind. It has never possessed a distinctively religious organisation. It never developed a specialised priesthood, priestly functions being performed by the head of the state or clan, or designated to scholar-officials. It possessed no credal statements nor authoritative doctrines. It frowned upon monasticism and asceticism. Its 'scriptures', though revered, were never thought of as 'revelation' in the same sense as the Bible, the Qur'an or the Vedas. There were no rites of initiation into a religious community. It is without a distinctive doctrine of the after-life and lacks an eschatology. Yet if religion is broadly defined as man's recognition of, belief in, and attitudes towards a higher spiritual power or powers, if religion is concerned with the ultimate meaning of human life and destiny, then Confucianism should be classed as a religion and not simply as an ethico-political philosophy. Throughout its history Confucianism has manifested a deep sense of man's dependence upon a supreme deity. It has fostered a sense of an intimate relationship between a transcendental spiritual world and the world of men. It has given expression to a sense of dependence on spiritual beings in elaborate rituals and heart-felt prayers.[4]

Before discussing the significance of Confucius for religion in China, it is necessary to ask what are the sources of our knowledge of his life and teaching, and to what extent are they reliable. The famous biography of Confucius by Ssŭ-ma Ch'ien[5] was not written till some 350 years after his death. Most of the works attributed to Confucius are now known to have reached substantially their present form in the Han dynasty. Anecdotes about him, references to him and quotations from his teachings are found in numerous Confucian, Taoist and Mohist publications of later times.[6] All this material needs to be treated with the utmost caution, for it is usually of a polemical or apologetical nature. There is substantial agreement among scholars that our earliest and most authentic source for Confucius and his teaching is the book called *The Analects of Confucius*.[7] Even the *Analects* did not come into being till some two generations after the death of Confucius, some time about the beginning of the fourth century BC. A second generation of Confucian disciples gathered together the scattered notes and memoirs of those who had been the immediate followers of the sage, and arranged them in twenty short chapters. A critical analysis of these twenty chapters reveals that as historical evidence for the life and teaching of Confucius they are of unequal value, and only books three to nine show any ordered arrangement and logical consistency. The *Analects* do not contain the *ipsissima verba* of Confucius, but only the substance of his teaching and a fairly vivid picture of the man and his character.

In this chapter we hope to show, mainly by reference to the *Analects*, that the lofty teaching of Confucius was grounded in religion; in a deep respect for the cultic practices by which the manes of the ancestors and other spiritual powers were worshipped and honoured, and also in a dominant concept of the 'Way of Heaven', where Heaven (*T'ien*) was conceived of as a supreme deity whose 'Way' was regulative for man's life and relationships.

Confucius is reputed to have lived from 551 to 479 BC. What we can glean from the *Analects* concerning his antecedents, and his personal history is sketchy and incomplete.[8] He grew to manhood in comparative poverty in the small but cultured state of Lu (now in modern Shantung) where he lived most of his life, and achieved some small measure of political success. In his day the ancient feudalistic form of society was breaking up, but sharp distinctions existed between the nobility and the mass of the people, between the governing class and the governed, between the great hereditary families and the peasants. But already the sharp edges of these distinctions were becoming blurred, as comparatively unknown adventurers and military opportunists arose to wrest power from dissolute and incompetent rulers. Old religious beliefs and ethical standards were breaking down in face of social, economic and political pressures. Yet at least the formal rituals and ceremonies of the ancient religion of China continued to play an important role in the lives of Confucius' contemporaries. As has occurred in many other ancient religions in the course of their development, there was a transition from ritual to ethical thinking, and in that transition Confucius played a crucial part.

Although comparatively neglected in his own day and with a very limited influence, Confucius stands out, first and foremost, as a great ethical teacher. He seems to have hardly concerned himself at all with metaphysical problems such as the nature and origin of the universe, or the nature and destiny of man. This cannot be used as an argument against Confucius' belief in a supreme divine being. When the *Analects* reports that Confucius did not speak of 'prodigies, feats of strength, disorders and spirits'[9] it simply means that he set his face against the superstitious beliefs and practices of his time. When his disciple Tzŭ Kung said that it was not possible to find out what Confucius really thought about the Way of Heaven,[10] he was indicating the fact that, though his master accepted the Way of Heaven as a tenet of his faith, he displayed a certain reticence in allowing his own personally held beliefs to become the subject of general discussion and argument. On rare occasions he did discuss this and kindred subjects, but preferred that men should deduce his religion from his manner of life.

The Master said, 'I do not wish to talk.' Tzŭ Hsia said, 'If the master does not wish to talk, how can your disciples record your words?' The master said, 'How does Heaven speak? The four seasons come and go, the hundred things come to birth. How does Heaven speak?' (*Ana.* 17: 9)

Undoubtedly Confucius' main concern was with man as he lives in this life, and with the fundamental principles which lie at the root of those relationships on which the stability, peace and prosperity of society, the family, and the individual ultimately rest. He was concerned to enunciate the basis of that inner integration and harmony of personality which results in good life and conduct. But that basis he found in obedience and conformity to the Way of Heaven. To suggest, as many scholars do, that Confucius found a satisfying solution in pure humanism, and that his ethics did not finally rest on deep religious insight and personal faith in *T'ien* is to discount many of the most pregnant sayings attributed to Confucius in the *Analects*.

Disappointed in a political career,[11] it was as an educator that Confucius found a niche for himself, training young men who showed promise for service at the courts of feudal princes. As a teacher he showed genius. He was probably one of the first in China to establish his own private school, attracting students solely by the force of his own personality and the quality of his teaching, and winning their loyalty and affection. He loved learning, believing that he was but selecting and passing on to others the best ancient wisdom, and never claiming to have an original message.

The master said, 'In a hamlet of ten houses you may be sure of finding someone quite as loyal and true to his word as I. But I doubt if you would find anyone with such a love of learning.' (*Ana.* 5: 27)

I have never grown tired of learning, nor wearied of teaching others what I have learnt. (7: 1)

I, for my part, am not one of those who have innate knowledge. I am simply one who loves the past, and who is diligent in investigating it. (7: 19)

The religion which Confucius inherited accepted belief in a supreme deity, *T'ien* or *Shang Ti,* which ruled over the cosmos and all other spiritual beings, and which concerned itself with men's welfare. The signs of *T'ien's* interest were there for everyone to see, but in particular *T'ien* revealed its will by means of its appointment, decree, commissioning or mandate. Confucius again and again reveals this sense of a divine commission.

> The master said, 'Heaven began the power [*Tê*] that is in me. What have I to fear from such a one as Huan T'ui?' (*Ana.* 7: 22)

> The master said, 'If it is the will of heaven that the Way shall prevail, then the Way will prevail. But if it is the will of heaven that the Way should perish, then it must needs perish. What can Kung-po Liao do against Heaven's will?' (14: 38)

> The master said, 'The truth is no one knows me . . . I do not accuse heaven nor lay the blame on men. But the studies of men here below are felt on high, and perhaps after all I am known; not here, but in heaven.' (14: 37)

> When the master was trapped in K'uang, he said, 'When King Wên perished, did that mean that culture [*wên*] ceased to exist? If heaven had really intended that culture such as his should disappear, a latter-day mortal would never have been able to link himself to it as I have done. And if heaven does not intend to destroy such culture, what have I to fear from the people of K'uang?' (9: 5)

Not until he was fifty years of age could Confucius say that he understood the decree of heaven (*Ana.* 2:4). A man could not be a truly 'noble' man unless he knew heaven's appointment (*Ana.* 20:3). The first thing that a noble character stands in awe of is the decree of heaven, and one who knows heaven's decree and does not reverence it is contemptuous (*Ana.* 16:8). The belief that life and destiny are ordained by heaven resulted in a tendency towards fatalism, a fatalism which is revealed in the writings of the Ch'un Ch'iu period, and in later disciples of Confucius whom Mo-tzŭ castigated. But Confucius' own views were not fatalistic. Heaven's ordainment is that man should walk in the way which heaven itself had laid down, but Confucius believed that man could choose to follow or reject heaven's ordainment. He was never in doubt that man could, in the exercise of his heaven-bestowed nature, walk in heaven's Way. That is what the sages of old, the *Shêng Jên,* had done, and on that account they were examples and models for men of later generations. The constant effort to walk in heaven's Way was the mark of the *chün-tzŭ,* or noble man. Thus in Confucius there was a strong sense of personal moral responsibility, and a belief that, in large measure, one's own destiny lies in one's own hands.

In seeking to conform himself to the Way of heaven the noble-hearted man is not merely conforming to human standards and laws, devised for the proper regulating of society, but is regulating his life in accordance with principles which are ordained by *T'ien* and which form the regulative principles of a cosmic order. Thus it is that the ethics of Confucius are rooted in religious belief. What really matters is that a man should be known by heaven (*Ana.* 14:37), and that 'Heaven gives birth to the power that is in him' (*Ana.* 7:22).

From his dominant concern with ethics, his reluctance to discuss the supernatural or life after death, and the infrequency of his references to heaven and the Way of heaven, it has been suggested that Confucius took the first step in divorcing ethics from religion,[12] and that his teaching is purely humanistic without any supernatural reference. Yet when we closely examine the basic concepts which underlie all his ethical teaching,[13] namely, the Way (*Tao*), Virtue (*Tê*), Love (*Jên*), Righteousness (*I*), and Propriety (*Li*), we find that these 'virtues' which characterise the 'perfect man' through whose influence and example society will move forward towards the ideal, are 'virtues' because they are the qualities which Confucius attributes to the governing and guiding principle of the universe. The cosmic order is what it is because of them. They are of the very nature of *T'ien.* Man becomes what he ought to be by modelling himself on *T'ien.* The teaching of Confucius is pervaded by a profound reverence for and belief in *T'ien.* He conceived *T'ien* as the author of his powers; found comfort in the knowledge that at least *T'ien* understood him though men failed to do so; and he called upon *T'ien* to vindicate him when he was subjected to calumny. He never seems to have had any doubt but that *T'ien* is righteous, and loving, and it is significant that Taoists of later times, in their attack on Confucianism, opposed Confucius on this very point by insisting that 'Heaven is not loving [*jên*], but treats all things as straw dogs'.[14]

If there is any one concept which we should consider as central in the teaching of Confucius it is the concept of 'The Way' (*Tao*). The character *Tao* meant originally a road or a path, and in that sense it is sometimes used in the *Analects* (9:11). Confucius, however, gives an extended meaning to this most important character, and it is significant that it is used more often in the *Analects* than in all the previous extant literature. A road is a way which a man travels in order to reach his goal or destination, and so becomes the way which one ought to travel in order to reach the heaven-ordained goal. For Confucius 'The Way' is not just a purely humanistic concept as some Chinese scholars have argued, that is 'The Way of Man', the Way laid down by earlier sages; but is fundamentally 'The Way of heaven', and consequently the way which heaven ordains for man to walk in. There is no thought here of the nameless, formless, self-existent, eternal principle which lies behind all phenomena, the metaphysical concept of the Taoists. The *Tao* of Confucius is the Way which wise and good men follow and always have followed as they sought to conform their lives to the will of heaven. It is therefore the way which all men of noble character should seek throughout their lives. The concept of the Way runs like a thread through the *Analects*: it is a Way characterised by love, righteousness, propriety and wisdom. It is the Way of reciprocity (*shu*) and loyalty (*chung*) in all human relationships. It is followed in perfect sincerity (*ch'êng*) and leads to harmony (*ho*).

If it is the will of heaven that the Way shall prevail, then the Way will prevail. (*Ana.* 14: 38)

Set your heart upon the Way, support yourself by its power, lean upon goodness, seek distraction in the arts. (7: 6)

In the morning, hear the Way; in the evening die content. (4: 8)

What I call a great minister is one who will only serve his prince whilst he can do so without infringement of the Way, and as soon as that is impossible, he resigns. (11: 23)

Wealth and rank are what everyone desires; but if they can only be obtained to the detriment of the Way he professes, he must relinquish them . . . never for a moment does a gentleman quit the Way of goodness. (4: 5)

Confucius had no doubt that a man could, if he so desired, follow the Way and attain to human perfection. There is in his thought no idea of a radical perversion of the will which could only be remedied by the grace of a saviour-god, nor of guilt so great that no personal amendment could wipe out its stain. He believed that man was by nature good and that *T'ien* itself had endowed him with that nature. Sin was man's failure to attain to a harmonious balance by means of which he could function as a perfect man, or else it was the disordered excess in the use of faculties and powers which needed to be kept ordered and disciplined.

Confucius did not teach, as some have supposed, that a man must rely entirely upon himself to attain perfection. *T'ien* was constantly before his eyes and on *T'ien* he could model himself. *T'ien's* way was written down for man to discover. Such discovery had already been made by ancient sages who in their day achieved perfection. They had left both example and precept for posterity to follow.

Though these sages, or *Shêng Jên,* were the supreme ideal of the perfect man, in the time of Confucius they were thought of as having attained divinisation, and Confucius himself never claimed to be of their rank. But he held up a practical ideal of perfection before men in the concept of the *chün-tzŭ* or princely man. Originally the *chün-tzŭ* were those who had been born into the hereditary nobility, but according to Confucius anyone might become a *chün-tzŭ* by self-cultivation and discipline. The *chün-tzŭ* was the man of noble or princely character, the true gentleman. In teaching this ideal of the *chün-tzŭ* Confucius developed his teaching concerning the cardinal virtues – love, righteousness, propriety and wisdom.

Confucius has sometimes been accused of being too much taken up by admiration of the great sages of ancient times, and of being too punctilious in respect of the narrow rules of conventional morality, ceremonial and etiquette. Yet again and again he gave proof of high moral courage and of a willingness to ignore convention if it conflicted with good feeling and common sense. The reason for this was the primacy which he gave to conscience and the stress which he laid on the inner quality of *jên* or the prompting of the heart as the source of right conduct, on motive rather than the outward act. He knew that among the ruling classes with whom he had to deal the greatest danger was the liberty which wealth, heredity and high rank gave them, a liberty which so easily turned to licence and self-indulgence. The powerful princes were a law unto themselves. Two things alone could restrain them from those excesses which would lead to the disintegration of society. Both these things receive great emphasis in the teaching of Confucius: *li,* which comprised a body of customary usage, the rules of propriety and decorum to govern all family and social relationships; and *jên,* that inner quality of the heart which gave serenity and poise, which integrated the inner personality, and resulted in the iron self-discipline of the princely man.

In setting forth his ideal as to how to attain to the Good Life in perfect accord with the will of heaven Confucius left no room for asceticism and self-mortification, nor did he believe that in the pursuit of personal perfection one should leave society and become a hermit or a recluse.

One cannot herd with birds and beasts. If I am not to be a man among other men, then what am I to be? If the Way prevailed under heaven, I should not be trying to alter things. (*Ana.* 18: 6)

An examination into Confucius' attitude towards and teaching about *li* and *jên* reveals the fundamental importance of religion to Confucius, both in its outward aspect of rites and ceremonies, and in its inner aspect of commitment to the will of heaven.

Though the character *li* has been variously translated as 'propriety, rites, ceremonies'[15] and the *li* of Confucius' day were the unwritten customary usages which regulated all the various relationships of society and family, an examination into the derivation of the character reveals that originally it was closely associated with the sacrificial cult by which the manes of the ancestors and the gods and spirits were worshipped and honoured. The books of rites which have come down to us, the *Li Chi,* the *I Li,* and the *Chou Li,* did not reach their present form till long after the time of Confucius,[16] and there is no doubt that in process of time simpler rites of an earlier age were much elaborated and adapted to changing circumstances. Yet these books may be trusted, in the main, to give us a true picture of the rites and ceremonies which were practised by the contemporaries of Confucius. Many of these rites were of a religious nature, particularly those appertaining to the ancestral temples, the earth altars, the cult of the dead, and the sacrifices which were made periodically to heaven, earth and the host of spiritual beings. All down through Chinese history from very early times the regular and correct performance of the rites has been considered essential for the peace and prosperity of the land and its people. That Confucius himself attached supreme importance to the performance of the *li* is witnessed to in the *Analects*. According to its teaching, the *li* provided guidance for the living, acted as a restraint on man's proclivity for evil, and provided a binding cement for society.

Yen Hui asked about Goodness [*jên*]. The master said, 'He who can himself submit to ritual [*li*] is Good. If [a ruler] could for one day himself submit to ritual, everyone under heaven would respond to his Goodness. For Goodness is something which must have its source in the ruler himself; it cannot be got from others.' Yen Hui said, 'I beg to ask for the more detailed items of this [submission to ritual].' The master said, 'To look at nothing in defiance of ritual, to listen to nothing in defiance of ritual, to speak nothing in defiance of ritual, never to stir hand or foot in defiance of ritual'.

(*Ana.* 12: 1–2)

In this quotation the *li,* which included all the religious ritual and ceremonial, is declared to be that by which the Goodness (*jên*) of man finds full expression. At the same time due observance of the *li* inevitably leads to a perfect control over all self-expression.

Courtesy not bounded by the prescriptions of ritual becomes tiresome, caution becomes timidity, daring becomes turbulence, inflexibility becomes harshness. (*Ana.* 8: 2)

While parents are alive, serve them according to *li.* When they die, bury them according to *li,* and sacrifice to them according to *li.* (2: 5)

To Confucius the sacrifices performed in the ancestral temple were so important that, if carried out improperly, he was not prepared to stay on after the libation had been poured out (*Ana.* 3:10). He believed that if anyone understood perfectly the significance of the rites he would be fitted to govern the whole land (*Ana.* 3:11). Princes must not think that it was sufficient to have sacrifices performed on their behalf in their absence. True sacrifices not only demanded one's own presence at the sacrifice, but also a sincere recognition that the ancestors or spirits to whom the sacrifices were made were also present (*Ana.* 3:12). When the disciple Tzŭ-Kung wished to dispense with the sheep which was presented in the temple on the first day of the new moon, Confucius said, 'You grudge the sheep, but I am concerned about the ritual' (*Ana.* 3:17). In all performance of the ritual sincerity and reverence were a *sine qua non.*

In the rites of mourning grief is more important than attention to detail.

(*Ana.* 3: 4)

Ritual performed without reverence and the rites of mourning performed without grief, – how can I look upon such things! (3: 26)

The master said, 'Ritual! ritual! Is it no more than the offering of jade and silk? Music! music! Is it no more than bells and drums?' (17: 11)

The master said, 'A man cannot be of truly noble character if he does not know heaven's commands. He will never be able to take his stand if he does not know the *li.*' (20: 3)

If the observance of *li* was the outward expression of the religious attitude of Confucius, the cultivation of *jên* was its inner dynamic. The character *jên* has been variously translated as 'love, goodness, benevolence, humaneness, man-to-man-ness', and in the *Analects* it is used in two senses; first, as one of the virtues, if indeed the greatest, in the sense of Love; and second, as the summation of all virtues, in the sense of perfect goodness. This was the quality which Confucius prized above all others, yet he was too humble to make any pretension to having attained to it (*Ana.* 7:33). Here was a supernatural grace, possessed only by *T'ien* and the divine sages of old. Yet, in a measure, all men could seek after it, and in so far as they lived by it they attained to the full stature of perfect manhood and fulfilled their appointed destiny as human beings.

It is *jên* which makes a neighbourhood beautiful. How can a man be called wise who does not settle in good [*jên*] surroundings? (*Ana.* 4: 1)

The master said, 'A man without *jên* cannot long abide in adversity, nor can he long enjoy happiness. Those who practise *jên* rest on *jên*, and the wise covet it.' (4: 2)

He who is bent on *jên* will do no evil. (4: 4)

I have never seen one who really loved *jên*, nor hated what was not *jên*. He who loved *jên* would esteem nothing above it; and he who hated what was not *jên* would practise *jên* and would allow nothing that was not *jên* to affect him. Is there anyone who for a single day is able to employ all his strength for *jên*? I have never seen one with insufficient strength. There may be such a person, but I have not seen him. (4: 6)

The master said, 'Is *jên* far off? I desire *jên* and *jên* is close at hand.' (7: 29)

Jên is self denial and a return to propriety [*li*]. For by self-denial and a return to propriety the whole world would return to *jên*. (12: 1)

Fan Ch'ih asked the meaning of *jên*. The master said, 'Love men'. (12: 21)

There may be a noble man [*chün-tzŭ*] who failed in *jên*, but never was there a mean man who possessed *jên*. (14: 7)

A man who possesses *jên* will not seek to preserve his life at the expense of *jên*. There are those who through death bring their *jên* to perfection. (15: 8)

Jên is of more importance to people than fire and water. I have seen men die through walking through water or fire, but I have never seen a man die through walking in *jên*. (15: 34)

Though these lofty sentiments by which Confucius spoke of *jên* may indeed characterise a humanism which is purely ethical and non-religious, when we take Confucius' teaching as a whole, with his emphasis on the will of heaven (*T'ien Ming*) on the Way (*Tao*), and on Love (*Jên*) as the summation of all virtues, we find that Confucius interprets these concepts as though they belonged to the nature of the spiritual power which lies behind and above the cosmic order. *Ming* is laid upon men at heaven's command; *Tao* is the Way which heaven ordains for men to walk in; *Jên* is the ideal goal of all men's striving because his heaven-born nature tells him that heaven is *jên*.

The teaching of Confucius is primarily an ethical philosophy which, if put into practice, will lead towards the ideal of a perfect man, the *chün-tzŭ* or *shêng jên*, and by extension to the final goal of universal harmony. But the original motive power for the transformation and the progress of human life lay in the directive principle of heaven's ordinance. Hence Confucius, in relating his own personal history, said 'At fifty I knew what were the biddings of heaven' (*Ana.* 2:4). Having reached that stage at which he was sensitive to the will of heaven for the direction of his own life he could proceed toward his goal of perfection. 'At sixty my ear was docile [to heaven's commands]. At seventy I could follow the dictates of my own heart, for what I desired no longer overstepped the boundaries of what is right' (*Ana.* 2:4). Though goodness was his supreme aim, he refused to dangle before men the expectation of reward for virtue either in this life or the next. As regards this life he knew from his own bitter experience that the pursuit of virtue may lead to suffering and poverty. As regards a life to come he seems to have been totally unconcerned. He was content to trust to all-virtuous *T'ien*. For him virtue was its own reward in the inner joy and contentment which it brought. Virtue must be practised for virtue's sake. It found its justification neither in the fear of punishment nor in the expectation of reward, but simply in the approval of heaven and one's own conscience.

If we define religion in broad terms, then Confucius was a deeply religious man. His ethical teaching and his humanitarianism were firmly based on the deepest religious insights of his own time. For him the rituals of the cultus had deep significance, and that is why he insisted that all ritual and ceremony were worthless without sincerity. He was convinced that there was a divine order which worked for love and righteousness, and taught that in obedience to that divine order man will find his highest good.

CHAPTER FOUR

CONFUCIAN INTERPRETERS: THE CHUNG YUNG; MENCIUS; HSÜN-TZŬ[1]

The teaching of Confucius was based, as we have seen, in a sincere reverence for heaven, a heaven which not only displayed its righteousness and benevolence in the harmonies of a cosmic order, but which conferred on man his moral nature, through the cultivation of which man could conform himself to the will of heaven. To attain such a state was 'sagehood' (*shêng jên*). The perfect sage not only attained to harmony, serenity, peace and joy in his own inner nature, but functioned, as heaven itself functions, so that his 'virtue' outflowed and pervaded the environment in which he lived, and exercised an influence throughout the whole sphere over which he ruled. Conforming to the 'will of heaven', and accepting the 'destiny' appointed to him by heaven, his inner life based on humanity and righteousness (*jên* and *i*) was reflected in all his external relationships in an absolute conformity to those standards of good behaviour (*li*) which tradition and customary usage had found to be conducive to the maintenance of a good society.

In the two and a half centuries immediately following on the death of Confucius the germinal ideas of this great teacher were destined to exert an ever increasing influence. His own disciples developed his teaching along several different lines, whilst rival systems, such as those of the Taoists and the Mohists, had to take account of him.

It happened with Confucius as with other great ethical and religious teachers that lesser minds took up various aspects of his teaching and over-emphasised or over-developed them to the obfuscation of other aspects which were equally important. According to the thirty-third chapter of *Chuang-tzŭ* a great number of schools grew up in the fourth and third centuries BC. Many of these, concerned with philosophical, ethical, social and political problems, are of great interest to the student but have little concern with religion as such. Some are frankly agnostic and even atheistical. They evidence practically no interest in or concern for the religious life and expression of the common people, except in so far as they reflect the scorn of the scholar class for beliefs and practices which they regarded as superstitious. Yet few of these writings deny the existence of a transcendental realm, a spiritual world, which men cannot afford entirely to neglect because its rulings impinge on human affairs and have a constant influence on human well-being.

Philosophical thought in these post-Confucian times was predominantly humanistic or naturalistic. The main concern was with the good life here and now. There is a remarkable absence of concern for man's destiny beyond the grave, a concern, however, which is far from being absent from the thought of ordinary people.

The *Chung Yung* (*Doctrine of the Mean*), attributed to Tzŭ Ssŭ, the grandson of Confucius, contains passages which are profoundly moving in their religious apprehension and mystical insight. The *Book of Mencius*, besides its lively discussion of human nature and its insistence on the prime importance of righteousness, recognises the all-pervading 'moving-force' of heaven. As Professor W. T. Chan writes, 'The *Doctrine of the Mean* is religious and mystical. It comes very close to the more mystical aspects of the *Book of Mencius*, and several passages are almost identical in the two works.'[2] Though Hsün-tzu was probably more responsible than anyone else for the humanistic or purely naturalistic bias of Confucianism as it developed, his doctrine of human nature and his emphasis on the rites (*li*) are of such interest to the student of religion that his teachings must be noted.

The Chung Yung[3]

The *Chung Yung*, or *Doctrine of the Mean*, is grounded in that deeply religious concept 'The Way of heaven', a Way which transcends time, space, substance and motion, and is at the same time unceasing and eternal.[4] The harmony which characterises the Way of heaven and which prevails throughout the universe is the same which underlies the moral nature of man. In fact, man and nature form a unity.

The *Chung Yung* recognises the omnipresence of spiritual beings, and therefore the importance of sacrificing to them.

> How abundant is the display of power of spiritual beings! We look for them but we do not see them. We listen to them but we do not hear them. They form the substance of all things and nothing can be without them. They cause all people in the world to fast and purify themselves and put on

their richest dresses to perform sacrifices to them. Like the spread of overflowing water they seem to be above and to be on the left and right.

(Chapter 16)

The ceremonics of sacrifices to heaven and earth are meant for the service of the Lord on high, and the ceremonies performed in the ancestral temple are meant for the service of the ancestors. (Chapter 19)

The doctrine of the unity of man with heaven and earth has always greatly impressed the Chinese. Much later it assumed great importance in the neo-Confucianism of the Sung dynasty.

Only those who are absolutely sincere can develop fully their nature. If they can fully develop their nature, they can fully develop the nature of others. If they can fully develop the nature of others, then they can fully develop the nature of things. If they can fully develop the nature of things, then they can assist in the transforming and nourishing processes of heaven and earth. If they can assist in the transforming and nourishing processes of heaven and earth, they can form a trinity with heaven and earth.

(Chapter 22)

It is interesting to find in the *Chung Yung* a reasoned justification of divination, which from earliest times occupied an important place in Chinese religion. Calamity or blessing to nation or individual were regarded as being in large measure due to the activities of spiritual beings which, however, give warning of what they intend to do by means of omens and extraordinary phenomena. Absolute sincerity gives one a spiritual power of discernment by which to prognosticate concerning these omens.

It is characteristic of absolute sincerity to be able to foreknow. When a nation or family is about to flourish, there are sure to be lucky omens. When a nation or family is about to perish, there are sure to be unlucky omens. These omens are revealed in divination and in the movements of the four limbs. When calamity or blessing is about to come [through divination] one can surely know beforehand if it is good or evil. Therefore he who has absolute sincerity is like a spirit. (Chapter 24)

The way of absolute sincerity is 'the Way of heaven and earth'. It is 'without doubleness, and so produces things in an unfathomable way'. It is 'deep, extensive, light, brilliant, infinite and lasting' (ch. 26). In the same way, 'The way of the sage is great. Overflowing, it produces and nourishes all things, and rises up to the height of heaven' (ch. 27).

The image of the perfect sage in the *Chung Yung*, set forth as the goal of all human attainment, cannot be understood in purely humanistic terms. It possesses a transcendental quality. The sage has risen to a height at which he understands heaven and co-operates in the divine processes by which the universe is sustained.

> Only those who are absolutely sincere can order and adjust the great relations of mankind, establish the great foundations of humanity, and know the transforming and nourishing operations of heaven and earth. Does he depend on anything else? How earnest and sincere – he is humanity! How deep and unfathomable – he is the abyss! How vast and great – he is heaven! Who can know him except he who has quickness of apprehension, intelligence, sageliness and wisdom, and understands the character of heaven?
>
> (Chapter 32)

Mencius[5]

Mencius was not primarily a religious teacher but, like Confucius before him, his ethical teaching, his political insights and his mysticism are grounded in a clear sense of mission and in a deep reverence for heaven. His distinctive doctrine of the goodness of human nature is based upon the belief that that nature is heaven-bestowed. The importance he attached to righteousness as a supreme moral value rested on the fact that he attributed righteousness to heaven.

It is said that Mencius studied under the disciples of the great Tzŭ Ssŭ, grandson of Confucius. As an interpreter of Confucius his stature grew with the process of time till, in the Sung dynasty, he was accepted as second only to Confucius himself, and the book which bears his name was studied, along with the *Analects*, the *Chung Yung* and the *Ta Hsüeh*, by every aspiring scholar. Of his reverence for Confucius there can be no doubt. He himself said, 'Now what I desire to do is to study to be like Confucius' (2a:22). The *Book of Mencius*, from which his teachings are derived, was compiled by the disciples of Mencius after his death. It comprises seven chapters, each divided into two parts.

Almost nothing is known for certain concerning Mencius' family or private life. He is reputed to have lived from about 372 to 289 BC. The *Shih Chi* of Ssŭ-ma Ch'ien records that he was a native of Tsou (in modern Shantung), and that he received his education from the disciples of Tzŭ Ssŭ. He travelled to serve King Hsüan of Ch'i, but the latter was unable to employ him. He went to the state of Liang, but

King Hui of Liang was insincere. At that time the state of Ch'in was employing the services of the Lord of Shang to enrich itself. Ch'u and Wei were employing Wu Ch'i to conquer weaker states. The kings Wei and Hsüan of Ch'i were employing the great military strategists Sun-tzŭ and T'ien Chi with the result that the feudal lords faced east so as to pay homage to Ch'i. The states of China were engaged in forming alliances, and held fighting as something worthy. Mencius, on the other hand, was intent on transmitting the virtues of T'ang, Yü and the three dynasties (Hsia, Shang and Chou), so that those whom he visited were not willing to listen to him. So he retired and with his disciples Wan Chang and others he put the *Shih Ching* and the *Shu Ching* in order, transmitted the doctrines of Confucius and composed the *Book of Mencius* in seven chapters.[6] From this we gather that Mencius, like Confucius, was a professional teacher, and that he reverenced the sage-kings of ancient times, and himself lived in a time of political and social ferment. The state of Tsou, where he was born, bordered on the state of Lu, and was reputed to be a centre of Confucian influence. The *Book of Chuang-tzŭ* refers to the Confucians as 'gentlemen and teachers of Tsou and Lu'.[7]

Mencius took up the theme of human nature as bestowed by heaven, but whereas Confucius had tacitly assumed that human nature is 'good', Mencius sought to prove that man is in his original nature 'good' and built his philosophy upon that premiss. His ethical and political ideals are based on this belief in the essential goodness of human nature. He taught that all political and social institutions are for the benefit of the people, and in this respect was much ahead of his times. He believed that the only one fit to govern was one who had nourished his heaven-bestowed nature so as to become a sage-king, and he deprecated government by the *Pa* or feudal tyrant.

He who uses force and makes a pretence of virtue is a *pa* [tyrant]. He who using virtue practises human-heartedness is a king . . . When one subdues men by force, they do not submit in their hearts and only submit because their strength is insufficient. When one subdues men by virtue, in their heart of hearts they are pleased and sincerely submit. (2a. 4)

The people are the most important element [in a state]; the spirits of the land and grain are secondary; and the ruler is least. Therefore, to gain the peasantry is the way to become king. (7b. 14)

He who outrages human-heartedness is a robber; he who outrages righteousness is a ruffian. (1b. 8)

In his exposition of love, loyalty and reciprocity Confucius had limited their applicability to the self-cultivation of the individual. Mencius extended their application to government and society. The ideal institutions of society constitute what Mencius calls 'the kingly way'. Such a way can only function if the inherent goodness of human nature is accepted.

All men have a mind which cannot bear [to see the sufferings of] others. The early kings, having this 'unbearing mind' produced an equally sensitive government. (2a. 6)

Treat as befits old age the elders of your family, so as to extend this treatment to the elders of others; treat as befits youth the young of your family, so as to extend this treatment to the young of others; do this, and the empire may be made to revolve in the palm of your hand. (1a. 7)

All men have a mind which cannot bear to see the sufferings of others. . . . If to-day men see a child about to fall into a well, they will without exception experience a feeling of alarm and distress. This will not be as a way whereby to gain the favour of the parents of the child, nor whereby they may seek the praise of their neighbours and friends, nor that they are so because they dislike the reputation of being unvirtuous. From this case we may perceive that he who lacks the feeling of commiseration is not a man; that he who lacks a feeling of shame and dislike is not a man; that he who lacks a feeling of modesty and yielding is not a man; and that he who lacks a sense of right and wrong is not a man. The feeling of commiseration is the beginning of love [*jên*]. The feeling of shame and dislike is the beginning of righteousness [*i*]. The feeling of modesty and yielding is the beginning of propriety [*li*]. The sense of right and wrong is the beginning of wisdom [*chih*]. Man has these four beginnings just as he has four limbs. When, having these four beginnings, he says he is incapable [of developing them] he is injuring himself. And when he says of his ruler that he is incapable, he is injuring his ruler.

Since all men have these four beginnings, let them know to give them their full development and completion, and the result will be like fire that begins to burn, or a spring that has begun to find vent. Let them have their complete development, and they will suffice to protect all within the four seas. Let them be denied that development, and they will not suffice for serving his parents. (2a. 6)

When Mencius affirms that human nature is good, he means that the natures of all men have within them the capacity for goodness, not that men's natures are entirely perfect. Men all possess the shoots of the cardinal virtues, and if those shoots are nourished and trained in the right way they will reach their full development in the perfect sage. When a man is not good, it does not mean that he is lacking in the basic material by which to become good. His badness results from the fact that he has not developed the shoots of goodness within him or has allowed them to be suppressed or warped.

But why should men develop these shoots of goodness? Mo-tzŭ, whom Mencius criticised, taught that such development brought benefit to the individual and to society. That is, he applies a pragmatic test: goodness in the long run is beneficial, and badness is harmful. Mencius taught that the shoots of goodness should be developed because it is through the exercise of virtues that man is 'human'.

> That by which man differs from the birds and beasts is but slight. The mass of the people cast it away, whereas the superior man preserves it. (4b. 19)

That which distinguishes man from animals is the human mind. A mind capable of reasoning is man's special prerogative, and this is 'what heaven has given to man'. It is the nobler part of his being. It is this which constitutes the part of man which Mencius calls 'great' (*ta t'i*). The senses – hearing, seeing, tasting, etc. – are shared by man in common with the animals. They constitute the part of man which is 'small' (*hsiao t'i*).

> Man's nature implies all that whereby man is human, and when this nature is lost, man becomes one with the beasts. (4a. 19)

Therefore man must accord with reason and righteousness so that he may follow that part of himself which is great. In this way he will preserve that heaven-bestowed nature which makes him human.

> The way in which a man loses his goodness of mind [*liang hsin*] is like the way in which trees are denuded by axes and bills. Hewn down day after day, can they retain their beauty? But there is a restoration of its [the mind] life every night, and in the calm atmosphere of early morning it feels to a degree those desires and aversions which are proper to humanity. But the feeling is not strong, and is fettered and destroyed by what takes place during the day. This fettering takes place again and again. The restorative influence of the night is not sufficient to preserve [the mind's natural goodness], and when

this proves insufficient it [the mind] becomes not much different from that of the irrational animals. (6a. 8, 2)

The supreme purpose of man is to serve heaven and to fulfil the destiny which heaven has conferred upon him. The heaven of Mencius is no longer the anthropomorphic deity of earlier times, yet heaven may be known and served. Heaven is righteous and preserves its own nobility, and ordains for man his destiny.

He who exerts his mind to the utmost knows his nature. He who knows his nature knows heaven. To preserve one's mind and to nourish one's nature is to serve heaven. Not to allow any double-mindedness regarding the longevity or brevity of life, but to cultivate one's person and wait for heaven's decree to take its course is to fulfil one's destiny. (7a. 1)

The acceptance of the doctrine of the fundamental goodness of human nature, and the belief that evil is due to lack of proper nourishment and care led Mencius to stress the importance of love (*jên*) and righteousness (*i*) in government, in education and within the circle of the family. As Professor W. T. Chan writes, 'In Mencius the ideal of righteousness assumed unprecedented importance. He was the first one to raise righteousness to the highest level in moral values.'[8]

Love, righteousness, propriety and wisdom are not drilled into us from outside. We originally have them in us. Only we do not think [to find them]. Therefore it is said, 'Seek and you will find it; neglect and you will lose it.' (6a. 1)

With proper nourishment and care everything grows, whereas without proper nourishment and care everything decays. (6a. 8)

I like life and I like righteousness. If I cannot have both of them, I shall give up life and choose righteousness. I love life, but there is something which I love more than life, and therefore I will not do anything improper to have it. (6a. 10)

Righteousness is man's path. Pity the man who abandons the path and does not follow it. (6a. 11)

According to Mencius true nobility consists of love, righteousness, loyalty and faithfulness, and these are characteristics of heaven. The 'nobility of heaven' is contrasted with the 'nobility of man'. The ancient sages, in seeking to cultivate the nobility of heaven, sought to perfect themselves in the cardinal virtues and thus they also achieved the nobility of man. Mencius scorned those who, having attained to rank, wealth and honour among men, forsook the nobility of heaven (6a. 16).

Mencius' firm belief in heaven is shown in his answer to the disciple, Wan Chang, when he asked, 'Is it true that Yao gave the empire to Shun?' 'No', replied Mencius, 'the emperor cannot give the empire to another person . . . heaven gave it to him.' 'By heaven's giving it to him, do you mean that heaven gave it to him in so many words?' 'No, heaven does not speak. It simply showed its will through Shun's personal character and his conduct of affairs . . . The emperor can recommend a person to heaven, but he cannot make heaven give that man the empire . . . Yao recommended Shun to heaven and heaven accepted him . . . He had him preside over the sacrifices and all the spiritual being enjoyed them. This means that heaven accepted him (5a. 5).'

When heaven is about to confer a great responsibility on any man, it will exercise his mind with suffering, subject his sinews and joints to hard work, expose his body to hunger, put him to poverty, place obstacles in his path, so as to stimulate his mind, harden his nature and improve him in that wherein he is incompetent. (6b. 15)

'It is difficult', writes Professor Chan, 'to say how strong the element of mysticism is in Mencius, but there is no doubt that it is present in him as it is in the *Doctrine of the Mean*.'[9] Mencius spoke of a 'strong moving force', a vital, active force which man is capable of nourishing. It is difficult for him to describe, for it properly belongs to the realm of the transcendental.

As power, it is exceedingly great and strong. If nourished by uprightness and not injured, it will fill up all between heaven and earth. As power, it is accompanied by righteousness and the Way. Without them it will be devoid of nourishment. It is produced by the accumulation of righteous deeds, but is not obtained by incidental acts of righteousness. (2a. 2, 13–15)

Mencius conceived of the sage as reaching to a stage of existence which is beyond our knowledge. He becomes 'a man of the spirit'.

When one is great and completely transformed, he is called a sage. When a sage is beyond our knowledge, he is called a man of the spirit. (7b. 25)

He who dwells in the wide house of the world, stands in the correct station in the world, walks in the great path of the world; one who practises virtues along with the people when he is successful, and practises the Way alone when he is disappointed; one whose heart cannot be dissipated by power, wealth and honours, who cannot be influenced by poverty and humble station, who cannot be subdued by force and might – such a person is a great man. (3b. 2)

Whenever a spiritual man passes through, transformation follows. Wherever he abides, there is a spiritualising influence. This flows abroad, above and below, together with heaven and earth. How can it be said that such an one mends society in a small way! (7a. 13)

Hsün-tzŭ[10]

In a chapter dealing with the development of Confucian religious ideas in the period between Confucius and the establishment of the Han dynasty, some attention must be given to Hsün-tzŭ. He belonged to the generation following that of Mencius and lived between 298 and 238 BC. He is perhaps responsible more than any other thinker for the trend in Confucianism towards a purely naturalistic or humanistic bias. He exerted a greater influence than did Mencius on the development of Confucianism during the great Han dynasty (206 BC–AD 220). He owed much to the Taoists and his concept of *T'ien* (heaven) in opposition to the views of both Confucius and Mencius was purely naturalistic.

We are told that Hsün-tzŭ was a native of Chao, a state which comprised the southern parts of present-day Hopei and Shansi. When fifty years of age he spread his ideas in Ch'i where, at three different periods, he was the official in charge of the sacrificial wine offerings. Being slandered in Ch'i, he went to Ch'u and became magistrate of the city of Lan-ling. His two most famous disciples, Han-fei and Li-ssŭ, were in large measure responsible for the rise of the state of Ch'in to a totalitarianism which for a time controlled the whole of China.

Hsün-tzŭ was a man of great intellect, a poet and a philosopher. He was particularly skilful in criticising other schools of thought. The people of his day 'gave their attention to magic and prayers, and believed in omens and good luck'. Against all forms of superstition Hsün-tzŭ raised the voice of protest. He honoured Confucius as a man whose learning was 'most complete, exhaustive and refined'. Whereas Mencius placed the supreme emphasis on love (*jên*) and righteousness (*i*) Hsün-tzŭ laid greatest emphasis on the rites (*li*) and on the necessity for education and training. Whereas Mencius was idealistic, Hsün-tzŭ was materialistic. His attitude to the great institutions of the Chou dynasty was conservative, for he believed that through them the people could be best controlled and educated.

The following quotations illustrate Hsün-tzŭ's attitude as regards *T'ien*.

If the right way of life [*tao*] is cultivated and not opposed, then heaven cannot send misfortune . . . but if the fundamentals for life are neglected and used extravagantly, then heaven cannot cause a country to be rich.

Book 17. (Dubs Transl., p. 173)[11]

Heaven has a constant regularity of activity. Respond to it with good government, and success will be the result. Respond to it with misgovernment, and calamity will result . . . To make complete without acting, and to obtain without seeking; that is what is meant by the activity of heaven. . . . Heaven has its seasons, earth has its material resources, man has his government. That is what is meant by forming a trinity. (Book 17)

Heaven cannot make a country poor; and if the supply of foodstuffs is complete and energy supplied at the right times, heaven cannot make the people sick; and if the right way is being cultivated, heaven cannot send down calamities. (Book 17)

If the people pray for rain and get rain, why is this? I answer: there is no reason for it. If the people do not pray for rain, it will nevertheless rain. When people save the sun or moon from being eaten [at an eclipse] or when they pray for rain in a drought, and when they decide an important affair only after divination, – this is not because they think in this way they will get what they seek, but only to gloss over the matter. Hence the prince thinks it is glossing over the matter, but the people think it is supernatural.

(Book 17)

In the above passages we see how Hsün-tzŭ is influenced by the Taoist teaching that the activity of heaven is to complete without acting and to obtain without seeking. He is quite sure that the most fervent prayers and sacrifices will do nothing to change the course of events. If rain is due, it will rain. No amount of divination will alter events which are pre-determined. Yet intelligent rulers, though they know this, still engage their diviners because they pander to the superstitions of their people.

Mencius believed that man's nature derived from heaven, and this formed the basis of his teaching that human nature is good. Hsün-tzŭ's heaven is naturalistic and contains no ethical principle, and so, though he too accepted the doctrine that man's mind, emotions and faculties are derived in the first place from heaven, he believed that there was no inherent tendency to goodness. In fact, human nature is originally evil, for a human being, following his inherent tendencies, seeks only self-advantage and pleasure. If men follow their original natures the result is inevitably anarchy and chaos, and hence mutual destruction. So men, to avoid destruction, learn by experience to order human societies, to give over control to intelligent and wise rulers, appointing them to govern and control. Men learn to value education. Though by nature evil, they have the intelligence to seek after the attainment of perfection, to educate themselves in love (*jên*) and righteousness (*i*), and place themselves under the kingly authority of those who have advanced farther than others on the road to perfection.

The nature of man is evil. His goodness is only acquired training.... To give rein to man's original nature, to follow man's feelings, inevitably results in strife and rapacity, together with the violation of etiquette and confusion in the proper way of doing things, and reverts to a state of violence. (Book 23)

In ancient times the sage-kings knew that man's nature was evil, selfish, vicious, unrighteous, rebellious, and of itself did not bring about good government. For this reason they created the rules of proper conduct (*li*) and justice (*i*); they established laws and ordinances to force and beautify the natural feelings of man, thus rectifying them. (Book 23)

Mencius maintained that the teachability of men means that their congenital nature is good. My reply is that this is not so. Mencius failed to understand man's nature, nor did he examine into the parts played respectively by the congenital nature and the acquired. What belongs to the congenital nature is from heaven. It cannot be learned nor can it be worked for: whereas the spirit of ritual-and-righteousness which the sage-kings brought into existence, that is what men have to learn if they are to become morally capable and arrive at completion. (Book 23)

Someone may put the question: if man's nature is evil, how do ritual-and-righteousness come to be? The answer is that all forms of ritual-and-righteousness are born of the acquired [character] of sage men, and do not have their origin in the nature of men. (Book 23)

If the authority of the ruler was removed and the transformation effected by ritual-and-righteousness, the strong would rob and maltreat the weak, the many would oppress and shout down the few. In no time there would be universal anarchy, everybody destroying everybody else. (Book 23)

Yet, though human nature is regarded as evil by Hsün-tzŭ, he did admit that men possessed a faculty of intelligence, and that they are capable of learning. Thus, though emotions (*ch'ing*) are the material of human nature, and desires are the reaction of emotions to external stimuli, man's intelligence leads him to consider and determine what desires are permissible, guiding but not wholly repressing them.

According to Hsün-tzŭ there is a standard or 'Way' (*tao*) to be followed which will lead to justice, virtue and proper conduct, and hence to human happiness. Man's intellect can be trained to weigh each possible aspect of benefit or harm. But how does man know the 'Way'? Because from birth he possesses a capacity for knowledge, and with this a power of memory to store things. Nevertheless, the mind is so constituted that the memory does not interfere with the reception of new impressions. The mind can also differentiate, yet underlying all the differentiation there is an essential unity. The mind is always active, even in dreams, yet this activity does not disturb the knowledge already gained. Behind all the activity there is a fundamental quiescence. The qualities of emptiness, quiescence and unity which characterise the mind make possible for man the attainment of a standard or balance by which to guide and restrain his desires, to choose the greater benefit and the lesser harm. Here Hsün-tzŭ reveals both Taoist and Mohist influence upon his thinking, and is pointing the way to that synthesis o various strands of thought which resulted in the orthodox Confucianism of the Han dynasty.

Hsün-tzŭ laid great stress on the ceremonies, rites, proprieties and customary laws (*li*) by which society is ordered and human relationships beautified. In some passages he equates *li* with *tao*, the principle by which heaven and earth unite to produce all things.

> *Li* is that whereby heaven and earth unite, whereby the sun and moon are bright, whereby the four seasons are ordered, whereby the stars move in their courses, whereby rivers flow, whereby all things prosper, whereby love and hatred are tempered, whereby joy and anger keep their proper place.
>
> (Book 19)

The *li* included, of course, the ceremonies, rituals and sacrifices by which spiritual beings and the spirits of ancestors were worshipped. Hsün-tzŭ himself acted as officer in charge of the sacrificial wine offerings in the state of Ch'i. As he did not believe in a personal or purposive heaven, nor in spiritual beings, nor in life after death, how could he justify the making of sacrifices and the offering of prayers to heaven and the spirits of the deceased ancestors? How far can sacrifice and prayer continue to have significance if one's intelligence denies that there are spiritual beings to accept the sacrifices and answer the prayers? The attempt of Hsün-tzŭ to deal with this problem is of great interest to the student of religion. Though Hsün-tzŭ claimed that reason leads men to deny the existence of spiritual beings and the possibility of life after death, their powerful emotions demand satisfaction. The *li* therefore have poetic significance in that by them men's emotions are controlled and satisfied. By them man's life is beautiful and enriched. From his entrance upon life at birth, and throughout his whole life until the curtain of finality is drawn over him at death, the appropriate ceremonies and rituals order his life in conformity to a natural law which regulates the whole universe of which he forms a part. The rites of worship are thus a poetic expression of man's conformity to the majestic processes of natural law, whilst the rites of death and mourning are a beautiful and deeply satisfying way of controlling and ordering those emotions of joy and sorrow, tenderness and grief which the memory of close human relationships inevitably calls forth.

> Birth is the beginning of man; death is the end of man; when the end and the beginning are both beautiful, the way [*tao*] of man is complete. Hence the superior man respects the beginning and venerates the end. (Book 19)

> All rites, if for the service of the living, are to beautify joy; or if to send off the dead, they are to beautify sorrow; or if for sacrifice, they are to beautify reverence; or if they are military, they are to beautify majesty. . . . Service of the living is beautifying their life; sending off the dead is beautifying their end; when the end and the previous life are both attended to, the way [*tao*] of the sage is completed. (Book 19)

> Sacrifice is because of the emotions produced by memories, ideas, thoughts, longings; it is the extreme of loyalty, faithfulness, love and reverence; it is the greatest thing of the rites [*li*] and of beautiful actions. (Book 19)

Hsün-tzŭ represents a strong naturalistic, rationalistic and empirical strain in Confucian ideology. His influence has been very great. Yet his attempt to explain away the cult of ancestors and the elaborate cult for the worship of heaven and all spiritual beings was not acceptable to the majority of the Chinese people. In spite of the purely humanistic tendencies of Confucian orthodoxy after the time of Hsün-tzŭ, the majority of the people held on to a belief in transcendental values and to a hope of personal significance beyond the grave. In the long run it was Mencius, rather than Hsün-tzŭ, who was recognised as the greatest interpreter of Confucius, whilst religious Taoism and Buddhism came to have an irresistible appeal to the common people.

CHAPTER FIVE

THE RELIGION OF MO-TZŬ

Mo-tzŭ or Mo-ti was undoubtedly one of the greatest of the religious and ethical thinkers of ancient China. Though there is no definite evidence from ancient Chinese sources respecting either the time or place of his birth, the consensus of scholarly opinion indicates that he was born in the state of Lu about or soon after the death of Confucius (479 BC), and that he died in the early years of the fourth century BC, some ten or more years before the birth of Mencius.[1] For some two hundred years after his death the followers of Mo-tzŭ were numerous and influential, but with the gradual triumph of Confucianism, Mohism as a cohesive movement died out. It is even doubtful if the Mohist scriptures would have been preserved had it not been for the interest taken in them by Taoists.

The neglect of Mo-tzŭ over the centuries seems surprising when we have regard to what some modern scholars have written concerning him. His teaching has been described as socialism. He has been called the anticipator of Rousseau's *Social Contract,* and of J. S. Mill's *Utilitarianism.* He has been called a puritan and a pacifist, and compared with the great Hebrew prophets of the eighth century BC. He was an ethical and political teacher of the highest rank. He was the exponent of universal love. As the great twentieth-century Chinese philosopher, Hu Shih, writes, he was 'the only Chinese who may be said to have founded a religion'.[2] Reference to him and his works are to be found in many ancient Chinese books: *Chuang-tzŭ, Mencius,* the *Huai-nan-tzŭ,* and the *Lü-shih-ch'un ch'iu.* Yet Ssŭ-ma Ch'ien in his famous *Historical Records* accords to him exactly twenty-four words.

A revival of interest in Mo-tzŭ took place in the eighteenth century with the publication of an edition of his works together with a commentary by Pi-yüan in 1783. Interest in Mo-tzŭ continued to grow through the nineteenth and early twentieth centuries, and many Western scholars saw in many of his teachings a remarkable likeness to Christian teaching. A standard edition and commentary by Sung-jang was published in 1894 and revised in 1907. An edition of his most significant works in English translation was made by Y. P. Mei, together with a book expounding his teaching.[3]

In his early years Mo-tzŭ studied under the Confucian scholar, Shih-chio, a man well versed in the rites and ceremonies which were carried out at the ancestral temples and at the border sacrifices. But Mo-tzŭ became extremely critical of the Confucians of his own day. He came to the conclusion that many of their rites served no useful purpose, that they were based on false doctrines and that, being wealth-consuming, they led to the impoverishment of the people. He developed his own distinctive teaching, the substance of which, as set down by Mo-tzŭ's disciples, is found in the fifty-three extant chapters of Mo-tzŭ's works.[4] The main ethical and religious teachings of Mo-tzŭ are contained in twenty-four so-called synoptic chapters, because in the majority of them the teachings of the Master are recorded in three different versions. This is probably due to the fact that, after Mo-tzŭ's death, his movement split into three factions each with its own leader. Five other chapters give us recorded sayings of Mo-tzŭ and anecdotes concerning him, very much after the style of the *Analects of Confucius*.

There is considerable evidence to show that Mo-tzŭ trained and bound in loyalty to himself a considerable body of disciples, who were well-disciplined and responsible to their leader, and gave to him their undivided allegiance. The *Huai-nan-tzŭ* says, 'Those who followed Mo-tzŭ were one hundred and eighty men, all of whom he could have made to enter fire or tread upon knife-blades, and whom even death would not have prevented from following one another.'[5]

Mo-tzŭ has been strongly criticised for his utilitarianism and for his emphasis on what was profitable or beneficial. It has been argued, not without justification, that for him the value of an action was not that it was intrinsically good, but in what it was good for. His great aim was to benefit mankind, and in consequence he deplored what was inimical to human well-being, and sought to promote what was conducive to human well-being. This attitude, however, grew out of his profound belief in a righteous and loving God (heaven), in the will of heaven and in the Way (*Tao*) of heaven. It is significant that the phrase *Tao Chiao* (the teaching concerning *Tao,* or the religion of the *Tao*) was first used by Mo-tzŭ. Confucius and the Taoists both spoke of *Tao,* and in the *Chung Yung* the two characters *Tao* and *Chiao* are first brought into close juxtaposition, but are not yet fused to become one term. 'What we call nature is decreed by heaven; what directs nature is *Tao*; and what cultivates the *Tao* is *Chiao*.'[6] In the *Works of Mo-tzŭ,* in the chapter 'Against Confucianism' it says, 'But the *Ju* [scholars] in regard to *Tao Chiao* are men who injure the whole land', and in the chapter entitled *Kêng Chu* it says, 'That by which all men live is the *Tao Chiao* of former kings'.[7] Here Mo-tzŭ is speaking of the religion of the rulers of ancient times. Y. P. Mei characterises the religion of Mo-tzŭ as 'a revival of the old orthodox cult of a personal God not only at the head of numerous other spiritual beings but also crowning the ethico-political hierarchy in the human world'.[8]

Mo-tzŭ has been called a pacifist because his works reveal an intense hatred of the offensive warfare so prevalent in his day, but instances are recorded in which he himself went to the defence of small states which were being unjustly attacked. He saw how constant warfare impoverished the common people whom he loved, and brought calamity to the whole land, calamity which he believed to be an expression of the anger of heaven. He spoke against the extravagance, ostentation and luxury of the princes with the passion of an Amos. He stood out against partiality and nepotism in the appointment of men to state office. He opposed the prevailing determinism which taught that fate controlled all things and therefore must just be accepted. His whole teaching is based on his belief in heaven, and along with this belief went a reverence for spiritual beings, which, he believed, under the supreme control of heaven, influenced the lives of men.

Some of the most moving passages in the *Works of Mo-tzŭ* are contained in the chapters on the will of heaven, from which the following quotations are taken.

I know heaven loves men dearly not without reason. Heaven ordered the sun, moon and stars to enlighten and guide them. Heaven ordained the four seasons to regulate them. Heaven sent down snow, frost, rain and dew to grow the five grains and flax and silk so that people could use and enjoy them. . . . Now heaven loves the whole world universally. Everything is prepared for the good man. *Ch. Will of Heaven* (2)

(See Y. P. Mei, *Works*, p.145)[9]

I know heaven is more honourable and wise than the emperor for a reason: When the emperor practises virtue heaven rewards, when the emperor does evil heaven punishes. When there are disease and calamities the emperor will purify and bathe himself and prepare clean cakes and wine to do sacrifice and libation to heaven and the spirits. Heaven then removes them. But I have not heard of heaven invoking the emperor for blessing. . . . Therefore, righteousness surely comes from Heaven. (2, pp. 141–2)

A proverb says, 'Sinning in broad daylight, whither can one flee?' Really there is nowhere to flee. For heaven clearly discerns it, even if it be in the woods, valleys or solitary caves, where there is no man. (1, p. 135)

Now what does heaven desire and what does it abominate? Heaven desires righteousness and abominates unrighteousness. Therefore in leading the people of the world to engage in doing righteousness, I should be doing what heaven desires. When I do what heaven desires, heaven will also do what I desire. (1, p. 136)

But how do we know that heaven desires righteousness and abominates unrighteousness? With righteousness the world lives and without it, it dies; with it the world becomes rich, and without it the world becomes poor. With it the world becomes orderly, and without it the world becomes chaotic. And heaven likes to have the world live, and dislikes to have it die. (1, p. 136)

To obey the will of heaven is to have righteousness as a standard. To oppose the will of heaven is to accept force as a standard. (1, p. 139)

The will of heaven is to me like the compasses of a wheelwright or the square of a carpenter. (1, p. 140)

Though Mo-tzŭ believed that heaven loves all men impartially, he traced the evils of his time to the fact that men do not love one another altruistically. Such love as they have is partial and selective. This partiality is shown by the Confucians in their dominant concern for family and clan. It must be replaced by universal love.

All the calamities, strifes, complaints and hatreds in the world have arisen out of want of mutual love. (*Universal Love*, 2, p.82)

As he loves his own family and not the families of others, the thief steals from other families to profit his own. (1, p. 79)

Suppose everybody in the world loves universally, loving others as oneself. Will there yet be any unfilial individual? When everyone regards his father, elder brother and emperor as himself, whereto can he direct any unfilial feeling? (1, p. 79)

Mo-tzŭ shows that the way to mutual love is one of regarding other people's lives and possessions with the same respect as one does one's own. But it was objected that this was only a distant and unattainable ideal. Mo-tzŭ countered this by the utilitarian argument that, if men consider their own proper interests, they will follow the way of love in order to benefit themselves. Also he claims that universal love is not impossible because in ancient times it was practised by Yü the Great and by King Wên and other worthies. Mo-tzŭ has been severely criticised because of his utilitarian approach, but we need to remember that he was dealing with rulers who had no other standard except self-interest.

When we try to develop and procure benefits for the world with universal love as our standard, then attentive ears and keen eyes will respond in service to one another, then limbs will be strengthened to work for one another, and those who know the *Tao* will untiringly instruct others.
(*Universal Love,* 2, p. 89)

Mo-tzŭ recognised that the application of his teaching did not always bring the benefits that he hoped for. The world was in such an appalling state that the results of his efforts might appear to be negligible. So one must look at a man's intentions. If his intentions are good, one must approve; if his motives are evil, one must condemn.

Wu-ma-tzŭ said to Mo-tzŭ: Though you love universally, the world cannot be said to be benefited: though I do not love [universally], the world cannot be said to be injured. Since neither of us has accomplished anything, what makes you then praise yourself and blame me? Mo-tzŭ answered: Suppose a conflagration is on. One person is fetching water to extinguish it, and another is holding some fuel to reinforce it. Neither of them has yet accomplished anything, but which one do you value? Wu-ma-tzŭ answered that he approved the intention of the person who fetches water and disapproved of the intention of the person who holds fuel. Mo-tzŭ said: [In the same manner] do I approve of my intention and disapprove of yours.
(*Kêng Chu,* pp. 213–14)

Wu-ma-tzŭ said: 'For all the righteousness that you do, men do not help you and ghosts do not bless you. Yet you keep on doing it. You must be demented.' Mo-tzŭ said: 'Suppose you have here two employees. One of them works when he sees you, but will not work when he does not see you.

The other one works whether he sees you or not. Which of the two would you value?' Wu-ma-tzŭ said: 'I would value him that worked whether he saw me or not.' Mo-tzŭ then said: 'Then you are valuing him who is demented.'
(pp. 214–15)

On his way from Lu to Ch'i Mo-tzŭ met an old friend who said to him, 'Now-a-days none in the world practises any righteousness. You are merely inflicting pain on yourself by trying to practise righteousness. You had better give it up.' Mo-tzŭ replied, 'Suppose a man has ten sons. Only one attends to the farm while the other nine stay at home. Then the farmer must work all the more vigorously. Why? Because many eat while few work. Now, none in the world practises righteousness. Then you should all the more encourage me. Why do you stop me?' (*Esteem for righteousness*, p. 222)

Because his religion was centred in the will of heaven Mo-tzŭ not only preached righteousness and the doctrine of universal love, together with man's accountability to heaven for what he did, but he upheld the ancient sacrificial system. He believed in a hierarchy of spiritual beings, and strongly objected to a tendency, already manifest in Confucianism, to depersonalise heaven by substituting for it a doctrine of an inexorable fate. As Y. P. Mei writes, 'His religion is a revival of the old orthodox cult of a personal God not only at the head of numerous other spiritual beings but also crowning the ethico-political hierarchy in the human world.' [10]

Mo-tzŭ had no doubts as to the existence of the manes of the ancestors and other spiritual beings. He claimed that the records from the past gave abundant testimony to their place and function in the religion of the ancient sage-kings. Belief in them and worship of them was almost universal in his own time.

The ghosts and spirits can reward virtue as well as punish vice. . . . Even in solitary caves, big ponds, woods and valleys, the ghosts and spirits are watching. And the punishments from ghosts and spirits cannot be evaded.
(*On Ghosts*, 3, p. 170)

Mo-tzŭ even argued that if one doubted, as many philosophers did, the existence of the manes and spirits, the sacrifices made to them were productive of blessing. For religious ceremonies and sacrifices are a means of social solidarity. Proper attention to the rites and ceremonies of worship was therefore essential for the well-being of the land and the people.

We should prepare clean cakes and wine reverently to do sacrifice. If ghosts and spirits do not exist, then it is to serve father and mother, elder sisters and elder brothers with food and drink. Is not this a great blessing? . . . Even if there were really no ghosts and spirits, a sacrifice will yet gather together a party and the participants can enjoy themselves and befriend their neighbours. (*On Ghosts*, 3, p. 173)

The sage-kings of old appreciated what heaven and the spirits desire and avoided what they abominate, in order to increase benefits and avoid calamities in the world. With purification and baths and clean wine and cakes they led the people to make sacrifice and libation to heaven and the spirits. (*Identification with Superior*, 2, p. 63)

Though Mo-tzŭ objected to lavish expenditure and ostentation in respect of the rites performed at the ancestral temples and in the mourning for one's parents, he deprecated niggardliness in the sacrificial offerings to the spirits.

The master of sacrifice of Lu offered one pig and asked for a hundred blessings. Upon hearing of it Mo-tzŭ said: 'This cannot be done. To give others little but to expect much from others would make them afraid of gifts. Now one pig is offered and a hundred blessings are asked of the ghosts and spirits. They would be quite afraid of a sacrifice of oxen and sheep. Anciently when the sage-kings worshipped the ghosts and spirits, they just offered them sacrifice and that was all. One would be better off to remain poor than become rich by offering a pig for sacrifice and asking for a hundred blessings.' (*Lu's Questions*, pp. 252–3)

The intense interest of the Mohists in the sacrificial cult is attested by P'an Ku, who speaks of the Mohists as caring for the temples or *ch'ing miao*. Those who were in charge of the temples were naturally the ones responsible for the organisation and correct performance of the sacrifices, and were regarded as religious leaders within the community.

As to Mo-tzŭ's attack on the doctrine that all was ruled by fate, Y. P. Mei writes, 'The conversion of heaven from a personal will to a cosmic law in Confucianism was just what Mo-tzŭ felt compelled to combat. The central difference between the will of heaven and fate lies in the interest of the former and the indifference of the latter in human affairs . . . The depersonalisation of the principle in the universe will leave only an iron law of nature, or fate', Mo-tzŭ insisted that man is a moral being and as such is master of his own destiny. 'Although', writes Y. P. Mei, 'there is a will of heaven, and both heaven and the spirits are ready to reward virtues and punish vice, man after all is to be the master of his own destiny. The spiritual beings are brought in not to perform miracles but to enforce the causal law in moral conduct and to ensure its proper consequences. The doctrine of fate is rejected because it is the doctrine of irresponsibility and is detrimental to industry and frugality and all other virtues.'[11]

Fatalism was an invention of the wicked kings and the practice of miserable men. It was not a doctrine of the magnanimous. Therefore those who practice magnanimity and righteousness must examine it and vigorously refute it. (*Anti Fatalism* 3, p. 199)

To adopt the fatalist's doctrine is to overthrow righteousness in the world. To overthrow righteousness in the world will establish fate, which is a temptation to the people. And to offer people temptation is to destroy the people. (1, p. 164)

How do we know that fatalism is the way of the wicked? In ancient times, the miserable people indulged in drinking and eating and were lazy in their work. Thereupon their food and clothing became insufficient and the danger of hunger and cold was approaching. They did not acknowledge: 'I was stupid and insolent and was not diligent in my work!' But they would say: 'It is but my lot to be poor'. (1, p. 187)

Mo-tzŭ was undoubtedly a product of his age who sought to measure his teachings to the desperate conditions of his time. It was an age of rapacity, violence, cruelty and licentiousness in which clan preyed upon clan and state upon state. He sought by his teaching and personal example to stem the tide of depravity and lawlessness. He held up before men the majesty and omnipotence of heaven, whose will worked for righteousness, peace, order and mutual love. In doing this Mo-tzŭ's teaching takes on a universality which is applicable in every age.

During the fourth and third centuries BC the followers of Mo-tzŭ were so numerous and influential that the Confucians grew apprehensive. Mencius complained that 'the words of Mo-tzŭ and Yang-chu fill the empire'.[12] Han-fei-tzŭ records that 'Confucianism and Mohism are the most distinguished systems of the time'.[13] Y. P. Mei, in writing of Mohism, says that it 'seems to embody all the main features of organised religion – a historic founder, a living leader, the scriptures and the community of like-minded followers'.[14] 'True to the ideals of its founder it emphasised the virtues of courage, loyalty, discipline and performing one's duty. The ascetic tendencies in the individual are in part revealed in the austere requirements of the community.'[15]

The writer of the thirty-third chapter of *Chuang-tzŭ* referred to Mo-tzŭ as an enthusiastic follower of the *Tao,* a well-meaning man, and one who might be called a genius. He praised him because he actually put into practice what he preached, but he argued that he pushed his system too far, carrying things to excess.

There was to be no singing in life, no mourning after death. He taught universal love and beneficence towards one's fellow men, without contention, without censure of others. Yet his views were not those of the ancient sages, whose music and rites he set aside. . . . He would have all men toil through life and hold death in contempt. But this teaching is altogether too unattractive. It would land mankind in sorrow and lamentation. It would be next to impossible as a practical system, and cannot be regarded as the *Tao* of the true sage. It would be diametrically opposed to human passions, and as such would not be tolerated by the world.[16]

This criticism of Mo-tzŭ has, in general, been accepted by the Chinese people. He was recognised as one who interpreted the teachings of the ancient sages but without due regard for the emotional needs of man's nature. It has been a cardinal tenet of Chinese philosophy throughout the ages that human relationships, and therefore the well-being and cohesiveness of society, are based on an appreciation of the differences in function and status as between one individual and another, and therefore Mo-tzŭ's altruism, proclaimed in his doctrine of impartial and universal love, was felt to be destructive of the hierarchical structure of family and state on which Chinese society was organised. As Hsün-tzŭ so aptly put it, 'Mo-tzŭ had insight about equality [universal love], but not about inequality [distinctions in human relations].'[17]

Though Mohism as a cohesive religious movement only flourished for a short time, 'as a habitual way of life it has taken deep roots in the soil of the nation and the fibre of the people'.[18]

CHAPTER SIX

THE CONTRIBUTION OF EARLY TAOISTS TO RELIGION

The origins of what is known as Taoism are lost in the mists of antiquity. In the latter half of the Chou dynasty Taoism developed along with Confucianism so as to form one of the main streams of philosophical and religious thought. It was only in the early centuries of the Christian era that Taoism developed as an organised religion, influencing the lives and claiming the allegiance of millions of the common people. Nevertheless, the beliefs and practices which characterise religious Taoism may be traced back, at least in germ, to much earlier times, to the activities of the shaman-diviner, the magico-religious techniques for the cure of sickness, and a concern for longevity and a post-mortem existence. Basic, however, to Taoist thought are two philosophical works of the greatest importance: the *Tao-tê-ching* and the *Book of Chuang-tzŭ.*[1]

These two works have always held a great fascination for the Chinese. The *Tao-tê-ching,* attributed to Lao-tzŭ, was traditionally assigned to the sixth century BC, thus antedating Confucius. Critical scholarship, on the whole, whilst willing to admit that the book contains material from earlier times, attributed the *Tao-tê-ching* to an anonymous writer who lived in the fourth or the third century BC.[2] The *Book of Chuang-tzŭ* is based on the teachings of a philosopher of that name who lived between 399 and 295 BC. Though much of the book is undoubtedly compiled later, the first seven chapters are generally accepted as from the hand of Chuang-tzŭ himself.[3]

The early beginnings of Taoism are to be seen in those men who, mistrusting an activist philosophy which sought to control human society for its own good, decided to escape from the attractions and dangers of political office and the responsibilities of social life in order to nourish their own inner life in communion with nature and in obedience to cosmic law. In pursuit of this object many became hermits or recluses. Believing that behind all the complex phenomena thrown up by the ceaseless transformations of cosmic process there was a Great Unity (*T'ai I*), or an eternal, unchanging principle called *Tao,* these men sought for the meaning of life in an understanding of and even a complete identification with *Tao*.

The *Analects of Confucius* speak of the *yin che,* that is, those who obscure themselves and seek escape from the world.

Chieh-ni [i.e. Confucius] said [to Tzŭ-lu, a disciple of Confucius]: 'Under heaven there is none that is not swept away by the same flood. Such is the world, and who can change it? As for you, instead of following one who flees from this man and that, you would do better to follow one who shuns this whole generation of men.' And with that he went on with covering the seed. Tzŭ-lu went and told his master, who said ruefully, 'One cannot herd with beasts and birds. If I am not to be a man among other men, then what am I to be? If the Way prevailed under heaven, I should not be trying to alter things.' (*Ana.* 18: 6)

Once when Tzŭ-lu was following [the master] he fell behind and met an old man carrying a basket slung over his staff. Tzŭ-lu asked him saying, 'Sir, have you seen my master?' The old man said, 'You, who with your four limbs do not toil, who do not sift the five grains, who is your master?' And with that he planted his staff in the ground and began weeding, whilst Tzŭ-lu stood by with his hands pressed together.

He kept Tzŭ-lu for the night, killing a fowl, and introduced him to his sons. Tzŭ-lu said, 'It is not right to refuse to serve one's country. The laws of age and youth may not be set aside. And how can it be right for a man to set aside the duty that binds minister to prince, or in his desire to maintain his own integrity to subvert the Great Relationship? A gentleman's service to his country consists in doing such right as he can. That *Tao* does not prevail he knows well enough beforehand.'

Next day Tzŭ-lu went on his way and reported what had happened. The master said, 'He is a recluse.' (18: 7)

However much early Taoism may have been influenced by these men, the writer of the *Tao-tê-ching* was certainly not one of them. The *Tao-tê-ching* as we possess it might almost be described as a political tract for the times, though in the depth of its philosophical insight it was certainly far more than this. It was, however, as much concerned with good government as was Confucius. Its teaching was not for the recluse but for the sage-king. It is scathing in its opposition to oppressive government, and the legal or moral attempts to make all men conform to a pattern. In its attempt to free men's minds from all man-made restraints and artificialities it taught conformity to nature, the relativity of good and evil, and the strength of non-action.

Two fundamental ideas characterised the early Taoists. They despised the pomp, glory, prestige, wealth and power for which other men strove. This can be illustrated by a story told of Chuang-tzŭ[4] who, when invited by Prince Wei of Ch'u to become his prime minister, smiled and said to the messengers

> You offer me great wealth and a proud position indeed; but have you never seen the sacrificial ox? When after being fattened up for several years, it is decked with embroidered trappings and led to the altar, would it not willingly then change places with some uncared pigling? . . . Begone! defile me not! I would rather disport myself to my own enjoyment in the mire than be slave to a ruler of a state. I will never take office. Thus I shall remain free to follow my own inclinations.

In the second place, the Taoists believed that life itself is the greatest of all possessions. Therefore it must be nourished and preserved so as to reach its natural term. In this respect the Taoists were probably greatly influenced by the teachings of Yang-chu, a contemporary of Mo-tzŭ, about whose life practically nothing is known. He and his followers stressed the importance of preserving one's own life and guarding one's own self-interest.

These ideas are illustrated again and again in Taoist literature. The *Lü-shih-ch'un-ch'iu* says,[5] 'Our life is our own possession, and its benefit to us is very great. Regarding its dignity, even the honour of being emperor could not compare with it. Regarding its importance, even the wealth of possessing the world would not be exchanged for it. Regarding its safety, were we to lose it for one morning, we could never bring it back.' The *Tao-tê-ching* has the same idea. 'He who in his conduct values himself more than he does the world, may be given the world. He who in his conduct loves himself more than he does the world, may be entrusted with the world' (chapter 13). 'Which does one love more, fame or one's own life? Which is more valuable, one's own life or wealth?' (chapter 44). And in *Chuang-tzŭ,* 'When you do something good, beware of reputation. When you do something evil, beware of punishment. Follow the middle way, and take this to be your constant principle. Then you can guard your person, nourish your parents, and complete your normal span of life' (chapter 3). 'Mountain trees are their own enemies, and the leaping fire the cause of its own quenching. Cinnamon is edible, therefore the cinnamon tree is cut down. Ch'i oil is useful, therefore the Ch'i trees are gashed' (chapter 4).

The fundamental concept of the *Tao-tê-ching* is that of *Tao,* but *Tao* has not the same connotation that it had for Confucius. For the Taoists, it is the unchanging unity underlying all the shifting plurality of the universe, the impetus giving rise to all forms of life and motion. In the *Tao* all opposites are blended, all contrasts harmonised. The highest type of men diligently practise *Tao,* they search after *Tao* as a life endeavour and becoming firmly established in *Tao,* they can never again be separated from it.

There is a thing, formless yet complete. Before heaven and earth it existed. Without sound, without substance, it stands alone unchanging. It is all-pervading and unfailing. One might think of it as the mother of all beneath heaven. We do not know its name, but we term it *Tao*. Forced to designate it, I should say that it is 'Great'. (*Tao-tê-ching,* ch. 25)

When the man of highest capacity hears *Tao,* he does his best to put it into practice. (Ch. 41)

Because *Tao* accomplishes all things, not purposefully but spontaneously, and is the ultimate standard of all things, those who model themselves on *Tao* must likewise learn to be natural and spontaneous. There is no need to strive nor to assert oneself.

The sage, putting himself in the background, is always to the fore; remaining outside, he is always there. (*Tao-tê-ching,* ch.7)

He does not show himself. Therefore he is seen everywhere. He does not define himself. Therefore he is distinct. He does not assert himself. Therefore he succeeds. He does not boast of his work. Therefore he endures. He does not contend. Therefore no one in the world can contend with him. (Ch. 22)

To what extent is it possible to call the philosophers of early Taoism religious? Certainly as regards the formal expression of religion, they were indifferent. They saw little value in those traditional rites and ceremonies beloved of the Confucians. They outraged the Confucian sense of propriety by their disregard for ceremonial. Their lack of respect for convention is illustrated in the case of Chuang-tzŭ, who, when his wife died, was found outside the door of his house singing and beating time on a wooden bowl.

'To live with your wife,' exclaimed Hui-tzŭ, 'and see your eldest son grow up to be a man, and then not to shed a tear over her corpse – this would be bad enough. But to drum on a bowl and sing; surely this is going too far!' 'Not at all,' replied Chuang-tzŭ. 'When she died I could not help being affected by her death. Soon, however, I remembered that she had already existed in a previous state before birth, without form or even substance; that while in that unconditioned condition, substance was added to spirit; that this substance then assumed form; and that the next stage was birth. And now, by virtue of a further change, she is dead, passing from one phase to another like the sequence of spring, summer, autumn and winter. And while she is thus lying asleep in eternity, for me to go about weeping and wailing would be to proclaim myself ignorant of these natural laws. Therefore I refrain.' (*Chuang-tzŭ*, ch. 18)

The above quotation is interesting in that it shows a belief in life as an incident in an eternal and constant process of transformation, and as Chuang-tzŭ elsewhere points out, the experiences of joy and happiness in this life give one faith and hope to believe that the experiences of future transformations will be equally joyous.

The Taoists were critical of the accepted standards of right and wrong, good and evil. They were agnostic as regards a personal deity and life after death, and they took refuge in an extreme form of naturalism. Yet in their search for perfect harmony with the *Tao* they entered, in all seriousness, on to what was of the nature of a religious quest. In pursuit of their goal they engaged in feats of self-discipline and asceticism, which at times seem to have resulted in deep mystical insight. They spoke of 'the fast of the mind', of 'sitting in forgetfulness' and of 'returning to the root' (*Tao*). There are passages in Chuang-tzŭ, for instance, not only famous for their lyrical beauty but revealing a mind which, faced by the inscrutable mystery of the universe, yet held on to the quest for serenity and inward peace, for the knowledge of the Eternal and the Absolute, and for ultimate perfection in *Tao*.

Wing-tsit Ch'an has suggested that the naturalism of Chuang-tzŭ is so strong that any personal God or one who directs the movement of things is clearly out of harmony with his philosophy.[6] Yet, though Chuang-tzŭ is agnostic, he does suggest that there is a Self which, though without physical form, manifests itself in human activity, and that, in the same way, there is a Self of the universe, a 'True Lord', which manifests itself within the activities of nature.

Without them [i.e. feelings of anger, pleasure, sorrow, joy, etc.] there would not be I. And without Me, who will experience them? They are right near by, but we do not know who causes them. It seems that there is a True Lord who does so, but there is no indication of his existence.

(*Chuang-tzŭ*, ch. 2)

H. A. Giles[7] writes of Chuang-tzŭ that he 'conceives of the soul as an emanation from God, passing to and from this earth through the portals of birth and death'. Several times he uses the term 'God' in his translation, as, for instance, 'We are embraced in the obliterating unity of God' (p. 46); 'He who knows what God is and what man is has attained. Knowing what God is, he knows that he himself proceeded therefrom' (p. 71); 'Verily, God is great! I wonder what he will make of you now. I wonder whither you will be sent.' (p. 80); 'Those of old who apprehended *Tao*, first apprehended God. *Tao* came next, and then charity and duty to one's neighbour' (p. 135); 'If my body is not my own, pray whose is it? It is the delegated image of God. Your life is not your own. It is the delegated harmony of God' (p. 212); 'Those who are constant are sought after by men and assisted by God. Those who are sought after by men are the people of God; those who are assisted by God are his chosen children' (p. 225); 'A man's knowledge is limited; but it is upon what he does not know that he depends to extend his knowledge to the apprehension of God. Knowledge of the Great One, of the great Negative, of the great Nomenclature, of the great Uniformity, of the great Space, of the great Truth, of the great Law, – this is perfection' (p. 246). Granted that the Chinese character translated by Giles is *T'ien*, which Chinese commentators have usually regarded as a purely natural principle, we have seen already that in the usage of Confucius and Mo-tzŭ this character denotes something that is not far removed from the anthropomorphic deity of the earlier religion, and in Chuang-tzŭ it is well-nigh impossible at times to give the character any other connotation than that of 'God'.

Though Chuang-tzŭ believed in the relativity of all knowledge and experience, and likens life to a dream, he seems to retain a hope that after death will come a great awakening. He teaches that there is no need to fear death, since it is a perfectly natural transformation.

How do I know that to love life is not a delusion? And how do I know that to dread death is not like a man who lost his home in childhood and does not know his way back thither? (*Chuang-tzŭ*, ch. 2)

Finally there comes the great awakening, and then we shall know that life is a great dream. (Ch. 2)

The pure man of old knew neither to love life nor to hate death. He did not rejoice in birth, nor did he resist death. Such being the pure man, his mind is perfectly at ease. (Ch. 6)

Death and life are destined, and that they are regulated like the succession of nights and days is due to heaven, beyond man's interference and of the nature of things. Some men regard heaven as a father and love it with their whole being. How much more should they love that which surpasses heaven! Some men regard the ruler as superior to themselves and for him are prepared to die. How much more should they be prepared to die for the true ruler [of the universe]! (Ch. 6)

It is a matter of special delight to have attained to the human form. But if a man's form went through ten thousand transformations without limit, how incomparable would such joy be! Therefore the sage roams freely in the realm where nothing is lost but all endures. Those who regard alike premature death, old age, beginning and end are followed by others. How much more should be followed that on which all things depend, and the cause of all transformations! (Ch. 6)

In the two previous quotations Chuang-tzŭ evidences a religious faith, a faith in One who controls the universe, but also the destinies of men. That Supreme Being should be the object of men's love, obedience and service, and the one being on whom men can absolutely depend. He then goes on to equate that Supreme Being with *Tao*.

Tao has reality and evidence, but is without action or form. It can be transmitted but not received. It can be obtained but not seen. Before heaven and earth came into being, *Tao* existed from all eternity. It gave divinity to spirits and to apotheosised kings. It gave birth to heaven and earth.

(*Chuang-tzŭ*, ch. 6)

The *Tao-tê-ching* reveals a sense of awe and wonder before the greatness of that which lies behind the universe, the majesty of the illimitable *Tao*. In the first chapter it speaks of the *Tao* as the Mystery, the Mystery of Mysteries, the Gate of all Wonders. The theme is continued by Chuang-tzŭ. Man is a puny creature, his life as evanescent as a dream. He must accept his destiny and seek to fulfil that destiny by acting always in conformity to *Tao*.

Here is a foundry-man casting metal. If the metal leaps up and says, 'I must be made into a specially tempered sword [*mo-yeh*]', the foundryman will regard it as metal of evil omen. Now in forming a man, suppose he cries out, 'Make me a man, make me a man', then the creator must regard such a one as evil. If we think of the universe as a great furnace and the creator as a foundry-man, can I object to the way I am turned out?

(*Chuang-tzŭ*, ch. 6)

There is an element of mysticism in Chuang-tzŭ, which grew out of his longing for spiritual freedom, spontaneity and perfect harmony with the cosmic forces which sustained and constantly transformed the world of nature. This mysticism, which characterised many of the early Taoists is exemplified in a story which the author of the *Book of Chuang-tzŭ* invents concerning Confucius. According to the story Tzŭ-kung, a disciple of Confucius, is shocked to find men singing and playing in the presence of death, and asks his master if such conduct can be in accordance with propriety.

'What sort of men are those?' asks Tzŭ-kung. 'There is nothing proper in their conduct, and they regard their bodies as external to themselves. They approached the corpse and sang without changing the colour of their countenance. I don't know what to call them. What sort of men are they?' Confucius replied, 'They travel in the transcendental world, and I travel in the mundane world. There is nothing in common between the two worlds. And I sent you there to mourn! How stupid! They are companions of the Creator, and roam in the universe of the one and original creative force [*chi*]. They consider life as a burden, like a tumour, and death as the cutting off of an abscess. Such being their views, how do they care about life and death, or their beginning and end? To them life is but a temporary existence of various elements in a common body which they borrow. They are unaware of sensations and emotions. They come and go and begin and end, and none will know when all these things will stop. Without any attachment, they stroll beyond the dusty world and wander in the original state of non-action'.

(*Chuang-tzŭ*, ch. 6)

The true sage dwells like a quail and feeds like a fledgling. He travels like a bird, leaving no trace behind. If there be *Tao* in the empire, he and all things are in harmony. If there be not *Tao,* he cultivates virtue in retirement. After a thousand years of this weary world, he mounts aloft, and riding upon the white clouds passes into the kingdom of God, whither the three evils do not reach, and where he rests secure in eternity. (Ch. 12)

The true sage, taking his stand upon the beauty of the universe, pierces the principle of created things. Hence the saying that the perfect man does nothing, the true sage performs nothing, beyond gazing at the universe. For man's intellect, however keen, face to face with the countless evolutions of things, their death and birth, their squareness and roundness – can never reach the root. There creation is and there it has ever been. (Ch. 22)

If *Tao* is the be-all and end-all of man's existence, the ground of his being and the goal of his striving, how can he attain to knowledge of the perfect *Tao*? This is a question to which the Taoists returned again and again. Chuang-tzŭ is certain that the question can only be answered after an intensive spiritual discipline and profound meditation. Man must learn to strip off the veil which hides the *Tao* and cast down the barriers which pride, self-esteem, conventional morality and propriety have erected against the *Tao*. He must become like an 'uncarved block', like a 'helpless infant'. He must 'return to the root'.

It is not from extensive study that this may be known, nor by dialectical skill that this may be made clear. The true sage will have none of these. It is in addition without gain, in diminution without loss, that the true sage finds salvation. Unfathomable as the sea, wondrously ending only to begin again, informing all creation without being exhausted, the *Tao* of the perfect man is spontaneous in its operation. (*Chuang-tzŭ*, ch. 22)

Purge your heart by fasting and discipline. Wash your soul as white as snow. Discard your knowledge. *Tao* is abstruse and difficult of discussion. (Ch. 22)

Tao cannot be heard. Heard, it is not *Tao*. *Tao* cannot be seen. Seen, it is not *Tao*. It cannot be spoken. Spoken, it is not *Tao*. That which imparts form to forms is itself formless. Therefore *Tao* cannot have a name. (Ch. 22)

CHAPTER SEVEN

FURTHER RELIGIOUS DEVELOPMENTS IN PRE-HAN CHINA

In the three previous chapters we have seen how Confucianists, Mohists and Taoists, in the period following the death of Confucius, made their distinctive contributions to the development of the religious ideas of ancient China. We have noticed that, in the main, philosophical thought tended towards naturalism and agnosticism and was highly critical of what were deemed to be the superstitions of the common people. Yet there was undoubtedly a deep concern, not only to explain the origin of the universe and of man in terms that would be comprehensible to the intelligent mind, but also to give some satisfactory account of human destiny.

The period under review was one in which the Chinese sphere of influence was continually expanding. Peoples unfamiliar with the 'doctrines of the sage-kings' were gradually being incorporated into the Chinese hegemony. Chinese civilisation had had its origins in the basin of the Yellow River and its tributaries, and this civilisation had accepted a view of history which was rooted in the belief in a common ancestry and in the teachings of divine sage-kings. During the latter half of the first millennium BC powerful states arose to the south and south-west. These states, incorporating vast territories, were now recognised as an integral part of China. But they contained peoples whose origin, customs and beliefs differed greatly from those of the closely knit tribes who had inhabited the Yellow River basin.

The recognition of the powerful states of Ch'u, Wu and Yüeh seems to have occurred during the Ch'un Ch'iu period. King Chuang of Ch'u (613–591 BC) had even been recognised as the last of the five *Pa* or tyrants who had usurped the authority of the Chou kings, and forced the numerous states of China to recognise their paramountcy. In chapter 49 of *Mo-tzŭ,* the author contrasts *Chung Kuo* (The Middle Kingdom, China) with Yüeh and speaks of 'going out' of the Middle

Kingdom to visit Yüeh.[1] China is compared favourably with the surrounding barbarian states and with the semi-barbarian states of Ch'u and Yüeh. Again in chapter 25 of *Mo-tzŭ* the author refers to tribes to the east of Yüeh and to the south of Ch'u who practised cannibalism, and tribes to the west of Ch'in who disposed of their dead by cremation.[2] Mencius speaks of 'the shrike-tongued barbarians of the south whose doctrines are not those of the ancient kings'.[3] To the east were the coastal peoples of Yen and Ch'i, whose concern for immortality led them to send out expeditions in search of the Isles of the Blest, whose inhabitants were believed to possess the secrets of immortality and perpetual youth. The gradual incorporation of many tribes who previously had been thought of as non-Chinese introduced the Chinese people to new mythological interpretations and religious practices.

It seems evident that throughout the ever-expanding territories of China during this period the common people were greatly influenced by shaman-diviners, mediums, exorcisers, rain-makers and other magicians, both male and female.[4] De Groot[5] claimed that the Chinese sorcerers, known as *wu,* were the real priests of China in the centuries immediately preceding our era, that in them the spirits were believed to be incarnated so that they acted as intermediaries between men and the gods. They practised magico-religious techniques, the arts of faith-healing, and claimed to be able to enter a state of trance in which they visited the transcendental world of the spirits and held communion with powerful gods, demons, fairies and deified cult-heroes.

A fair picture of the religious beliefs and expression of the Chinese people during the closing centuries of the Chou dynasty and the foundation of the Chinese empire under the Ch'in and Former Han may be obtained from a study of the *Poems of Ch'u,*[6] the *Book of Rites* (The Li Chi)[7] and the references to cosmological ideas in the *Book of Divination* (I Ching).[8] Referring to this period, R. Wilhelm writes:

> Another fresh factor was the penetration of influences from the border states in the south, producing a remarkable revival in mythology. The famous poem of Ch'ü Yüan, 'On Encountering Sorrows', opens up a new world. The atmosphere is densely packed with spirits and gods – no longer just nameless forces, which even Confucianism recognised, but individual beings endowed with consciousness and will, who live and move behind the scenes. It is difficult to estimate the extent of Indian influence in those early days. These religious-mythological ideas were exploited by the ranks of the *Fang-shih* [magicians] who played an important part in court life, since more

than one emperor hoped to solve with their help the problems of transmuting gold and achieving immortality. These magicians seized upon and interpreted in their own light the old natural religion of China. They appropriated Taoism in the same way, for the metaphors and personifications of Chuang-tzŭ afforded numerous points of contact.[9]

The poems of Ch'u

These poems, attributed to the fourth and third centuries BC, reveal the magico-religious beliefs and practices which, with local variations, were ubiquitous throughout the states which made up the Chinese hegemony. The religion of the period was a mixture of ancestor worship and animism. Everywhere shaman-diviners engaged themselves in ritual dances and incantations designed to bring back the spirits of the sick and of the dead, or to induce trances in which they wandered freely in the spirit world, or drew down the gods of stars, rivers and mountains to their assistance. As Professor Hawkes writes in his introduction to a translation of the *Ch'u Tz'ŭ*,[10] the poet who composed the *Li Sao* (On Encountering Sorrows)

> is, or aspired to be, a magician. He feels that he belongs to a supernatural environment more pure than this earthly one, in which he feeds on nothing less ethereal than the dews and vapours of heaven, in which he can summon gods and immortal spirits to do his bidding, and can roam at will to the uttermost ends of the universe. His is the frustration of an immortal spirit condemned to exile in the world of men.[11]

The short collection of poems known as the *Nine Songs* (Chiu Ko) are believed to be songs used in an erotic liturgy in which male and female shamans 'having first purified and perfumed themselves, and dressed up in gorgeous costumes, sing and dance to the accompaniment of music, drawing the gods down from heaven in a sort of divine courtship'.[12] The gods mentioned seem to have been gods of local cults, but they include *T'ai I,* the Great Unique, and *Ssŭ Ming,* the Master of Destinies, who both feature prominently in later Taoist religion.

The famous poem *Chao Hun,* or 'The Summons of the Soul',[13] is based on the belief that the soul of man can, for various reasons such as sickness, madness or coma, leave the body. It was one of the arts of the shaman, trained as he was to wander in comparative immunity within the spirit-world, to entice back such souls to their earthly abode. In the *Chao Hun* it seems as though the shaman-priest performed his rituals on behalf of a king who was very sick, and that he did this at the express command of the supreme God. 'The Lord said to Wu-yang,[14] "There is a man on earth below whom I would help, for his soul has left him. Make divination for him." Wu-yang therefore went down and summoned the soul, saying, "O soul! come back!" '[15] In the *Li Chi* (*Book of Rites*) this calling back of the soul seems to have been a popular practice in the case of one who has just died.[16] The followers of Mo-tzŭ, in their attack upon the Confucians, refer to their practice of searching for the soul of a dead man. 'When his parent dies he first lets him lie there without dressing him for burial. He climbs on the roof, looks into the well, reaches into the rat-holes and searches into the washing basins to look for the dead man.'[17] The Mohists poured scorn on such practices, but from their criticism it is reasonable to deduce that some Confucian scholars were not averse from engaging in them.

A primitive cosmology is to be found in the *T'ien Wên,* a poem of doubtful authorship, attributed by Professor Hawkes to the fourth century BC.[18] The poem refers to many early Chinese concepts concerning the nature of the universe and the origin of things. Heaven is conceived of as like a tent (*vvs.* 9–10) upheld by a central pole and by eight pillars round the circumference, great towering mountains. There is a gap to the south-east caused by the demi-urge, Kung-kung, who in his rage butted his head against the north-west pillar, causing the earth to tilt and the sky to fall in that region, and upsetting the symmetry of the universe. Heaven is thought of as having nine divisions (*vvs.* 11–14) and the twelve zodiacal signs rule over the 'houses of heaven'. In them the stars are interspersed, whilst the sun, moon and planets wander through them (*vvs.* 15–18). The sun daily performs his journey from the Valley of Dawn to the Valley of Darkness, and nightly makes his return journey through the underworld, an idea familiar in other primitive religions. The moon dies, but comes to life again and grows, and so the dying and resurrection of the moon become connected with the idea of immortality (*vvs.* 23–34). The earth was formerly covered by floods, but through the massive labours of K'un and Yü, who were assisted in their labours by a winged dragon, the waters were enclosed within bounds and the nine lands appeared (*vvs.* 35–55). The earth is surrounded by a nine-fold wall, with gates on its four sides, and whenever the north-east gate is opened a great wind passes through (*v.* 56). Shên-i, the divine archer, saved the world from being burnt to a cinder by shooting down nine of the ten suns.

Many of the religious and mythological ideas of the times are reflected in Ch'ü Yüan's most famous poem, the *Li Sao*.[19] In referring to his own birth, in verse one, the author speaks of 'descending', suggesting the belief that his spiritual nature was pre-existent in heaven. Verse two reveals the custom of consulting the horoscope at the birth of a child, followed by the careful choosing of an auspicious name. Verse eleven speaks of the taking of a solemn oath by the nine heavens, indicating the common belief that heaven had nine tiers or stages. Verse seventeen refers to the teaching, frequently found in Taoist literature of later times, that the drinking of dew and the eating of flowers is a sign of purity. Towards the end of the poem, the author tells of how, after bitter tears and dark despair, he kneels on a spread-out mat to address his complaint to heaven. Thereupon he receives a dazzling revelation of the path which stretches out before him.

The wide-spread dissemination of this shamanistic religion among the common people is indicated by the frequent expression *wu chia* or 'shaman-family', suggesting that the profession was often hereditary. In the state of Ch'i (North Shantung) 'among the common people the eldest daughter was not allowed to marry. She is called "the shaman-child" [*wu êrh*] and is in charge of the family's religious rites'.[20]

From what little we have been able to glean from these early *Poems of Ch'u* concerning the magico-religious ideas and practices of the closing centuries of the Chou dynasty we gain the impression that the world of gods, demons, fairies, nature-spirits and immortalised ancestors was very near to the ordinary people, who believed that their happiness and well-being, both here and hereafter, depended upon maintaining a right attitude through appropriate channels to a host of spiritual beings whose activities strongly influenced for good or ill the lives of men. Reading the extant pre-Han philosophical texts, one would hardly realise that this popular religion existed. With the establishment of Confucianism as a state religion in the second century BC there was a tendency for the governing class roundly to condemn the gross superstitions, extravagant beliefs and crude religious practices of the shaman-priests, and to expunge from their texts everything that could not be fitted into the pattern of Confucian orthodoxy. Yet, as we shall see in the next section, Confucianism itself, being firmly based on a religious apprehension of reality, came to demand the rigid observance of minute ritual prescriptions for the service of God, the spirits and the deceased ancestors.

The Li Chi

The *Li Chi,* or 'Records on Ceremonial', was compiled during the first century BC from documents of varying age which had been transmitted from the Chou dynasty. It contains sections which are identical with parts of the *Works of Hsün-tzŭ,* and there seems to be little doubt that these passages were copied into the Classic from that philosopher's work. The *Li Chi* is undoubtedly heavily indebted to him. It also contains much that is transparently legalistic or Taoist, and it also incorporates theories of *Yin* and *Yang,* and of the five elemental forces which make up the universe. Thus the Classic illustrates the syncretistic tendencies of the Han dynasty, when Confucian orthodoxy took up into its system leading ideas from other schools of thought.

It is from the *Li Chi* that we gain an insight into the ceremonial usages, ritual practices and religious beliefs which were current in official circles during the last few decades of the Chou dynasty.

The *Li Chi* refers to the ritual obligation laid upon a king to make a tour of inspection through his domain once every five years. It was as 'Son of heaven', vice-regent of God on earth, that he performed this duty. One important object of this inspection was to examine into the relation between the spirit-world and men, to correct any acts of irreverence and in appropriate places to make sacrifices to the gods.

The Son of heaven, every five years, made a tour of inspection through the land. In the second month of the year he visited those on the east, going to the honoured mountain of *T'ai.* There he burnt a great pile of wood and announced his arrival to heaven; and with looks directed towards them, sacrificed to the hills and rivers. If any of the spirits of hills and rivers did not receive attention, it was deemed to be an act of irreverence.

(*Li Chi,* 3: 2; 13–15)

In the second month, on a lucky day chosen by divination, the people were given orders to sacrifice to the earth spirits. (4: 2; 1, 7)

Orders were given [in the second month of summer] to the officers to pray for the people, and to offer sacrifices to the spirits of the hills and streams and all springs. This was followed by the great summer sacrifice for rain to God, when all the instruments of music were employed. Orders were given throughout all districts to sacrifice to [the manes of] various princes, ministers, officers who had benefited the people, praying that they may have a good grain harvest. (4: 2; 2, 8)

In the first month of winter, the son of heaven prays to the honoured ones of heaven for the coming year; sacrifices with an ox, a ram and a boar at the public altars to the spirits of the land, and at the gates of towns and villages; offers a sacrifice three days after the winter solstice with the spoils of the chase to all ancestors, and at the five [household] sacrifices.

(4: 4; 1, 19)

The son of heaven issues orders to the proper officers to pray and sacrifice to [the spirits presiding over] the four seas, the great rivers with their famous sources, the deep tarns, and the meres, wells and springs. (4: 4; 2, 10)

The above quotations are sufficient to illustrate the strong belief that human life and well-being were intimately bound up with a populous and ubiquitous world of spirits whose goodwill had to be maintained by appropriate rites and sacrifices.

As the sacrificial system with its elaborate rituals was of benefit to the whole land, it was necessary that the common people should understand what was being done on their behalf by the ruler.

The ancient kings were troubled lest the ceremonial usages should not be understood by those below them. They therefore sacrificed to God in the suburb [of the capital] and thus the place of heaven was established. They sacrificed on the altars of earth inside the capital, and thus were initiated the benefits derived from earth. Their sacrifice in the ancestral temple gave their fundamental place to the sentiments of humanity. Those at the altars of hills and streams served to mark their intercourse with the spirit breathing [in nature]. Their five sacrifices [of the home] prove a recognition of the various businesses that had to be done.

For the same reason there are officers who attend to prayer in the ancestral temple; the three ducal ministers at the court; the three classes of old men in the college. In front of the king there were the sorcerers, and behind him the recorders, the diviners by the tortoise-shell and by the stalks, the blind musicians and their helpers were all on his left and right. He himself was in the centre. (*Li Chi*, 7: 4; 2)

The altars erected for the worship of the spirits of the land and grain (*shê chi*) seem to have been the focal point for those religious ceremonies which were performed in order to ensure the prosperity of the states. On the enfeoffment of a vassal lord, he received from his king a sod to incorporate in his *shê* altar. If the state was for any reason destroyed, the altar was covered over so that it could no longer receive the beneficent influences of heaven and earth.

At the *shê* altar they sacrificed to the spirits of the land . . . The great *shê* altar of the son of heaven was open to receive the hoar frost, dew, wind and rain and allow the influences of heaven and earth to have full development upon it. For this reason the *shê* altar of a state that had perished was roofed in, so that it was not touched by the brightness and warmth of heaven.

In the sacrifices at the *shê* altar they dealt with the earth as though it were a spirit. The earth supported all things, while heaven hung out its brilliant signs. They derived their natural resources from the earth; they derived rulers [for their courses of labour] from heaven. Thus they were led to give honour to heaven and their affection to the earth. (*Li Chi*, 9: 20–1)

The close connection between good government and the worship of heaven and the host of spiritual beings is indicated in the following passages.

Government is the means by which the ruler keeps and protects his person, and therefore it must have a fundamental connection with heaven. Heaven uses a number of ways in sending down the intimations of its will.

(*Li Chi*, 7: 2; 12)

The sage forms a ternion with heaven and earth, and stands side by side with spiritual beings, in order to the right ordering of government.

(7: 2; 13)

The processes by which the universe is ordered and governed are fixed and determined. Everything follows its ordained pattern and sequence. The height of wisdom is, therefore, for the ruler to lead his people to an understanding of and perfect conformity to those processes. The *Li Chi* is greatly influenced by two theories which, though probably having their origin in dim antiquity, found philosophical formulation during the fourth century BC. The one is the theory of the Five Agents or Elements which form the basis of the cosmos. The other is the theory of two primal and complementary forces, the *Yin* and the *Yang*, out of whose constant interaction all phenomena proceed.

According to the Five Agents theory (*wu hsing*), the basic constituents of the universe are, wood, fire, earth, metal and water, and these succeed one another in exercising a dominating influence over both human and natural events. As Wing-tsit Chan writes:[21]

Each of the five agents succeeds the others according to its official function by fulfilling its capacity. Thus wood occupies the eastern quarter and controls the forces of spring. Fire occupies the southern quarter and controls the forces of summer. Metal occupies the western quarter and controls the forces of autumn, and water occupies the northern quarter and controls the forces of winter. For this reason wood controls production, metal controls destruction, fire controls heat, and water controls cold . . . Earth occupies the centre and is the natural benefactor . . . Thus among the Five Agents and the four seasons, earth includes them all.

The philosophy of *Yin* and *Yang* was taken up into Confucian orthodoxy, because it supplied a simple but profound explanation of the world, embracing every aspect of life, from the physical constitution of the universe to man's personal, social and political life. The *Yin* is the female principle, negative, receptive, passive, quiescent; the *Yang* is the male principle, active, positive and aggressive. All life is in constant flux, and derives from the blending and harmony of these two forces. The *Yin* and the *Yang* alternate in cycles, so that one is dominant while the other is recessive.

In the religious life of the Chinese people two periods of the year were of special significance; the summer and the winter solstices. For it was at these periods that the *Yang* and the *Yin* respectively, having reached the maximum of their influence, began to give way to the other. These times were regarded as of exceptional danger to mankind, and consequently men must take extraordinary precautions.

In this month [the second month of summer] the longest day arrives. The influences in nature of darkness and decay [*Yin*] and those of brightness and growth [*Yang*] struggle together; the tendencies to death and life are divided. Superior men give themselves to vigil and fasting. They keep themselves retired in their houses, avoid all violent exercise, restrain their indulgence in music and beautiful sights, eschew the society of their wives, make their diet spare. (*Li Chi*, 4: 2; 2, 15)

There shall be nothing done [in the second month of winter] in works of earth; care should be taken not to expose anything that is covered, nor to throw open apartments and houses, and rouse the masses to action, that all may be kept securely shut up. Otherwise the genial influence of earth will find vent, which might be called a throwing open of the house of heaven and earth. In that case all insects would die; and the people be sure to fall ill with pestilence, and various losses would ensue. (4: 2; 2, 7)

The practice of divination which had become ingrained in the Chinese from earliest times, in spite of the scorn of the more rationalistic of the Confucian scholars, finds justification in the *Book of Rites*.

The ancient kings made use of the stalks of the divining plant and the tortoise shell; arranged their sacrifices; burned their offerings of silk; recited their words of supplication and benediction; and made their statutes and measures. (*Li Chi*, 7: 2; 1)

In the various articles of tribute the tortoises were placed in front of all other offerings, because the shell gave knowledge of the future. (9: 7)

In all cases of divining about a day, whether by tortoise shell or stalks, if it is beyond a decade [the ancient week of ten days], it is said, 'On such and such a day'. For matters of mourning a distant day is to be preferred; for festive matters a near day.

It is said, 'For the day we depend on thee, O great tortoise shell, which dost give the regular indications. We depend on you, O great divining stalks, which give the regular indications'.

Divination by the shell or the stalks should not go beyond three times.

Divination by the shell is called *pu* and by the stalks *shih*. The two were the methods by which the ancient sage kings made the people believe in the seasons and days, revere spiritual beings, stand in awe of the laws and orders; the method by which they made them determine their perplexities and settle their misgivings. Hence it is said, 'If you doubted, and have consulted the stalks, you need not think you will do wrong. If the day be indicated, boldly do it [on that day].' (1: 1; 5, 6 (23–7))

Belief in the close correspondence of human affairs with the processes of nature is reflected not only in the fact that through divination man can understand and in a measure predict future happenings, and through his supplications and sacrifices call to his assistance the mighty influences of heaven, earth and the host of spiritual beings, but through his ceremonial acts he can actually impose on the world around him a measure of harmony and co-operation which is conducive to human happiness.

The quality which set a virtuous king far above all his fellow men was this power of ritual action by which heaven and earth and all nature were induced to respond to his wishes.

When the Great Man (the sage ruler) uses and exhibits his ceremonies and music, heaven and earth will in response to him display their brilliant influences. They will act in happy union, and the energies [of nature] now expanding, now contracting, will proceed harmoniously. The genial air from above and the responsive action below will overspread and nourish all things. Then plants and trees will grow luxuriously; curling sprouts and buds will expand; the feathered and winged tribes will be active; horns and antlers will grow; insects will come to light and revive; birds will breed and brood; the hairy tribes will mate and bring forth; the mammalia will have no abortions and no eggs will be broken or addled; and all will have to be ascribed to the power of music. (*Li Chi*, 17: 3, 3)

By means of the ceremonies performed in the suburb all the spirits receive their offices. By means of those performed at the altar of earth, all things yielded by the earth receive their full development. (7: 4; 3)

A ruler stood with his face towards the south to show that he would be [in his sphere] what the influence of light and heat is [in nature]. (9: 14)

Rules and ceremonies must be traced to their origin in the Great Unity. This separated and became heaven and earth. It revolved and became the dual forces. It changed and became the four seasons. It was distributed and became the breathings [thrilling in the universal frame]. Its lessons transmitted to men are called its orders; the law and authority of them is in heaven. (7: 4; 4)

It is in the ceremonies connected with death and mourning that the *Li Chi* clearly indicates many of the religious ideas which animated the minds of the Chinese in this period prior to our era. Immediately upon death the body was laid upon the earth, to indicate that it was from the great nourisher and sustainer of all things that man came forth, and to it he must return. The soul, on the other hand, left the body on death, but might possibly be recalled before it journeyed away to some celestial home. Several sections of the *Li Chi* are devoted to meticulous regulations for the burial of the dead, the rites of mourning, and the sacrifices appropriate to the manes of parents and ancestors. In sacrificing to the spirit of a parent the custom was still in vogue of providing a living representative of the dead parent, if possible a grandson, but it became a customary practice to provide a wooden tablet on which were written the name and rank of the deceased. This spirit-tablet was set up on or near the coffin, and after interment it was buried and another permanent tablet was made. Before this tablet the family made sacrifices at appropriate times so long as the family remained an entity.

Just before death, the body was laid upon the ground. A change of clothing was made. A man was not permitted to die in the arms of a woman or vice versa. The body was then transferred to a couch. (*Li Chi*, 19: 1)

When one died, they went upon the housetop, and called out his name in a prolonged note, saying, 'Come back, so and so'. After this they filled the mouth of the deceased with uncooked rice and set forth offerings of packets of raw flesh. Thus they looked up to heaven [whither the spirit had gone], and buried the body in the earth. The body and the animal soul [*p'o*] go downwards; and the intelligent spirit is on high. Thus also the dead are placed with their heads to the north, whilst the living look towards the south.

(7: 1; 7)

Calling the soul back is the way in which love received its consummation, and has in it the mind expressed by prayer. The looking for it to return from the dark region is a way of seeking for it among spiritual beings. The turning of the face to the north springs from the idea that the north is the dark region.

(2: 2; 1, 22)

An inscription with the surname, name and rank of the deceased was prepared and fastened up under the eaves on the east. Meanwhile a tablet of wood, 'the first spirit-tablet', was prepared and the inscription transferred to it. It was set up on, or by, the coffin, now having the corpse in it. Later it was moved to the east of the burial pit where it remained till after the interment. After the interment this tablet was buried and a permanent tablet [*shên chu*] was made, before which the family sacrifices are offered from generation to generation. (2: 2; 1, 25)

After the interment the spirit-tablet was placed, with great ceremony, next to that of the grandfather. (2: 2; 1, 38)

Tsêng-tzŭ [a disciple of Confucius] asked, 'Is it necessary that there should be a representative of the dead in sacrifices? Or may he be dispensed with, as when the satisfying offerings are made to the dead?' Confucius replied, 'In sacrificing to a full-grown man for whom there has been the funeral rites, there must be such a representative, who should be a grandson, and if a grandson be too young, someone must be employed to carry him in his arms. If there be no grandson, someone of the same surname should be selected for the occasion.' (5: 2; 20)

In connection with the burial, objects, vessels and utensils were prepared for the use of the deceased in the after-life, but these objects were only representational and could not be used by the living. In the burial of the nobility these included representations of wives, concubines, servants, guards as well as favourite horses and other animals. We have seen that in the Shang dynasty a deceased king or noble was accompanied into the next world by a host of immolated retainers. By the closing years of the Chou dynasty this barbaric custom had practically died out, and the authority of Confucius was cited for a more humane practice. Even the use of lifelike wooden dolls with movable parts was frowned upon, because of the danger that such use might lead again to the sacrifice of living men and women.

Confucius said, 'He who made the vessels, which are so only in imagination, knew the principle underlying the mourning rites. They were perfect to to all appearance and yet could not be used. Alas! If for the dead they had used the vessels of the living, would there not have been danger of this leading to the interment of the living with the dead?' They were called 'vessels in imagination', the dead being thus treated as spiritual intelligences. From of old there were the carriages of clay and the figures of straw . . . Confucius said that the making of straw figures was good, and the making of wooden automata was not benevolent. Was there not a danger of its leading to the the use of living men? (*Li Chi*, 2 : 2; 1, 44–5)

The belief that man is compounded of two 'soul' elements, the *p'o* which after death became the *kuei* which descended with the body to the grave, and the *hun* which became the *shên* and ascended to the spiritual world above, seems to have been fairly generally accepted at this time. Later on these ideas were to be much elaborated in religious Taoism.

Tsai-wo [a disciple of Confucius] said, 'I have heard the names of *kuei* and *shên*, but I do not know what they mean.' The Master [Confucius] said, 'The intelligent spirit is of the *shên* nature, the animal soul is of the *kuei* nature. It is the union of the *kuei* and the *shên* that forms the highest exhibition of doctrine. All the living must die, and dying return to the ground; that is what we call the *kuei* nature. The bones and the flesh moulder below, and, hidden away, become the earth of the fields. But the spirit issues forth and is displayed on high in a condition of glorious brightness.'
(*Li Chi*, 21 : 2; 1)

The words above, put into the mouth of Confucius, show how necessary it was felt to claim the authority of Confucius for views concerning human nature, death and immortality which had gained currency even among the orthodox in the closing decades of the Chou dynasty.

From this short study of passages taken from the *Li Chi* or *Book of Rites* we gain the impression of a people whose minds were greatly exercised with what were fundamentally religious ideas and problems. The elaborate ceremonial in the ancestral temples and at the earth altars, the familiar worship of the spirits of the land and grain, the hills and streams, and the homage paid to the household gods all tended to emphasise the pervasive influence of the spirit-world. Peace, prosperity and happiness in this life and a meaningful existence in the life beyond depended upon the promotion of a harmonious relationship with a spiritual realm ruled over by high heaven and filled with a vast host of spiritual beings. Yet, Confucian orthodoxy taught that 'it is only the sage who can sacrifice to God, and only the filial son who can sacrifice to his parents'. This dictum led to the interesting result that, throughout Chinese history, as far as the official religion was concerned, the vast bulk of the people were merely passive spectators of rites performed on their behalf. Indeed it was an offence of the gravest magnitude for any but the 'Son of heaven' to perform the sacrifices due to heaven, and for any but the eldest male representative of the family to perform the sacrifices due to the ancestors.

The I Ching or Book of Changes

We cannot end this chapter without some reference to the cosmological ideas contained in the *I Ching*, a book which, perhaps more than any of the other Confucian Classics, was to exercise a profound influence on subsequent Confucian thought in respect of the origin of man's nature and his place and status in the universe. Though not completed in its present form until well on in the Han dynasty, the *I Ching* contains material gathered from very early times. Many Chinese scholars accept that it was well known to Confucius and was studied by him. Already in the Ch'un Ch'iu period (*c.* 720–479 BC), according to the *Kuo Yü*[22] and the *Tso Chuan*,[23] the eight trigrams were being thought of as symbols of heaven and earth, mountains and marshes, wind, fire, water and thunder. The cosmologies of the *I Ching* based their speculations respecting the origin of all things in the universe on the analogy of the conception of human beings. A primeval unity manifested itself in two complementary forces, namely the *yin* and the *yang*. They, by their constant interaction, produced all things. As Fung Yu-lan wrote:[24]

> The greatest things in the universe are heaven and earth. In heaven the most noteworthy objects are the sun and moon, wind and thunder. On earth, the most noteworthy objects are mountains and marshy lowlands. Of most use to men are fire and water. These objects were thought to constitute the universe. Hence the objects symbolised in the trigrams were the basic constituents of the universe.

The character *I* in the title of the *I Ching* has the primary meaning of transformation or change. But it is change which is based on constancy and regularity, which are the very essence of the eternal and invariable principle *Tao*. This *Tao* by the simple and spontaneous interaction of the *Yin* and the *Yang* produces all the changes and transformations in the universe. Everything in the universe results from this transformation, and is still in process of transformation. By a study of the eight trigrams and the sixty-four hexagrams which were derived from them man can attain to a thorough understanding of the phenomena which they signify, the mutual relationships under which they subsist, and the patterns of transformation and change which they inevitably obey. Man has thus in the *I Ching* a blueprint from which he can read the whole universe. But man can do more. He can so learn to model his own life and conduct on the guiding principles revealed in these symbols that he puts himself in perfect harmony with cosmic process. Thus a work which began as a Chou dynasty treatise on divination, by the end of the Chou dynasty came to have great ethical and metaphysical significance.

We have already noted a tendency among scholars in the period immediately preceding our era to seek for a synthesis between Taoist and Confucian thought. This tendency is particularly evident in the *Third Appendix* to the *I Ching*. The author of this work, a product of the Han dynasty, in line with the naturalistic tendency of Taoism, conceived of heaven as a cosmic force. But whereas Taoism, in its effort to follow the spontaneity of nature, poured scorn on human wisdom, morality, art and culture, the *I Ching* in this *Third Appendix* identifies the 'Way' (*Tao*) of man with the Way of heaven, and attributes the development of society, morality and civilisation to the fact that sage-kings modelled themselves on the Way of heaven by studying the symbolic representations of all that heaven produces. Thus in a truly Confucian manner[25] the *Third Appendix,* in describing the ideal man, says of him:

The great man, in his attributes, is in harmony with heaven and earth; in his brightness, with the sun and moon; in his orderly procedure, with the four seasons; and in his relation to the good and bad issues, in harmony with the spiritual agents. He may precede heaven, and heaven will not act in opposition to him; he may follow heaven, but will only act as heaven at the time would do. If heaven will not act in opposition to him, how much less will man! how much less will spiritual beings![26]

Here is presented a 'way of life' which in its main emphasis differs fundamentally and characteristically from those religious systems which arose in India and in the Semitic world. Chinese indigenous thought was not indifferent to the radical imperfections which appertained both to individuals and to society, but it conceived of 'salvation' as the attainment of the status of the 'perfect sage'. This was a state of being which it was possible for all men to reach through an enlightened understanding of 'the nature of things', and on the basis of that understanding to a harmonisation of one's own nature with that of the cosmos. There was no need to postulate a personal God. The whole of nature was 'spirit-fraught', and the spiritual worked through and manifested itself in the processes of nature. There was no need for a Saviour or for radical conversion, because the root of goodness was in all men and only needed 'natural' development. In spite of the emphasis on the cult of ancestors, there was little or no concern for the hereafter, since 'change' was inherent in the nature of all things, even in what lay beyond our ken. All that really mattered was that the transformations which took place within ourselves, and for which we were morally responsible, should be in perfect harmony with the spontaneity of the *Tao*.

That such a philosophy should make an appeal to the highly intellectual and agnostic scholar is understandable. But it failed to satisfy the deep-felt religious needs of the multitude of ordinary men and women who, as we shall see in the following chapters, found satisfying answers to those needs in religious Taoism and in Buddhism. Both these 'faiths' came into prominence in China during the early centuries of our era.

CHAPTER EIGHT

RELIGIOUS ECLECTICISM IN THE HAN DYNASTY

The rise of the great Han dynasty marks the end of what has been called the Classical Period of Chinese religious, ethical and philosophical thought. The short-lived Ch'in dynasty (221–206 BC), execrated on all sides, ended in large-scale revolts and bloodshed. Most of the great aristocratic families were either exterminated or so seriously decimated as to be incapable of exerting a dominating influence over government. Consequently, when order was restored under the unified rule of the Han emperors, there was need for a large number of officials and administrators who were drawn from the scholar class. Thus men trained in the Confucian tradition came into their own. Through their influence Confucianism became the ideology which governed state policy, and the basis of an elaborate state cult. There was manifest a great concern to preserve and study those writings from the past which Ch'in Shih-huang-ti had sought to destroy. Extensive work was done in collecting, editing and compiling the Confucian classics, and the six Confucian disciplines of Poetry, History, Rites, Music, the *Book of Changes* and the *Spring and Autumn Classic* became the required study of all who wished to enter upon an official career. Chinese official life and thought became predominantly Confucian, and social and individual life was based on the ethical principles derived from Confucius. It was a Confucianism, however, strongly influenced by other schools of thought, tinged with Taoist and Mohist ideas and seeking to interpret the universe and man in terms of the *Yin-Yang* and the Five Elements philosophies.[1]

When the Han emperor Wu-ti (140–87 BC), himself greatly influenced by Taoism, carried out the plan of the Confucian scholar Tung Chung-shu, who asked that 'all not within the field of the six disciplines or the arts of Confucius should be cut short and not allowed to progress further', Confucianism came to its own, and from that time continued to mould Chinese official attitudes right down to the twentieth century. As W. T. Chan writes, 'Tung Chung-shu (*c.*179–*c.*104 BC) was chiefly instrumental in making Confucianism the state doctrine in 136 BC. This supremacy excluded other schools and lasted until 1905.'[2]

The state cult relied not so much on belief in a personal god, omniscient and omnipotent, as on belief in an ordered cosmos which followed a pre-ordained way, and this involved appropriate attitudes to heaven, earth and the ancestors, and the honouring of them by elaborate rites, in which music and ritual, dances and offerings and prayers encouraged such a correspondence between man and nature as to ensure fertility and prosperity which all men desired.

Tung Chung-shu was probably the most influential and representative Confucian of the Former Han dynasty. In his *Ch'un Ch'iu Fan Lu*[3] he manifests those eclectic tendencies which characterised what became later known as the New Text School of Confucianism. The following brief quotations from his writings will give some indication of his thought.

Nothing is more refined than the [*Yin* and *Yang*] ethers, richer than earth, or more spiritual than heaven. Of the creatures born from the refined essence [*ching*] of heaven and earth, none is more noble than man. Man receives the Decree [*Ming*] of heaven, and therefore is loftier [than other] creatures. [Other] creatures suffer trouble and distress, and are unable to practise love [*jên*] and righteousness [*i*]: only man is capable of practising them. [Other] creatures suffer trouble and distress and are unable to match themselves with heaven and earth; only man is capable of doing this.

(*Ch'un Ch'iu Fan Lu*, ch. 56)
(See Fung Yu-lan, *A History of Chinese Philosophy*, Vol. 2, p. 30)

What produces man cannot [itself] be man, for the creator of man is heaven. The fact that men are men derives from heaven. Heaven indeed is man's supreme ancestor. This is why man is to be classed with heaven above.
(11:1. Fung, p. 32)

Heaven, earth and man are the origin of all things. Heaven gives them birth, earth nourishes them, and man perfects them. (6:12. Fung, p. 32)

The beautiful expression of love [*jên*] lies in heaven, for heaven *is* love. Heaven protects and shelters all creatures, generates and produces them, nourishes and forms them . . . If we examine the purpose of heaven [we see that] it is boundless and infinitely loving. Man, receiving his life from heaven [likewise], receives from it love and is thereby himself loving.

(11: 9. Fung, p. 32)

In the above quotations, Tung Chung-shu reveals himself as a true Confucian, but one who seems to have imbibed something from Mo-tzŭ. In his writings he stresses the paramountcy of the three virtues, love, righteousness and wisdom. Yet Tung Chung-shu is concerned to explain a constantly evolving universe in terms of cosmic law, and to do that he has to fall back on the teachings of the *Yin-Yang* and the Five Elements Schools, which he attempts to synthesise into a coherent philosophy. He sees everything being produced by the constant interaction of *Yin* and *Yang,* but with this he combines the idea of the Five Elements (*Wu hsing,* or Movers), i.e. wood, fire, earth, metal and water, which, presiding in orderly sequence over all the forces of nature, also preside over the affairs of man. For him man is the microcosm of which nature is the macrocosm, and there is detailed correspondence between the two.

Within the universe exist the ethers [*ch'i*] of the *Yin* and the *Yang*. Men are constantly immersed in them, just as fish are constantly immersed in water. (*Ch'un Ch'iu Fan Lu,* Ch. 81. Fung, p. 20)

Heaven has five elements: the first wood, the second fire, the third earth, the fourth metal and the fifth water. Wood is the starting-point of [the cycle of] the five elements, water is its conclusion, and earth is its centre. Such is their heavenly sequence . . . Each of the five elements circulates according to its sequence; each of them exercises its own capacities in the performance of its official duties. (Ch. 42. Fung, pp. 20–1)

Collected together, the ethers [*ch'i*] of the universe constitute a unity; divided they constitute the *Yin* and the *Yang;* quartered, they constitute the four seasons; [still further] divided, they constitute the five elements. These elements represent movement. Their movements are not identical. Therefore they are referred to as the five movers [*Wu hsing*]. These movers constitute five officiating powers. Each in turn gives birth to the next and is overcome by the next in turn. (Ch. 13: 7. Fung, pp. 21–2)

One can see from a study of the *Po Hu T'ung*[4] that these theories concerning the nature of the universe and of man became fairly generally accepted by the scholars of the former Han period (206 BC–AD 8). They provided a philosophical justification for the belief in portents and prophecies, magic and miracles, accepted not only by the population at large but in the intimate court circles which surrounded the emperors themselves. A whole mass of apocryphal material came into existence so as to interpret the Confucian Classics in such a way as to justify these ideas.

The attempt was now made to reverence Confucius, not only as the supreme Sage, but as 'uncrowned king' appointed by heaven, and even as a god. Though this tendency to deify Confucius was reversed during the first century AD through the influence of the Old Text School and by the scathing attacks on popular superstitions of Wang Ch'ung (AD 27–*c*. 100). In his *Lun Hêng* or *Critical Essays*,[5] Confucius continued to hold a unique place as China's greatest Sage, as is seen even in the writings of the great Taoist commentators, Wang Pi AD 226–49) and Kuo Hsiang (who died in AD 312), who admitted that Confucius had attained to the perfection which Lao-tzŭ and Chuang-tzŭ were striving after.

In the first century of our era Taoism was becoming an increasing force in intellectual circles. Wang Ch'ung used Taoist naturalism to attack the superstitions of his day, and throughout the Later Han period many scholars interested themselves in a neo-Taoism known as *Hsüan-hsüeh* or 'Mysterious Learning'. It was, however, in a great popular movement which swept over China in the second century AD that Taoism became established as one of the most significant religious movements, to exert a permanent influence on the Chinese people.

The Han period was one of great imperial expansion. The boundaries of China were extended westward and southward, and more and more aboriginal and non-Chinese tribes were brought under the control of the Chinese emperor. Trade contacts were increasing with countries to the west, and it was along the great trade routes through central Asia that Buddhism began to infiltrate into China. What began as an insignificant movement, confined mainly to foreign traders, became within a few centuries the dominant faith of the majority of the Chinese people.

In the following chapters we shall trace the development of religious Taoism, Buddhism and the state cult of Confucianism from the Han dynasty up to the eleventh century AD. These subjects must of necessity be considered separately, but it is important to bear in mind that there was not only constant interaction but extensive mutual borrowings. Institutional religion in China was always relatively weak, and was never so rigidly organised as to exclude tendencies to eclecticism and syncretism.

CHAPTER NINE

THE RISE AND DEVELOPMENT OF RELIGIOUS TAOISM

In chapter six we considered the contribution of early Taoism to religion in the writings of the *Tao Tê Ching* and the *Book of Chuang-tzŭ*. We have also noted the influence of Taoism in the development of a Confucian ideology and in the formation of the *Li Chi* and the *I Ching*. We now take up the theme of religious Taoism as it arose during the Han dynasty, and as it continued to influence Chinese life and thought down to the present day.

Taoism is usually included among the world's religions, but to call it a religion may be misleading, for it includes many other elements. As Holmes Welch writes, it included 'the science of alchemy; maritime expeditions in search of the Isles of the Blest; an indigenous Chinese form of yoga; a cult of wine and poetry; collective sexual orgies; church armies defending a theocratic state; revolutionary secret societies; and the philosophy of Lao-tzŭ.'[1]

Our primary source for the study of religious Taoism is the *Tao Tsang* or the Taoist Canon,[2] comprising some 1,120 volumes which have been compiled over some fifteen centuries. Most of these volumes are not dated, nor do they bear the names of their authors.[3] Many are written in an esoteric language which only the initiates were expected to understand. Some of the books claim to be divine revelations made to Taoist adepts while in a state of trance. The researches of H. Maspero indicate that some 194 books, of which we possess the titles and numerous extracts, were in existence by the seventh century AD. [4] Of these, the *Classic of the Yellow Chamber* (Huang T'ing Ching), an extremely cryptic and esoteric production of the second century AD, and *The True Classic of the Great Mystery,* (Ta-tung chên ching) appear to be the most ancient. Much of the Taoist literature from the fourth to the sixth centuries was based on ideas derived from these works.

Four main streams converged to form Taoism, and they appear to

1 Oracle bones of the Shang dynasty

2 Confucius traditionally depicted, from a Chinese engraving

3 Confucius, from a stone rubbing of the Yüan dynasty, 1280–1368

4 Temple of the Auspicious Year, at the Altar of Heaven, Peking

5 A Taoist priest

6 Paradise of Amitabha Buddha. A painting on silk from Tun Huang, 8th century

7 Kuan Yin, as the guide of souls. A painting on silk from Tun Huang, 10th century

8 A Buddhist monk lighting incense in the temple at Ningpo

9 A Lama priest in full canonicals, outside the temple

10 Image of Mani, in a small former Manichaean temple near Ch'üan Chou

(a)

Early Western religious influences in China
11(a) ancient Muslim tomb, probably of the Yüan dynasty

(b)

11 (b) part of a Nestorian gravestone, discovered in 1946. It represents a pearl-studded cross, surmounting the Lotus, to which flying angels offer their gifts. The inscription is in Syriac

11 (c) the gravestone believed to be that of Bishop Andrew of Perugia, appointed to the see of Zaiton in 1322. The inscription, almost indecipherable, is in Latin.

11 (d) a Manichaean (or Nestorian) gravestone. These four gravestones were all discovered at Ch'üan Chou, Fukien Province, which in the Sung and Yüan dynasties possessed a large and influential foreign community, and where Muslims, Christians and Manichaeans had their places of worship and their own burial grounds

(c)

(d)

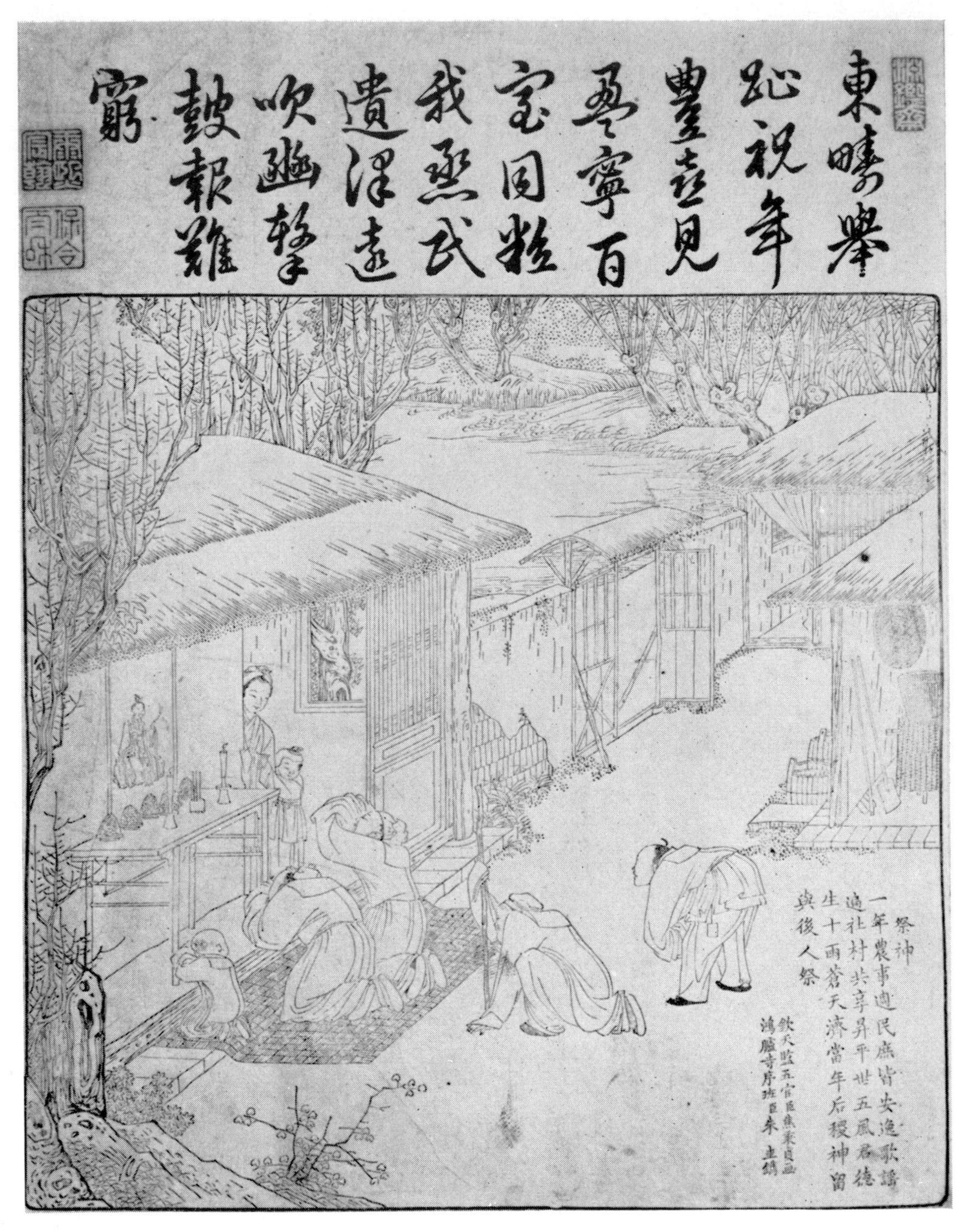

12 A Chinese family returns thanks for Harvest before the household shrine. Taken from the Kêng Chih T'u, an illustrated book on agriculture and sericulture, published in 1696

have come into prominence from about the fourth century BC. First, there was philosophical Taoism which we have already discussed in chapter six. Secondly, there was a 'hygiene school', which cultivated longevity by means of breathing exercises and the control and exercise of the body. Thirdly, there was an intense interest in the search for an elixir of life. Finally, there were expeditions organised and sent out from the north-east coasts of China in search of the Isles of the Blessed, where, it was believed, grew the plant which could renew a person's vitality and maintain life perpetually.[5] Three of these movements were concerned primarily with immortality, but with immortality or perpetual life conceived of in very different terms from those accepted in Christianity. Early Taoism was above all a religion which had as its aim the attainment of endless life. Since life was thought of as due to the harmonious relationship of material elements appertaining to the *Yin* and the *Yang,* which before birth were invisible and without form, then if those elements, which normally dispersed at death, could be held together in perfect harmony, life would be prolonged indefinitely. Unfortunately, that interior harmony was continually being disturbed by evil conduct, by passion and appetite, and by taking into the body disruptive elements which were the material cause of sickness and death. The complete elimination of such materials by discipline, dieting, fasting, breath-control, etc., would lead to the prolongation of life indefinitely.

By the time of the Han dynasty, in face of the logic of inevitable death even to those Taoist adepts who most consistently practised these techniques, the teaching concerning immortality had to be modified. There developed the idea that one must seek to grow within oneself an invisible, immortal 'embryo'. This 'embryo', properly nourished and growing stronger throughout life, was the real 'self' of which the body was but a shell. At death it emerged as a butterfly from its chrysalis or as a snake from its sloughed-off skin, to wander at will in perfect freedom through the universe, or make its way to the realm of the blessed *hsien* (immortals). Though the Taoist adept seemed to die, what was buried in the tomb was not his true body but only a resemblance. Fantastic stories were current which told of tombs being opened up, to reveal nothing but a dried up stick or a bundle of cast-off clothing.

These various strands were brought together during the century between 220 and 120 BC, and those mainly responsible were the *fang-shih* or magicians who gained an influential position at the courts of the emperors. The first emperor, Ch'in-shih-huang-ti, who united China in 221 BC seems, in his latter years, to have been completely under their influence, so that he went to incredible lengths to preserve his own immortality.[6] One of these *fang-shih,* Li Shao-chün by name, gained the confidence of the Han emperor, Wu Ti (140–87 BC) and emphasised that it was possible for a man to become a *hsien* or an 'immortal', and to acquire magical powers such as invisibility. He made experiments in alchemy and persuaded the emperor to seek immortality by transmuting cinnabar into gold.[7] Li Shao-chün became recognised as a classic example of the Taoist adept. In his *Historical Memoirs* (*Shih Chi*), a contemporary historian, Ssŭ-ma Ch'ien, says of Li Shao-chün:

> He abstained from cereals, escaped old age, knew the method to avoid dying, and transmuted cinnabar. When he died, it was said that he had been transformed and, on opening his tomb several years later, they found no corpse there but only his cap and clothing.[8]

In the alchemistic processes, such as transmuting cinnabar, the first important action was to sacrifice to the god of the stove. This god, Tsao chün, was soon to rank as one of the most important divinities of Taoism. By the third century AD he had acquired a niche in almost every home. Under the title *Ssŭ Ming* or 'Master of Destinies' he kept a register of every man's good and evil deeds, and the length of a man's life was determined on his recommendation to heaven. Tsao Chün is the first clearly identified divinity to be associated with Taoism.[9]

Another ancient divinity, mentioned in the *Ch'u Tz'ŭ* of the fourth century BC, was *T'ai I* or 'The Grand Unity'. In 122 BC the magician Miu Chi recommended to the emperor that *T'ai I* should be worshipped as the greatest of all gods. Not much later a triad of gods were worshipped, associated together in control of the whole universe. They were *T'ai I,* the 'Grand Unity'; *T'ien I,* the 'Heavenly Unity'; and *Ti I,* the 'Earthly Unity'. Before very long Taoist invention and imagination were to people the universe with innumerable spiritual beings, Taoists adepts, deified heroes and natural forces. These formed a divine hierarchy, controlling the universe on the analogy of a state bureaucracy and presided over by the supreme triad.

During the former Han dynasty several of the emperors had leanings towards Taoism. Wên-ti (179–157 BC) was probably a Taoist, and the religion influenced him in abolishing mutilating punishments and the extermination of the families of great criminals. For a while he abolished the land tax which bore heavily on the peasants, and he pursued a pacific policy towards the barbarian tribes on the borders of China. His son, Ching-ti (156–140 BC) was the first emperor to recognise the *Tao Tê Ching* as a classic.[10]

The interior gods Hygiene School[11]

Although this school was primarily concerned to achieve immortality by the practice of breath-control, by alchemy and dietetics, it laid great stress on acts of virtue. Ho Kung, the reputed author of the Taoist classic, the *Pao P'u Tzŭ*,[12] wrote:

> Those who do not perform acts of virtue but merely content themselves with the practice of magical techniques will never attain to immortality.
> (*Pao P'u Tzŭ*, 3: 8b)

> Someone asked the Master, 'Is it not true that those who practise the Tao ought to begin by acquiring merit'. He replied, 'Yes. . . those who practise the Tao perform meritorious actions by saving those in danger, by rescuing them from misfortune, by shielding them from sicknesses, and preventing them from premature death. Those who desire to become immortals should take the five virtues as a foundation.'
> (3: 8b)

Han dynasty Taoism laid great stress on the virtues of caring for orphans, maintaining roads, repairing bridges and tending the aged and infirm. Voluntary poverty was encouraged and the distribution of alms to the poor. As H. Maspero writes:

> To practise virtue and avoid transgression, to confess and repent of one's faults, to perform good works, to feed the hungry and clothe the naked, to succour the afflicted and distribute one's wealth to the poor, to do good in secret without boasting of it, these are virtues well recognised by us and with which we are familiar. But, in the China of Han times, this was something new. In face of Confucianism, for which man is never more than a cog in society, Taoism virtually gave to the Chinese a sense of individual morality.[13]

In pursuit of immortality, the adepts of the interior hygiene school developed techniques to ward off the dissolution of the body in death, and to produce within oneself an ethereal and immortal body. They represented the human body as a microcosm reflecting the macrocosm of the universe. Every man had three sections to his body, each with its vital centre. These were located in the head, chest and abdomen.

They were called the 'Fields of Cinnabar'. Within these 'Fields of Cinnabar' dwelt thirty-six thousand gods, the same gods which under a supreme head control the universe. The Three Unities each presided over one of the 'Fields of Cinnabar', and supreme over all was *T'ai I* or 'The Grand Unity' who lived in one of the nine compartments of the head. Near to him resided *Ssŭ Ming,* the 'Master of Destinies' who kept two registers, one for the immortals and one for mortals. The object of the 'hygiene' was to get one's name transferred to the register of the immortals.

The thirty-six thousand gods within the body were thought of as necessary to sustain life. Another aim of the 'hygiene' was to keep them happy at their posts. As they detest the smell of wine and meat, these had to be avoided. Man is also host to three transcendental beings known as the 'three worms', one in each 'field of cinnabar'. They are the principal cause of old age, sickness and infirmity. They are evil spirits who seek to impede man's struggle to attain immortality. As they are sustained by the five cereals which formed the main Chinese diet, the adept must learn to refrain from eating cereals:

> The five cereals are the shears which cut off life, they rot the five internal organs. Owing to them life is shortened. If one grain enters the mouth, do not hope for immortality. Keep yourself free from eating cereals if your hope is not to die. (*Ta Yu Ching,* 3: 1b[14])

So the adept entered upon an impossible task. Refraining from cereals, meat and wine, he gradually restricted his diet until, in theory, he existed only on breath and saliva. He purified his body by never eating solid food, by performing gymnastics and by respiratory techniques by means of which he believed he could circulate the breath through all three 'fields of cinnabar'. He sought for an interior vision which would enable him to see the gods within his body. By uniting the breath with semen in the lower 'field of cinnabar' he formed 'the mysterious embryo' which, nourished on breath, developed a new and pure body within the old one, and this new body, released on death, was immortal.

Under the influence of Buddhism, the aim of Taoism came to be not mere longevity or physical immortality. With Buddhism there was introduced the concept of a soul as something differing from the material body. It was this soul that was immortal, and after death it proceeded to an existence in some heaven or hell, according to its merits. The main concern now came to be, not how to survive, but how to ensure for oneself a happy existence in heaven rather than having to endure the sufferings of hell. And as the hells were considered to be places where one suffered a just retribution for sins committed in life, it might be possible to have some at least of one's sentence remitted through the intercession of some merciful deity.

If religious Taoism had only been represented by these searchers after immortality, it would probably have remained an esoteric cult confined to comparatively few Taoist scholars, who, under the guidance of skilled 'masters' practised alchemy, interior meditation, abstinence and physiological disciplines. Taoism would never have attained to recognition as one of the main religious systems of China. It was only by the popularisation of Taoist teachings, and by linking them to the semi-religious, semi-political mass movements of the second century AD that a Taoist cultic organisation came into being.

The development of a Taoist cultic organisation

The slow disintegration of the great Han dynasty throughout the second century AD was accompanied by widespread misery and suffering, leading to unrest and disaffection among the peasantry. Here was a fertile field for the preaching of millennarist and apocalyptic hopes and the promise of the establishment of an era of peace which would be brought about not by military force alone but by the intervention of supernatural agencies. Two movements, widely separated, arose about the middle of the second century and rapidly grew to incredible proportions. They were both revolutionary and religious in character. They attracted the peasants in tens and hundreds of thousands. Nearly all the leaders connected with the early history of the Taoist church bore the name Chang, which has occasioned some confusion, as these Changs belonged to at least three different families.[15] One movement started in Szechuan and southern Shansi; the other in Shantung.

In Szechuan, towards the middle of the second century AD, a Taoist master, credited with magical powers, started a health cult which attracted a considerable following. He healed the sick, and either as payment for the cure or as cult dues he demanded from each family five pecks of rice a year. He gave himself the title *T'ien Shih* or 'Celestial Master' and expounded his doctrines in a book which cannot now be identified. He was succeeded in his office by his son and grandson. The latter, Chang Lu, had considerable military ability and the governor of Szechuan gave him charge of an army, sending him to the north to attack the governor's enemies. There he linked up with another successful war-lord, Chang Hsiu, who also ran a health cult and followed similar practices. Chang Hsiu, as part of his health cult, insisted on the expiation of sins and penances. The sins and penances were written on three pieces of paper. One of these pieces of paper was buried in the earth, one exposed on a mountain top and one cast into a river, thus notifying the spiritual beings who controlled the universe. To minister to his numerous following, Chang Hsiu organised an elaborate hierarchy of priests, called 'libationers'. One of their duties was to see that the teachings of the *Tao Tê Ching,* grossly misinterpreted, were observed and practised. The priests were also officers in the army, and the new converts were called *kuei-tsu* or 'demon soldiers', and the faithful were the 'demon people' or *kuei-min*. Conversion was also recruitment. Under the 'libationers' were officers who assembled the people for prayer and ceremonies of healing and confession, as sickness was thought to be the direct result of sin. Chang Hsiu was head of the hierarchy under the grandiose title *T'ien Shih Chün* or 'Heavenly Instructor'.

Chang Lu and Chang Hsiu rebelled; later on Chang Lu had Chang Hsiu executed, and took over his organisation and health cult as being superior to his own. He kept the title 'Heavenly Instructor', organised a theocracy, and taught his followers the duties of honesty and trustworthiness. For thirty years he ruled over a large border domain, and finally in AD 215 he surrendered to the warlord Ts'ao Ts'ao who awarded him high honours.

Meanwhile, in Shantung, a little known figure called Yü Chi, well versed in sorcery and medicine, began to preach and heal. In curing the sick he used holy water and incense. He is believed to have incorporated his teachings in a book, now lost, called *T'ai P'ing Ch'ing Ling Shu* or 'The Book of Grand Peace and Purity'.[16] Though executed in AD 197 (his head was exhibited in the market place), his followers continued to believe in him, and claimed that he had become an immortal. About AD 175 his influence inspired Chang Chüeh to found a new movement in Shantung known as the *T'ai P'ing Tao* or 'The Way of Grand Peace'. Chang Chüeh sent missionaries throughout east and central China to convert the people. He held vast public ceremonies, highly dramatic, in which the sick were healed by magic and faith-healing, confessing their sins. He too organised his followers into a church hierarchy, and was himself the head under the title 'Heavenly General'. People flocked to his ceremonies in thousands and there were scenes of intense religious fervour. By AD 184 the movement had spread through eight provinces, and the government decided to take active measures towards its suppression. The Taoists, warned in advance, decided on rebellion, and a vast number, estimated at some 360,000, put on yellow kerchiefs as a signal of revolt, thus giving rise to the name 'Yellow Turbans'. It took many years to suppress the rebellion, though Chang Chüeh and his two brothers were caught and executed.

H. Maspero claims that the aim of this organisation was not simply to replace the imperial government by a government of Taoist functionaries, but to direct the faithful into a religious life, and lead them stage by stage in the performance of such practices as would ensure for them immortality. This religious life was open to people of both sexes, and women were given a prominent place in the hierarchy.[17]

The Taoist hierarchy continued to minister to the faithful, and the 'libationers' became hereditary priests or *Tao Shih*. The movement adopted the *Tao Tê Ching* as its scripture, Huang-Lao as a supreme god, the five elements theory as a science, and breath-control, dieting and fasting as means to the attainment of a pure life. Healing was dramatised. The believer was taught that by expiating sin his disease could be cured. All over the country elaborate corporate ceremonies were held, rituals performed, and instruction given by the priests. Some ceremonies were organised as needed, others took place at the equinoxes and solstices. In certain districts collective sexual orgies took place which scandalised the Confucians and the Buddhists, but their fundamental aim seems to have been the prolongation of life.

Largely as a result of these movements Taoism became a popular religion, highly organised among the masses.

Neo-Taoism and the School of Pure Conversations (Ch'ing T'an)

Whilst religious Taoism was gaining a hold over the masses and competing with Buddhism for their allegiance, a revival of philosophical Taoism was taking place among the intellectuals. This movement between AD 220 and 420 has been characterised as an escape from reality by men who found it impossible to serve under corrupt governments, and who withdrew themselves from office to find freedom and security in a search for transcendental values. It was far more than this. It was a protest against the arid scholasticism of Han dynasty Confucianism, and an attempt to promote critical study, free inquiry and independent thinking. It was an attempt to escape from conventional value, and to seek for oneself the meaning of ultimate reality.

The School of Pure Conversations (*Ch'ing T'an*) is best exemplified in the Seven Sages of the Bamboo Grove (*c.* AD 210–63) who lived in Honan and met together to converse, drink, make music and write poetry in utter disregard of normal social conventions. One of them, by name Chi K'ang, had a luxurious estate in which was a magnificent grove of bamboos where he and his friends would often walk and talk. They repudiated all worldly position, honour, fame and ambition, and sought spontaneity of action by following the impulse of the moment. They engaged in conversation till, as they put it, they reached the Unnameable, and then 'stopped talking and silently understood each other with a smile'. They cultivated the belief that one's personal integrity depended upon conformity to nature. They advocated becoming one with the universe and transcending all distinctions of right and wrong, wealth or poverty, high or low social status.

This impulsiveness and unconventionality, this repudiation of ordinarily accepted standards of morality, was often accompanied by a great sensitivity to nature in all her moods. This aspect of Taoism was to be the inspiration of some of the finest lyrical poetry and some of the greatest painting.

The revival of philosophical Taoism is associated with the work of Wang Pi (d. AD 249), Ho Yen (d. AD 249) and Kuo Hsiang (d. AD 312). Wang Pi, who wrote famous commentaries on the *Tao Tê Ching* and the *I Ching,* found the ultimate reality in original 'non-being' (*pên wu*). This 'non-being' is in perfect accord with a fundamental principle which overrules and unites all particular objects, concepts and events. Kuo Hsiang, enlarging and developing a previous commentary on *Chuang-tzŭ* by Hsiang Hsiu (AD 221–*c.* 300) saw in nature (*tzŭ jan*), with its spontaneous transformations, the only reality. He denied the existence of a Creator and pushed Taoist naturalism to its logical conclusion. Each thing in nature acted according to its own principle and was sufficient to itself.

These men took up the old Taoist theories concerning following nature, spontaneity, determinism and relativity and gave to them a new interpretation. They attacked the idea of a 'sage' becoming a hermit or a recluse. The true sage remains in the midst of affairs, but responds to them with perfect naturalness and spontaneity. Confucius, rather than Lao-tzǔ or Chuang-tzǔ, was their ideal of a perfect sage, because, while they talked of non-being, he realised it. As W. T. Chan writes:

> Neither Wang Pi nor Kuo Hsiang considered Lao-tzǔ or Chuang-tzǔ a sage. Instead their sage was Confucius. This seems amazing, but the reason is really not far to seek. For to Kuo Hsiang especially the ideal person is a sage who is 'sagely within and kingly without', and who travels in both the transcendental and mundane worlds. According to the neo-Taoists, Lao-tzǔ and Chung-tzǔ travelled only in the transcendental world, and were therefore one-sided, whereas Confucius was truly sagely within and kingly without.[18]

The contribution of these neo-Taoists was very great, for they provided Taoism with an intellectual and metaphysical basis which no religious system can do without. Their ideas undoubtedly had a considerable influence on Buddhism as it developed in China, and later on, the neo-Confucianism of the Sung dynasty took up and developed many of their fundamental concepts.

The further development of religious Taoism

Taoism as a religion became established at a time when Buddhism was infiltrating into China. At first Buddhism seems to have been accepted as a foreign teaching with great similarities to Taoism. Friendly contacts grew up in which Taoists assisted in the translation of Buddhist texts, and Taoist terms were taken over to explain Buddhist concepts. But as the influence of Buddhism rapidly grew friction and hostility increased. The leaders of both religions, keenly alive to the fact that freedom to propagate their respective faiths, to attract the populace and to build temples and monasteries was in large measure under the control of the political authority, sought by every means within their power to win the patronage and active support of superstitious emperors. Often they engaged in acrid controversy, seeking to prove the superiority of their own system over that of their rival. The Taoists were not averse to exciting persecution of the Buddhists and could point to Buddhist beliefs and practices which were inimical to the Chinese way of life.

At the same time Taoism was not averse to borrowing extensively from Buddhism. The Mahāyāna schools of Buddhism had adopted the belief in a continued personal existence, either by transmigration into animals or other living entities, or by translation into one of the numerous heavens or hells, where souls were recompensed in accordance with their conduct while on earth. This concept of a future state was seized upon by the Chinese mind, and incorporated into Taoism. Taoism thus borrowed the general framework of its underworld from Buddhism. The number of infernal judges was fixed at ten, one of whom sat at the entrance to the next life to direct each soul to its appropriate place of torment, eight presided over the different hells, whilst a tenth sat at the exit in judgment and sent off those who had completed their penance along the various paths of transmigration.

Faced with the Buddhist teaching that there were innumerable Buddhas and bodhisattvas whose mercy encouraged the faithful and whose merit guaranteed to them salvation, the Taoists proclaimed that their immortals were divine instructors, who taught the Taoist adepts to follow in their footsteps. They now began to people their universe with a hierarchy of innumerable gods who would match up to the Buddhist pantheon.

The Taoists, in order to prove the antiquity and therefore the superiority of their religion, placed the birth of Lao-tzŭ before the creation of heaven and earth. They claimed that creation resulted from his departure from chaos, and that, like the Buddha, Lao-tzŭ had been through several incarnations. As they had no gods of mercy who answered the prayers of the people for protection and salvation, the shadowy figure of Huang-Lao was replaced by a triad of 'Celestial Honoured Ones' (*T'ien Tsun*), who were raised far above the human sphere and had never been incarnated as men. The greatest of these was *Yüan Shih T'ien Tsun* who was concerned for the salvation of all men. Under these 'Celestial Honoured Ones' were a whole host of superior and inferior divinities each with his or her appropriate station — gods, genii, deceased heroes, good men and virtuous women, the spirits of stars, of elementary forces such as thunder and lightning. All these became objects of worship, even to the goddesses of smallpox and measles. All received their share of attention.[19]

Though Taoism, like Buddhism, had no permanent central authority to which all believing Taoists submitted, Taoism was organised into districts presided over by priests or *Tao Shih*. Some of these priests were itinerant, but during the fifth and sixth centuries monastic life became increasingly the rule. The priests could marry and have children and their office became hereditary. Under the priests small groups of 'elders' assisted in performing the cermonies and in collecting dues. The support of the priests came mainly from two sources, the 'banquet' held annually and also on special occasions such as birth or death, when the priest was presented with a fixed amount of money, and the 'Celestial rice tax' of five pecks of rice presented on the seventh day of the seventh month.

It was in the course of the fifth century that a Taoist named K'ou Ch'ien-chih gained the favour of the emperor of the Northern Wei dynasty, T'ai Wu Ti (AD 424–52), and was able to institute several reforms, purifying Taoism of some of its grosser elements and emphasising the importance of good works and hygiene. He assumed the ancient title *T'ien Shih* or 'Celestial Master', and under his influence Taoism was proclaimed as the official religion of the empire in AD 444.

During the sixth century, in imitation of Buddhism, those Taoist priests who lived in monasteries became celibate, and nunneries were established for women. Taoist monasteries began to issue certificates which attested that the holder was an ordained monk who had attained to a certain proficiency. Such certificates, which were also issued by Buddhist monasteries, were of great importance, since monks were exempted from military service, *corvée* and most forms of taxation. Inevitable abuses in the issue of these certificates led the government in the T'ang dynasty to assume control over ordination and the issue of certificates.

When Li Shih-min founded the T'ang dynasty in AD 618, the Taoists were not slow to suggest that he was a descendant of Lao-tzŭ, who possessed the same surname of 'Li'. The Taoists gained a measure of imperial favour and had precedence at court, and though Li Shih-min himself was inclined towards Buddhism, many of his successors became active patrons of Taoism. They conferred titles and dignities on Lao-tzŭ, and Hsüan Tsung (AD 712–56) ordered that a Taoist temple should be built in every city, and that every noble family should possess a copy of the *Tao Tê Ching*.[20] During his reign the *Tao Tê Ching*, *Chuang-tzŭ* and *Lieh-tzŭ* were regarded as classics, and for a time were accepted as suitable studies for the civil service examinations. When in AD 840 Wu Tsung came to the throne, it was not long before he came under the influence of Taoist priests and alchemists. Largely through the machinations of Taoist advisers, Wu Tsung instituted a most virulent persecution of all 'foreign' religions, and especially Buddhism.

The pattern of the Taoist religion was by this time fully established, and few fundamental changes were to take place in subsequent centuries. During the Sung dynasty (*c.* 960–1280) *Yü Huang* or the 'Jade Emperor' came into prominence as the supreme Taoist deity, and his image gradually began to take a central place in the main hall of the Taoist temples. The reputed descendant of Chang Ling[21] was honoured as *T'ien Shih* or 'Celestial Master' and given a large hereditary estate on the Dragon and Tiger mountain in Kiangsi. One large and influential sect of Taoism continued to recognise his descendants as the titular head of the Taoist church right down to the twentieth century. The Sung emperors patronised the compilation of the Taoist Canon, which was catalogued in the tenth century and printed in the year 1019. It was probably, also, in the eleventh century that one of the most popular Taoist works was composed, known as the *T'ai Shang Kan Ying P'ien,* a short precis of Taoist morality. Charitable societies and monasteries considered it to be a work of merit to distribute this short treatise free. It pointed out that man's virtues and sins are regularly reported to heaven, and that man's life is drastically shortened by sin. By the performance of numerous good actions, life was not only prolonged, but one had the assurance of becoming an immortal.

Although some eighty-six Taoist sects have been recorded, Taoists priests can be divided roughly into two groups. There are those who seek 'perfect realisation' by withdrawal from the world, by emphasis on hygiene techniques, meditation, rigorous asceticism, and the practice of gymnastics and breath-control. These priests in theory live a celibate life, are vegetarian and abstain from alcohol. Then there are the followers of the Celestial Masters of the Dragon and Tiger Mountain, who do not live in monasteries, but go among the masses performing religious ceremonies, selling charms, telling fortunes and demonstrating magical arts. They marry and hand down their office and their arts to their children. They are believed to be great sorcerers, and so are called in by the superstitious peasants in cases of sickness or misfortune.

With the rise of neo-Confucianism. Taoism as a religion began to lose whatever hold it had had over the upper classes. W. T. Chan goes so far as to write, 'During the last millennium there has been no outstanding Taoist priest, philosopher or teacher.'[22] The scholars continued to study the philosophical works of Taoism, but they looked down on Buddhism and religious Taoism as superstitions fit only to delude the common people. Gradually, at least as far as the peasant religion was concerned, Buddhism and Taoism lost much of their distinctiveness. They became merged in an incoherent mass of peasant beliefs and practices in which the worth of a god or his priestly representative was measured by the result obtained. Yet Taoism still maintained some hold through its lay vegetarian societies, promoted for mutual encouragement in the religious life, meditation, study and good works, and in its secret societies among the peasants giving a religious sanction to revolutionary activity in times of trouble. Most of the Taoist priests, with their faith-healing, spiritism and fortune-telling are little more than ignorant charlatans, though there are still many notable exceptions.

CHAPTER TEN

BUDDHISM IN CHINA

Introduction of Buddhism and early development

The introduction of Buddhism into China was one of the great events of Chinese history, yet most of the Buddhist accounts of that event are legendary and the actual date of entry is unknown. Later Buddhist apocryphal literature, in seeking to demonstrate for propaganda purposes the early existence of Buddhism in China, refers to the arrival of Buddhist priests at the capital of Ch'in Shih-huang-ti between 221 and 208 BC, and to the existence of Buddhist monks at Ch'ang-an in the second half of the second century BC, but there are no means of verifying such stories.[1] The apocryphal character of the story of the 'official' introduction of Buddhism under the emperor Ming (AD 58–75) has only recently been recognised. H. Maspero regarded it as a pious fiction[2] whilst the Chinese historian T'ang Yung-t'ung believed that there might be some basis of fact behind this tradition.[3] According to this tradition, the emperor Ming had a dream of a golden image in the west and consequently sent emissaries to India requesting that Buddhist teachers might be sent.

The evidence seems conclusive that Buddhism was 'unofficially' represented in China from about the beginning of the Christian era, being confined to scattered groups and settlements of foreigners. It infiltrated into China from the north-west along the two branches of the continental silk-road through central Asia, and entered China at what was to become the celebrated Buddhist centre of Tun-huang. The biography of prince Ying of Ch'u, who in AD 52 went to live at P'êng-ch'êng, the capital of Ch'u in north Kiangsu, mentions pious laymen and monks, and implies the existence of a Buddhist community in that city.[4] A memorial presented to Emperor Huan in AD 166 mentions a joint sacrifice made to Huang-Lao and the Buddha performed by the emperor and contains two quotations from the *Sūtra in forty-two sections,* thus showing that this sūtra in some form was in circulation at that time, and that Buddhism was already beginning to influence the court circles in the capital, Loyang.[5]

Until the close of the Huan dynasty (*c.* AD 220) Buddhism in China was largely the religion of foreigners, but at least three important centres were already in existence, namely P'êng Ch'êng, Loyang and Chiao Chou (now in Vietnam). Very early on Loyang became a centre for the translation of Buddhist scriptures, a work organised by foreign monks, the most famous being An Shih-kao, a Parthian prince who, after his arrival (*c.* AD 148), spent more than twenty years as a Buddhist missionary in China. He is the first undoubtedly historical character in Chinese Buddhism.[6]

Early allusions to Buddhism in China refer to its association with the Taoist cult of Huang-Lao.[7] Several factors contributed to this Buddhist-Taoist mixture. It was found that Buddhist ideas could only be successfully conveyed to the Chinese mind through the medium of Taoist terms. Many of the assistants to the early translators were drawn from the ranks of Taoist scholars. There was a certain similarity in the ceremonies of the two religions, and in both worship was carried on without the aid of the animal sacrifices. There was a similar emphasis on concentration and meditation, on abstinence from certain foods, and a concern for immortality. It must be remembered that early Buddhism in China was regarded by the Chinese as teaching the indestructibility of the human soul and the possibility of rebirth in the Brahmā-heavens, whereas at this time the Taoists sought immortality in a heaven of grand purity. The famous historian, Yüan-hung (AD 328–76) AD in his *Hou Han Chi* summarises the Buddhist teachings of the Han dynasty:

They also teach that when a man dies his soul does not perish, but will be reborn and assume another form. The meritorious and evil deeds performed during this life-time will have their rewards and punishments. Therefore they value the practice of meritorious deeds and the cultivation of the Way, so as to discipline the soul. By doing so they attain to Nirvāna and become Buddha.[8]

The Buddhists taught the suppression of the passions by concentration and meditation and by the observance of the rules laid down in the *Patimokkha*. They stressed charity, compassion, harmlessness and the merit of donating worldly possessions to the monastic community. In a temple built by a local official, Chai-jung, in AD 191 in north Kiangsu Buddhist worship was combined with a social programme and community welfare.[9] In this way Buddhism was attracting the populace. Yet in a Taoist work known as the *T'ai P'ing Ching,* and attributed to Yü Chi (*fl.* AD 126–44) Buddhism is criticised under four heads: (a) it is unfilial, (b) it encourages celibacy and results in the neglect of wives and children, (c) it permits the eating of impurities, i.e. the taking of cow's urine as medicine, (d) it promotes begging. All these were considered by the orthodox Chinese as unnatural.

As far as we know early Buddhism in China was an urban phenomenon. The foreigners gravitated to the cities for business. It was in the cities that wealthy patrons and devotees could most easily be attracted, scholars gathered together for the translation of scriptures and Buddhist teachings most easily disseminated. As E. Zürcher writes, 'The history of the Buddhist Church before *c.* 290 is still ninety per cent a history of translations.'[10] Yet according to Demieville, it was not until AD 286 that translations were made giving literate Chinese access to the speculative ideas of the Mahāyāna.[11]

Around the middle of the third century AD, when the disturbances occasioned by the fall of the Han dynasty began to abate, Buddhist travellers from China began to explore central Asian countries in search of sacred scriptures. Chu Shih-hsing is the first recorded case of a Chinese making the ardous journey to Khotan in quest of Buddhist scriptures.[12] He succeeded in obtaining the Sanscrit text of the *Prajña-páramitá* in twenty-five thousand verses, and this work 'perhaps more than any other scripture would come to play a dominant role in the formation of Chinese Buddhist thought'.[13] About this time Ch'ang-an came to overshadow Loyang as the chief stronghold of Buddhism, and in that city an unprecedented period of development occurred under the inspiration and leadership of Dharmaraksha (Fa Hu, *fl. c.* 266–308), who completed a translation of *The Lotus of the True Doctrine (Saddharmapundarīkasūtra)*,[14] with its doctrine of the one Buddha vehicle which opens the way of Buddhahood to all believers, and which stresses the eternity and omnipotence of the Buddha. The translation of this scripture completed a series of five Mahāyāna sūtras whose teachings were of fundamental importance for the development of the great Mahāyānist schools of Chinese Buddhism.[15]

The growth and domestication of Chinese Buddhism

The downfall of the Han dynasty in AD 220 brought weakness and disunity. It led to the invasion of north China by non-Chinese peoples from the north and west. For almost three hundred years the control of north China was lost to the Chinese. The famous cities of Ch'ang-an and Loyang were captured by the Hsiung-nu in the early decades of the fourth century, and the year 311, which marks the sack of Loyang, might be regarded as a turning-point in Chinese history. It led to a great exodus of scholars, officials and learned monks to the south, where they helped in the establishment of the Eastern Chin dynasty (AD 317–420). For a long period the development of Buddhism in the north and south followed very different lines.

In the north the Buddhists sought the protection of the ruling princes, who looked favourably on the religion and controlled it in the interests of the state. Buddhist monks became political, military and diplomatic advisers, and also gained a great reputation among the people through their skill in thaumaturgical and magical performances. Fo T'u-têng (d. 349) was the most influential Buddhist monk of this period, being court-chaplain to the Hsiung-nu emperors. He became celebrated for his shamanistic and magical practices. He seems to have been indefatigable in preaching the Buddhist faith in its most elemental form, seeking thereby mass conversion. He established numerous monasteries, introduced a more complete set of monastic rules, and is said to have taken the initiative in establishing an order of nuns on Chinese soil.[16]

In Ch'ang-an itself a famous school of translators worked under the guidance of Kumārajīva (AD 344–413). Born in Kucha of a Brahmin father and a Kuchean princess, he studied Buddhism in Kashmir, after which he returned to Kucha and was ordained. There followed twenty years of study of the Mahāyāna before he was taken to China. He arrived at Ch'ang-an in 401. 'Kumārajīva's distinctive work,' writes E. R. Hughes,[17] 'was to enable Buddhism to stand on its own feet in China, and claim with some success to be a universal religion and the one and only means of salvation for the individual.' He made a new translation of the *Lotus Scripture,* which from this time onwards gripped the Chinese mind by its imaginative and religious appeal. He introduced the teachings of Nāgārjuna, who in the second century AD had taught in India a 'middle path' (*Mādhyamika*) between the two extremes of existence and non-existence, affirmation and negation, pleasure and pain, and related this middle path to the doctrine of dependent origination. 'Nothing comes into existence, nor does anything disappear. Nothing is eternal, nor has anything an end. Nothing is identical or differentiated. Nothing moves hither or thither.' In this way the truth of *śunyatā* (the void) was underlined. With remorseless logic Nāgārjuna insisted that any contradiction is an infallible proof of error. He then proceeded to find contradiction in every concept. He argued that comprehension of the unreal, the void, the relative nature of all phenomena leads to *prajñā* (intuitive wisdom or non-dual knowledge). When we reach *prajñā* we gain absolute truth, which is *śunyatā,* that which is beyond cause, thought or conception. But this absolute truth is only reached by going through a relative or worldly level of truth. Kumārajīva and his followers opened up to the minds of Chinese scholars the great ideas of the Indian masters of Mahāyāna Buddhism, and their teachings had a profound influence. Kumārajīva had a most attractive personality, being honest, loyal, humane and self-sacrificing. Among his disciples Sêng Chao (374–414) became an outstanding master of Mādhyamika.

The famous monastery of Tun-huang lay to the far north-west at a strategic point on the central Asian trade route. Though a Buddhist community existed here at the end of the third century, the first of the famous cave-temples is dated AD 366. Here a treasury of murals painted on the walls of the caves reveals nearly one thousand years of Buddhist history, from the fourth century to the end of the Sung dynasty.

In 399 Fa-hsien[18] left Ch'ang-an on his famous pilgrimage to India. Thus was inaugurated a pilgrim movement to the great centres of Indian Buddhism, for study under great masters, to visit well-known shrines, to bring back sacred texts and relics, and to persuade Indian missionary teachers to return with the pilgrims to China.

In the south of China, where a purely Chinese dynasty had been set up, the fourth century witnesses to the penetration of Buddhist doctrine into the highest gentry circles, and the development of what is known as 'gentry Buddhism'. The cultured classes were keenly interested in the new teachings. They became patrons of the sangha, founding monasteries and temples, supplying the monks with all necessities, and often paying for the translation of sacred texts. Though few of the highest rank became monks, many educated and wealthy people joined the ranks of the Buddhist laity, accepting the five Buddhist rules of morality, paying frequent visits to monasteries to pray, burn incense, listen to sermons, or hold conversations with learned monks. Famous exponents of Buddhist doctrine were often invited to the imperial court, and came to act as advisers in secular affairs.

Buddhism in the south developed two different trends. There was an emphasis on the *dhyāna* school of meditation, control of the mind and suppression of the passions, a school which was Hīnayānist in inspiration. On the other hand there was the *prajñā* school, interested in questions concerning the nature of ultimate reality, the translation of the great Mahāyānist sūtras, and in fostering closer relations between the sangha and the literati. To the cultured classes the Mahāyāna had a great appeal. It brought a new perspective to the handling of those fundamental problems which had been the concern of the neo-Taoists. The Prajñā sūtras taught that the nature of all phenomena (*dharmas*) was *śunyatā* (void). Dharmas do not possess their own self-nature. Nothing conditional exists of itself, but everything is the result of many causes. Individuality and entity have no existence for the assumption of any duality is erroneous. There is no dualism between subject and object, affirmation and negation, *samsāra* and *nirvāna*. This teaching seemed to tie in well with the Taoist teaching of *wu-wei* (non-activity) and the Taoist concept of the eternal Tao.

The central figure in all the main developments of Buddhism in China throughout the middle decades of the fourth century was Tao-an (312–85).[19] Born in north China, his early years as a monk were spent in ardent propagation of the faith and in the study of the Dhyāna-sūtras which had been translated by An Shih-kao. Tao-an had a genius for bibliography and for collecting sacred scriptures on which he wrote numerous commentaries. He possessed extraordinary gifts as a teacher, scholar and organiser. Under his guidance a flourishing and famous centre of Buddhism grew up at Hsiang-yang in northern Hupei. Here his interest shifted from the Hīnayānist inspired *dhyāna* to the Mahāyānist *Prajñāpāramitās,* from Buddhist yoga to Buddhism gnosticism with its background of Chinese *hsüan-hsüeh* (mysterious learning).[20] His exposition of the *Perfection of Wisdom* attracted large numbers of scholarly monks and laymen. He also laid great stress on the devotional aspects of Buddhism, and in particular on the cult of the future Buddha, Maitreya. This great Buddha was believed to reside in the Tushita heaven, and from there, in obedience to Śākyamuni's special commission, descend to the earth as Buddha and inaugurate a great era of peace.

In governing a large and growing community Tao-an exercised strict discipline, but soon realised the need for a competent translation of the Vinaya rules, a need which was fully supplied later by Kumārajīva's translation. During his latter years at Ch'ang-an, Tao-an was instrumental in setting up a large group of translators who rendered the literature of the Sarvāstivādins into Chinese.

The most famous of Tao-an's disciples was Hui-Yüan (334–416) who, absorbed in metaphysical speculations and *prajñā* philosophy, resorted to the concepts of philosophical Taoism to make the meanings of the sūtras clear to his audiences. He was attracted to Lu-shan, a mountain famous for its glorious scenery and haunted by traditions of Taoist hermits of antiquity. Here he established what was to be for centuries the most famous Buddhist centre in south China. To his beautiful monastery countless lay visitors were attracted. In the year 402 he assembled a large group of monks and laymen before a statue of Amitābha, there to make a collective vow to be born in the Western Paradise. On the basis of this tradition Hui-yüan is regarded as the founder of the Pure Land (*Ching-t'u*) school, and its first patriarch. In his exposition of Buddhist truth his wide reading in Confucian and Taoist classics stood him in good stead.

Another great figure who made a highly significant contribution to the development of Chinese Buddhist thought was Tao-shêng (*c.* 360–434). His great interest was the *Nirvāna sūtra,* which emphasised the eternal, joyous, personal and pure nature of Nirvāna, and claimed that all sentient beings, possessed as they were of the Buddha-nature, will eventually attain to Buddhahood. The emphasis on 'being' seemed to be heretical to Buddhists familiar with the *śunyatā* doctrine of the *Prajñā sūtras* and the Taoist theory of non-being, and those who taught that Nirvāna is an impersonal state of emptiness. But Tao-sheng believed that the *Prajñā sūtras* and the *Nirvāna sūtra* taught the same lesson, that the ultimate truth of Buddha-nature is without characteristics, transcending forms and symbols, and is realisable instantly and completely. To realise it one must know his 'true-self', the reality of the Buddha-nature which is in each individual. Tao-shêng contended that since the Buddha-nature is within us there is no Pure Land to go to, nor can meritorious deeds expect a reward. Buddhahood is achieved by a sudden and complete enlightenment.

In the work of these great Buddhist masters of the latter part of the fourth century and the early decades of the fifth century we can see in germ the ideas which were to develop into the great Mahāyānist schools of Chinese Buddhism. As Chinese Buddhist thinkers, familiar with the teachings of the Confucian and Taoist classics, assimilated the teachings of the great Indian Buddhist interpreters, Ashvaghosha, Nāgārjuna, Vasubandhu and Asanga, there slowly emerged a distinctive Chinese Buddhist tradition, which was to come to flower in the *T'ien T'ai,* Pure Land, *Hua Yen* and *Ch'an* sects of the T'ang dynasty.

It is estimated that before the end of the Eastern Chin dynasty there were 1,786 temples and 24,000 monks and nuns in China. The growing wealth and influence of the Buddhist clergy were bound to give rise to criticism and anti-clericalism. Monks were not averse to meddling in affairs of state. Many were entering the *sangha* from impure motives. Though for the time being the relation between the *sangha* and the state was settled in favour of the monks who were considered to have transcended society and worldly affairs, the problem of the relation of the monasteries to the state was to grow more and more acute. The monasteries were governed by their own monastic laws. They were largely exempted from taxation. The monks were freed from observing the usual formalities of reverence due to secular rulers. The following two centuries mark the continued progress of Buddhism in China, but at the same time a gathering storm of opposition.

The development of a Chinese Buddhist tradition

During the period of political disunity known as the Northern and Southern Dynasties (420–589) Buddhism in China continued to develop on lines laid down in the previous century. In the south it gained a strong following in the aristocratic circles connected with the court. The emperor Wu of the Liang dynasty (*c.* 502–49) was an ardent Buddhist. There was great activity in temple construction, and under imperial patronage Buddhism spread rapidly among the populace. Imperial patronage, resented by Confucians and Taoists alike, led to strong protests by non-Buddhist writers, who were sometimes vitriolic in their attacks. One such critical attack on Buddhism was made by Hsün-chi, a disappointed scholar who failed to receive office under the emperor. He wrote a memorial against Buddhism entitled the *Lun-fo-chiao-piao*[21] in which he charged Buddhist monks with sedition, immorality and hypocrisy and claimed that they presented a serious economic liability. He believed that Buddhism was reducing the Confucian code of social behaviour and relationships to a state of confusion.

Emperor Wu welcomed to the court the famous Indian monk

Paramartha, who arrived in Canton in 546. It was through his translations of the sūtras belonging to the Vijñānavādins that Paramartha made available to the Chinese the idealistic teachings of Asanga and Vasubandhu, thus paving the way for the great idealistic school of the T'ang dynasty and the works of Hsüan-tsang and K'uei-chi.

In the north, the most powerful state was the Northern Wei Dynasty founded by a To-pa people whose origin was probably Turkic. By the year 440 this people controlled the whole of north China, and gradually adopted Chinese civilisation and culture. In 446 anti-Buddhist persecution broke out, engineered by a Confucian named Ts'ui-hao, and a Taoist K'ou-ch'ien-chih. A proclamation from the Wei emperor ordered that 'all stupas, paintings and foreign sūtras are to be beaten down and burned utterly; the sramanas without distinction of age are to be executed'.[22] Though the persecution did not last long, Buddhism in the north received a temporary check. This persecution was followed in 574 by another in which Buddhism was proscribed as unfilial, wealth-consuming, rebellious, and a foreign religion. In spite of these persecutions Buddhism continued to develop with amazing vigour. The building of temples went on on such a massive scale that early in the fifth century it was estimated that in the northern capital of Loyang, with a population of about half a million, there were 1,367 temples. The great rock cave temples of Yün-kang and Lung-men were begun about this time, to become magnificent and permanent symbols of devotion to the Buddha. At this time the most popular objects of devotion were Śakyāmuni (Chinese: *Shih-chia-mo-ni-fo*) and Maitreya, (Chinese: *Mi-lo-fo*). The former, though regarded as the historic Buddha, was from the earliest days of Buddhism in China spoken of as the glorified, heavenly Buddha and given such titles as *Ju-lai,* 'he who appears in this manner', or 'the norm which has appeared', or *chen-ju* ('the true norm'). These Buddhist deities were to give place later in popular esteem to Amitābha (Chinese:*O-mi-t'o-fo*) and Avalokiteśvara (Chinese: *Kuan-yin*), as the Pure Land school of Buddhism became increasingly popular. Buddhism made a strong appeal to the rulers, and at the same time was adapting itself to the needs of the Chinese people by an increasing stress on filial piety, and by coming to terms with the cult of ancestors by directing that prayers should be chanted for the well-being of the departed. The devotional aspects of Buddhism were being increasingly stressed as Buddhism was becoming *the* religion of the common people.

In the year 581 Yang-chien, one of the most remarkable men in Chinese history, unified both north and south to form the Sui dynasty, and he greatly relied on Buddhism to help in the unification and consolidation of his empire. He initiated a series of measures to promote Buddhism, establishing Buddhist monasteries at the foot of each of the five sacred mountains, and also on the sites of famous battles.

The growth of Buddhism was achieved in spite of the fact that in several respects its ideas and teachings were opposed to indigenous culture. The Chinese held the view that life is good and to be enjoyed, and this went counter to the Buddhist teaching that all is suffering and illusion. The Buddhist practice of celibacy was inimical to the Chinese emphasis on family life and the need for numerous progeny. The mendicant monk was an object of scorn to those who believed that all able-bodied people should be engaged in productive labour. The concept of a monastic community possessing its own government and laws was entirely unacceptable to the Confucian, who believed in the unity of the empire under one supreme ruler. Yet in a time of lawlessness and confusion it was the monastery that provided refuge for the disillusioned scholar and the multitude who sought escape from the difficulties and burdens of life. Buddhism offered an irresistible appeal just where Confucianism failed. It satisfied religious aspirations, brought solace in sorrow and disappointment, offered divine assistance through ever-compassionate Buddhas and bodhisattvas, reward for meritorious living in some heaven of supreme bliss, whilst its concept of inevitable punishment for sin acted as a deterrent. The idea that all creatures possess the Buddha-nature and are capable of attaining to Buddhahood, linked to the doctrine of *karma* and the belief in rebirth, was attractive to rich and poor alike. Buddhist scholars were all the time seeking to interpret their religion in such a way as to make it attractive to the Chinese.

Buddhism in China reaches its maturity

The great T'ang empire (618–907) was on the whole favourable to the progress of Buddhism, although the early T'ang emperors, claiming descent from Lao-tzŭ, favoured Taoism. The expansion of the empire into central Asia and the opening up of trade relations with peoples in the far west of Asia brought many foreigners into China. The early years of the T'ang dynasty saw the introduction into China of Nestorian

Christianity, Islam and Manichaeism. Buddhism, constantly being renewed and revitalised by contacts with India and the Buddhist countries of western Asia, had now been in China for more than half a millennium and was assuming a more Chinese character. Schools such as *T'ien T'ai* and *Ch'an* reflected many Chinese characteristics.

The T'ang rulers saw it expedient to bring the Buddhist *sangha* under the strict control of the state. Serious crimes committed by monks were now judged by the civil authorities. Throughout the eighth century a number of measures were introduced to regulate and control Buddhism, prohibiting monks and nuns from wandering about the countryside to preach and sell Buddhist scriptures and images. In 747 entry into the monastic order was restricted by the granting of government certificates to ordained monks. But the religion was too well established to be seriously affected by these measures. The imagination of the people was held captive by the rich imagery, the beautiful rituals, the magnificent festivals and dazzling spectacles, and the processions when Buddhist images and relics were carried in pomp through the streets. In or near all the great cities temples of great architectural beauty witnessed to the strength of the Buddhist faith, temples in which nature and art combined to bring solace and peace of mind. The extensive temple lands, usually exempted from taxation, the vast accumulation of temple treasures, the powerful influence of the higher clergy and the widespread appeal of Buddhism to the common people aroused in Confucians and Taoists alike strong anti-Buddhist feeling. In 621 Fu-i, a leading Taoist, presented a memorial attacking Buddhism on nationalistic, economic and intellectual grounds. Later in 819 the famous Confucian scholar Han-yü presented his well-known anti-Buddhist memorial in which he vented the utmost scorn on the idolatrous veneration of Buddhist relics. Though he was degraded and punished, the seeds were sown which were to culminate in the great persecution of 845.

During the T'ang dynasty there was a large increase in Chinese Buddhist pilgrims to India. The most famous of these pilgrims was Hsüan-tsang (*c.* 596–664) who left China in 629 to visit in turn the famous Buddhist centres in India. He studied Sanscrit and the Vijñānavāda doctrines at the university of Nalanda. Arriving back in China in 645, after an absence of many years, and loaded with Buddhist sūtras and relics, he was given a hero's welcome. He settled down to a prodigious work of translation, and left for posterity an account of his pilgrimage known as the *Hsi-yu-chi*. In 671 another famous monk, I-tsing, took the sea-route to India from Canton, and besides his translations he left for posterity two famous books: *A Record of Buddhist Kingdoms in the Southern Archipelago*, and his *Biographies of famous monks of the T'ang Dynasty who sought the Dharma in the Western Regions*.

The great monastic foundations of the T'ang dynasty were deeply involved in economic activities. They employed vast numbers of free laymen and temple slaves to cultivate their estates and to provide labour for water-powered rolling-mills, oil presses, hostels, pawnshops, etc. The slaves were recruited in a variety of ways. Some were criminals who were released on condition that they became attached to a monastery, some were orphans brought up by the monks, others were drawn from the ranks of the dispossessed and unemployed who sought for security in the monastery.

Religious instruction was given in the monasteries to postulants and novices, and attempts were made to train a literate body of monks conversant with the sacred texts of Buddhism. Through public lectures, debates, story-telling and drama the truths of Buddhism were disseminated among the masses.

The monasteries served as charitable institutions caring for the aged and the sick. Monasteries ran dispensaries and hospitals, established bath-houses and rest-houses, arranged for the feeding of the hungry and engaged in communal projects such as road-mending, bridge-building, digging wells and planting trees. These were ways in which merit might be accumulated to ensure entrance into Amitābha's paradise.

By the middle of the ninth century Buddhism in China had reached the peak of its influence, its power and its splendour. The government became fearful for its own authority, and cast envious eyes on the tremendous wealth owned by the monastic communities. It finally decided to strike a heavy blow at what had virtually become an 'imperium in imperio'. The emperor Wu-tsung struck first against the Manichaeans, and in 843 their temples were surrendered to the government and their foreign priests excluded. In 845 a census was taken of all Buddhist monastic communities. It revealed that there were some quarter of a million monks and nuns, 4,600 temples and over 40,000 lesser shrines. The order went out to destroy all Buddhist establishments except for one temple in each of the major prefectures and four temples in each of the capital cities. The majority of monks and nuns were forced to take up secular life. Though the persecution did not last long it had a disastrous effect from which Buddhism in China never completely recovered. This was particularly noticeable in respect of some of the great monastic foundations with their architectural beauty, their priceless treasures of art and their extensive libraries, which perished in the flames of destruction.

The schools of Chinese Buddhism

Though the various schools of Chinese Buddhism are seen best in their period of fullest development under the T'ang dynasty, the roots of most of them go back to the fifth and sixth centuries and even earlier.

It must be borne in mind that, when Buddhism became firmly established in China, Indian Buddhism had been flourishing for about a thousand years. All the great works of the Hīnayāna and Mahāyāna canons were already in existence. 'The Chinese, with their deeply ingrained confidence in the written word, accepted the Buddhist scriptures in Chinese translation as the literal word of the Buddha. They treated all the Buddhist scriptures, including the Hīnayāna canon, as the record of the forty-odd years of Šākyamuni's preaching career.'[23] The rise of the different Buddhist sects in China resulted largely from the fact that the volume of translated Buddhist scriptures had grown so vast that few scholars could hope to be reasonably familiar with them all, and the teachings contained in them were so extremely diverse as to appear at times to be contradictory. Furthermore, as the writings of the great Indian Mahāyānist writers became familiar in Chinese translation, their distinctive interpretations of the Buddhist *dharma* were avidly seized upon by Chinese Buddhist scholars, stimulating new currents of thought.

Though all the scriptures were treated as canonical, schools arose under distinguished teachers who adopted widely different interpretations of Buddhist truth, and claimed that they presented the quintessence and perfection of the Buddha's message. A Buddhist master would accept some particular work as of paramount importance, considering the rest of the canon as introductory teaching leading up to the supreme truth. This supreme truth he believed to be revealed and expounded in the scripture of his choice. Out of an intense study of the great Indian texts by minds already impregnated by Confucian and Taoist thought there grew up a truly Chinese form of Buddhism very different from its Indian parent. 'Most of the Chinese Buddhist sects were founded during the period of unity under the Sui and T'ang dynasties from the end of the sixth century through to the eighth.'[24]

The following eight schools of Chinese Buddhism have had practical importance, and they all flourished and exerted a powerful influence in the T'ang dynasty. They are tabulated with the approximate date of their founding:

1 *Ching T'u,* or Pure Land, *c.* fourth century.
2 *San Lun,* or the School of Three Treatises, Mādhyamika, *c.* 400.
3 *Ch'an,* a Meditation school, *c.* 520.
4 *T'ien T'ai,* an attempt at harmonisation, *c.* 550.
5 *Hua Yen,* the Garland school, *c.* 600.
6 *Wei Shih,* or *Fa Hsiang,* the Mere Ideation school, *c.* 650.
7 *Lü,* a school of discipline, Hīnayānist, *c,* 650.
8 *Chen Yen,* or *Mi Tsung,* Tantric, *c.* 720.

Of these schools of Chinese Buddhism, some had already absorbed into themselves minor schools which had arisen and persisted for a while. San Lun and Wei Shih were too academic to exist for long independently, but their metaphysical teachings were kept alive in the monasteries and the neo-Confucianism of the Sung dynasty was greatly influenced by them. *T'ien T'ai* and *Hua Yen* were merged into the great *Ching T'u* or Pure Land form of Buddhism. The *Lü Tsung* or Legalistic school, emphasising the more severe and ascetic aspects of Buddhism, had a pervasive influence in other schools, and continued as a small sect down to present times.[25]

Though the various schools of Chinese Buddhism flourished for a while in China, and some of them, having been transplanted to Japan, had a brilliant history in that country, a continuous process of syncretism gradully obliterated the salient features of doctrine and practice. It is not possible, within the limits of this chapter, to give more than a very brief account of each of these eight schools, pointing out the most important features.

The Ching T'u or Pure Land Sect. Of all the great Mahāyāna sects of Chinese Buddhism the Pure Land sect was destined to exert a pervasive and dominating influence over the lives of the common people. Probably the oldest of all the schools, it was also the least philosophical. Yet certain tenets were basic in the mind of its founder: 'a concept of the Buddha's infinity, a firm belief in the indestructibility of the human soul, a belief in *karma* or retribution, and a strong belief in the universality of the Buddha-nature in all creatures.'[26]

Early in the third century Chih-tun had been influenced by Pure Land ideas, but it was Hui-yüan who is considered to be the founder of the sect in 402. He and his successors took as their principal scripture the Greater *Sukhāvatī-Vyūha Sūtra (Wu-liang-shou Ching)* which proclaimed the doctrine of salvation by faith in Amitābha (O-mi-to-fo) and contained vivid descriptions of the Pure Land over which he ruled. Two other great sūtras beloved by the sect proclaimed the same doctrine and extolled the infinite compassion of Amitābha. They proclaimed the way by which the human soul might reach his land of perfect bliss. These two sūtras were the smaller *Sukhāvatī-Vyūha sūtra (O-mi-to Ching)* and the *Amitā Yurdhyāna sūtra (Kuan-wu-liang-shou Ching)*. Later the teachings of the sect were condensed in the famous *Awakening of Faith in the Mahāyāna (Ch'i Hsin Lun)*[27] which became 'a source of greatest blessing to many of the best educated people in the East'.[28] and 'standard for Buddhists down to the present day'.[29] A single act of faith in the saving power of Amitābha would ensure rebirth in his Pure Land. In his saving activity Amitābha is assisted by two great powers, the bodhisattva Avalokiteśvara (*Kuan-yin*), known as the goddess of mercy and representing Amitābha's infinite compassion, and Mahāsthama (*Ta-shih-chih*) who represented Amitābha's omnipotence and wisdom.

Hui-yüan, who really established the Pure Land sect, was a zealous Taoist who, having been converted to Buddhism, entered upon a lifelong quest for a real understanding of the Mahāyāna faith.[30] About the year 380 he settled at a famous monastery which had been built on the Lu-shan, 'a mountain haunted by the memory of famous Taoist hermits of antiquity'.[31] This became one of the most important centres of Buddhism, attracting monks and laymen alike.

One of the greatest exponents of Pure Land doctrine was Shan-tao (613–81) who realised that men, as long as they live in the world, are bound in a vicious circle of sin and error through the three poisons of greed, anger and stupidity. They have little power to save themselves, but enlightenment is guaranteed for all who make a sincere vow of faith in Amitābha, filling the mind constantly with thoughts of him and accepting his mercy and merit. Reichelt thinks that Shan-tao may have been influenced by Nestorian Christianity which was being introduced into China at about this time.[32]

The Pure Land school with its emphasis on salvation by faith alone and its teaching of devotion to the Buddhas and bodhisattvas is comparable with the bhakti developments of Hinduism. It opposes the idea that salvation is gained solely by self-effort which results in an 'enlightenment' in which the mind is set free from all the entanglements of the phenomenal world. Pure Land accepted the orthodox Buddhist teaching that life is sorrow and disillusionment, but it directed the mind to the infinite host of Buddhas and bodhisattvas who offered to the believer the assistance which only infinite power, grace and merit could give. As the *Awakening of Faith* puts it:

> Let those who doubt and desire to give up meditate on this wise. All the Buddhas and bodhisattvas of the ten quarters have attained great spiritual and unhindered perception, and are able by means of excellent and skilful acts of merit to rescue all distressed beings. Having thus meditated, let them make a great vow that they will with single mind think only of the Buddhas and bodhisattvas, so as to produce in this way a settled conviction. Then at the end of life they will attain entrance into the Buddha's realm, and perceiving the Buddhas and bodhisattvas with perfected faith they will be everlastingly freed from evil conditions. As a sūtra says 'If good men and good women would think only on Amitābha in his perfectly blessed world in the western region, and direct all their root of merit towards him, and desire to be borne there, then they will assuredly be born there'. Faith increases through a constant beholding of the Buddhas, and there would never be a relapse. Through hearing the Dharma one comes to comtemplate the Dharmakāya of the Buddha, and by persistent discipline one enters into a state of Truth.[33]

San Lun. The school of the Three Treatises. It was Kumārajīva (344–413) who first translated the great philosophical treatises of the Mahāyāna in a manner comprehensible to the Chinese, and gave the inspiration for the growth of a systematic development of Buddhist philosophy in China. Two of Nāgārjuna's writings and one attributed to Āryadeva and Vasubandhu formed the basis of the Mādhyamika school of thought which became known in China as the *San Lun* or Three Treatises school.

Taoist thought in China had been exercised for a long time over the relation of non-being to being, (*chên-ju*) of quiescence to movement, of non-activity to activity. Buddhists also had been concerned with similar problems: the relation of the Absolute being (*chên-ju*) to the temporal, of nirvāna to Samsāra. The exponents of Mādhyamika believed that it was impossible to describe the nature of ultimate reality. Seek to define the infinite and it no longer remains infinite. Sêng-chao (384–414), who was closely associated with Kumārajīva, was the first great teacher of *San Lun,* combining the Mādhyamika philosophy with neo-Taoist thought.

The central concept of the school is Emptiness [*šunyatā*] in the sense that the nature and character of all *dharmas,* together with their causation, are devoid of reality. Thus all differentiations, whether being or non-being, cause or effect, or coming-into-existence or going-out-of-existence are only 'temporary names' and are empty in nature. The only reality is emptiness itself, which is Absolute, Ultimate Void.[34]

Under Chi-tsang (549–623) the *San Lun* school was systematised and reached its highest peak of development. He developed the doctrine of two levels of truth. On the level of common or relative truth things exist provisionally as dependent beings or temporary names, but on the level of absolute truth all *dharmas* are empty. The approach of the school, following Nāgārjuna, was nihilistic and destructive. Though everything and every event may be thought of as possessing a temporary reality, in the last resort there is 'no production or extinction, no permanence or annihilation, no unity or diversity, no coming or departure'. Such philosophical nihilism proved unacceptable to the Chinese mind and the school rapidly declined in the ninth century to become merged in the Ch'an or Meditation school.

Ch'an, or the Meditation School. Ch'an Buddhism is undoubtedly one of the most distinctive and original products of the Chinese mind. 'The Chinese genius, working on the raw material of Indian thought, with contributions from Confucianism and Taoism with Bodhidharma as midwife, produced the essentially Chinese school of Ch'an.'[35] It has been described by the philosopher, Hu-shih, as a 'reformation or revolution in Buddhism'.[36]

The character *Ch'an* is derived from the Sanscrit word for meditation, *dhyāna,* and hence the school was designated the Meditation school. But it uses meditation as a means of direct enlightenment of the mind. It is not contemplative in the sense that it precludes activity. It is a radically mystical sect of Chinese Buddhism, aiming at a mystical experience in which subjectivity and objectivity are transcended, a state of being in which there is no duality. The goal is referred to as *prajñā, nirvāna, bodhi,* etc. *Ch'an* taught that the only reality is mind, the Buddha-mind. 'It seeks an immediate awareness of Reality, which cannot be attained by philosophic or religious thought, meditation or the practice of ritual or magic. It cannot be taught or transmitted by books or teachers. All a teacher can do is to speak, write, paint or act in such a way as to arouse the faculty of direct knowledge or intuition, a kind of spiritual illumination which comes only when thought and sense perception have ceased.'[37]

The early Hīnayānist schools taught that the way to enlightenment was through 'radical abandonment'. The *klesas,* that is the defilements and depravities of mind due to anger, greed and stupidity, were to be entirely abandoned. The four noble truths were to be embraced. The five *skandhas* or constituents of personality were to be dissolved. *Samsāra* was annihilated and *nirvāna* achieved. The early Mahāyānists laid stress on 'transformation' rather than 'abandonment'. The *klesas* were transformed into *bodhi,* and the mind was transformed by leading it through *samsāra* to *nirvāna.* Ch'an in China, and Mahāmudra in Tibet stressed 'realisation' and linked it to the concept that the only 'reality' is Buddha-mind, and everything is but a manifestation of that mind. Hence *Samsāra* IS *nirvāna,* my mind IS the Buddha-mind, pure consciousness IS wisdom. Buddhahood is achieved, neither by superseding the mind nor by the accumulation of knowledge, but through direct identification of the limited human consciousness with the Buddha-mind. As a *Ch'an* saying expresses it, 'I and all the Buddhas of the past, present and future breathe through one nostril,' and as Hui-nêng, the sixth patriarch of *Ch'an,* says, 'Without closing your eyes or ears to shut out the external world, you may reach Buddhahood directly.' *Ch'an* declared that the teachings of all the Buddhas are given for the sole purpose of helping one to 'unfold one's own mind'.

Though Tao-an and Hui-yüan had early emphasised the importance of *dhyāna* exercises, it was with Bodhidharma (Ta-mo) that the *Ch'an* school dates its beginnings. Yet little is known about this important figure of Chinese Buddhism. His biography is largely legendary, and filled with miraculous stories. Even the date of his arrival, which is traditionally given as AD 520, has been hotly disputed.[38] He seems to have spent some time in Nanking and then proceeded to Loyang, where 'scorning the worship of images and disregarding the study of scriptures, he taught by precept and example that the best way to achieve the Buddhist goal of escape from life's chains was simply to concentrate on the Buddha-nature within one's own heart and mind.'[39] He was reckoned to be the twenty-eighth patriarch from Śākyamuni Buddha and the first patriarch of the *Ch'an* school in China. The following famous lines are ascribed to him:

> A special transmission outside the scriptures,
> No dependence upon word or letters,
> Direct pointing to the soul of man,
> Seeing into nature and attainment of Buddhahood.

According to tradition, Bodhidharma emphasised the teachings of the *Lankāvatāra sūtra,* which focused attention on the centrality of ultimate reality, and emphasised the doctrine of inner enlightenment and the transcending of all mental discrimination and all duality. But with Hung-jên (601–74), the fifth patriarch and his two outstanding disciples, Shên-hui (605?–706) and Hui-nêng (638–713), *Ch'an* Buddhism began to develop divergent tendencies. Since the basic tenet of *Ch'an* is that the Buddha-mind is everything, that *nirvāna* is identical with the Buddha-nature which is in all men so that all can become Buddha, divergencies arose over interpretation and method. Shên-hui and the Northern School distinguished the pure, undifferentiated mind from the false mind which differentiates, and taught the need to eliminate all false and erroneous thinking, and reach a point of absolute quietude. They taught that the goal of attainment was, in general, only reached gradually. Hui-nêng and the Southern School refused to make this distinction between pure and false mind. They believed that all activities of the mind are functions of 'Thusness' (True Reality). The Buddha-mind is everywhere and in everything, and therefore if the individual sees his own true nature he becomes a Buddha. This realisation can happen at any moment. One can suddenly and in a flash become aware of Absolute Truth.

The influence of this teaching of Hui-nêng was immense. According to his followers his superior grasp of the fundamental principles of *Ch'an* was recorded in a stanza on the wall of the monastery where he and Shên-hui were disciples of Hung-jên. Contending for the position of patriarch in succession to Hung-jên, Shên-hui first wrote the stanza:

This body is the bodhi tree
The soul is like a mirror bright,
Take heed to keep it always clean
And let no dust collect upon it.

In the middle of the night, while the rest of the monks were sleeping, Hui-nêng wrote a second stanza:

Bodhi is not like a tree,
The mirror is nowhere shining;
As there is nothing from the beginning,
Where can the dust collect?

The next morning, according to the story, Hung-jên saw the two stanzas, and at once recognised in Hui-nêng a supreme master, and later on he secretly handed over to Hui-nêng the insignia of his office.

Hui-nêng is credited with the production of the only Chinese Buddhist writing to be honoured with the rank of sūtra (*ching*). The famous *Platform Scripture of Hui-nêng (Liu-tsu-t'an Ching)* became a basic text of *Ch'an* Buddhism. As W. T. Chan writes:

Everything other than the cultivation of the mind, such as reading scriptures, making offerings to Buddha, reciting his name, joining the monastic order, are regarded as unnecessary. The total effect is to minimise, if not to wipe out, the whole Buddhist organisation, creed and literature and to reduce Buddhism to a concern for one's mind alone. The logical conclusions are that everyone can achieve enlightenment and become a Buddha, since everyone possesses the Buddha-nature, that he can do so immediately and that he can do so 'in this very body.' No matter how one looks at this movement, it was revolutionary in the true sense of the word.[40]

Soon after the death of Hui-nêng the meditation hall came into use in *Ch'an* monasteries and has been a prominent feature ever since. At the same time Buddhist laymen and lay women learned to practise *Ch'an* meditation in their own homes. By the tenth century the *kung-an* or *koan* came to be recognised as a device for the attainment of sudden enlightenment. The *koan* is an enigmatic phrase insoluble by the intellect. It is meant to 'baffle, excite, puzzle and exhaust the intellect until it is realised that intellection is only thinking *about*; it will provoke, irritate and again exhaust the emotions until it is realised that emotion is feeling *about*, – and when the disciple is brought to an intellectual and emotional impasse, it bridges the gap between second-hand conceptual contact with reality and first-hand experience'.[41] *Ch'an* did not object to conceptual knowledge as such, but to clinging to intellection, which actually acted as a barrier to enlightenment. *Ch'an* enlightenment was the direct experience of beholding, unfolding or realising the Mind-essence in its fullness.

As *Ch'an* developed it led to a great outpouring of creative art as men sought direct communication with the inner nature of things, and sought to express the vision of a world beyond all opposites.[42] It exerted a great influence upon the idealistic neo-Confucian movement of the Sung dynasty, whilst its influence in Japan as Zen has provided many of the basic elements of life and culture.

T'ien T'ai. An attempt at harmonisation. T'ien T'ai became the most influential of the sects of Buddhism during the T'ang dynasty, exerting a powerful influence on the thought and practice of other schools. In their rituals and rules for living they reveal considerable dependence upon the teachings of *T'ien T'ai.*

It was established by Chih-i or Chih-k'ai (538–97) in a famous monastery on the T'ien T'ai mountains of Chekiang province. The basic text of the school was the *Lotus Sūtra (Saddharmapundarīka Sūtra)*[43] which teaches that Śākyamuni was but an earthly manifestation of the eternal Buddha. Chih-i taught that while the Buddha was alive he suited his teachings to the needs and capacities of his hearers. Faced with the mass of Buddhist scriptures with their divergent teachings, he divided the main Buddhist scriptures into five periods of the Buddha's life, and taught that, although they all have value, they lead forward step by step to the quintessence of Buddhism which is contained in the *Lotus Sūtra*. 'T'ien T'ai was a prodigious attempt to bring order and system out of a mass of contradictory ideas, and an endeavour to understand the evolution of Buddhist thought.'[44] It taught that as soon as the Buddha became enlightened he preached the abstruse doctrines of the *Hua Yen Sūtra (Buddhavatamsaka-mahāvaipulya sūtra)* in which he set forth the contents of his perception exactly as he perceived them. But this profound teaching could not be grasped by disciples who were still at an elementary stage, and so the Buddha preached the Hīnayānist scriptures. From them the disciples were led on to the more elementary concepts of Mahāyāna, then to the more advanced teachings of the *Prajñāpāramitās (Ta-pan-jo Ching)* which set forth the doctrine of *Śūnyata* or the Void. Finally the Buddha, in his old age, revealed to a few of his more intimate followers the doctrines of the *Lotus Sūtra* and the *Mahāpārinirvāna Sūtras.*

Chih-i relied extensively on the theories of Nāgārjuna as they were transmitted through the translations of Kumārajīva. He emphasised the idea of totality and mutual identification, the whole and its parts being identical. The whole cosmos and all the Buddhas were present in a grain of sand. Absolute mind embraces the universe in its entirety and all things depend on this mind for their existence. In its substance, absolute mind is the same; in its functioning, it is differentiated.

Chih-i sought to link the practical expression of religion with spiritual cultivation and the pursuit of wisdom by concentration (*chih*) and insight (*kuan*). 'He stressed the weakness of wisdom without practice, and the dangers of religious practice lacking the eye of wisdom.'[45]

As a result of Chih-i's work a remarkable spirit of tolerance pervaded Chinese Buddhism, for no interpretation of the Buddha's teaching was so strange as to be unable to find a place in his great scheme. Indeed, as K. L. Reichelt writes, 'it was only a sign of Amitābha's endless grace that he had so many different kinds of "vehicles" for suffering and struggling humanity, suited to each country and each individual's need.'[46]

The *Lotus Sūtra,* which contributed so much to the popularity of *T'ien T'ai,* came to be treasured by most of the sects of the Mahāyāna. It was of paramount importance for the development of a rich Buddhist mythology in China, in which the eternal Buddha, represented in innumerable forms, was working out his purposes which included the salvation of all suffering humanity. As W. E. Soothill writes:

We find the *Lotus Sūtra* to be unique in the world's religious literature. A magnificent apocalypse, it presents a spiritual drama of the highest order, with the universe as its stage, eternity as its period, and Buddhas, gods, men, devils as its dramatis personae. From the most distant worlds and from past aeons, the eternal Buddhas throng the stage to hear the mighty Buddha proclaim his ancient and eternal Truth . . . On earth he had assumed human form with all its limitations. Now he reveals himself, *sub specie aeternitatis,* as the Eternal, Omniscient, Omnipotent, Omnipresent Buddha creator-destroyer, recreator of all worlds.[47]

Hua Yen. The Garland School. According to W. T. Chan 'the Hua Yen philosophy represents the highest development of Chinese Buddhist thought. It is the most syncretistic, and with the philosophy of T'ien T'ai forms the basis of Chinese Buddhism in the last millennium.'[48] This sect appealed to the intellect, basing its principal teachings on the

Avatamsaka sūtra (Hua Yen), which was reputed to be an account of the Buddha's most recondite teachings, and which sets forth the practices of a bodhisattva. Tu-shun (557–640) is reputed to be its first Master, followed by Chih-yen (602–68) and Fa-tsang(643–712). It accepted as its most important doctrine, in common with other schools, that all beings without distinction possess the Buddha-nature. In process of time this doctrine became a fundamental article of faith common to all Chinese Buddhists. Hua Yen expressed the dissatisfaction of many Chinese Buddhists with the 'negative expressions of emptiness and substancelessness so essential to Mahāyāna Buddhism'.[49] It taught a theory of causation by the universal principle (*li*), and the interpenetration and mutual identifications of all phenomena. Phenomena are manifestations of the universal principle. Thus, by its affirmation of 'reality' it brought Buddhism into line with fundamental Chinese thought.

The Hua Yen sect prohibited the eating of meat, and this too became accepted as a necessary discipline by almost all Chinese monks.

Wei Shih or Fa Hsiang. The 'Mere Ideation' School. Fa Hsiang was based on the writings of Asanga and Vasubandhu of the fourth century AD, who taught that only ideation exists. The external world is only a fabrication of our consciousness. *Fa Hsiang* analysed the mind into eight consciousnesses – the five senses together with a sense-centre, a thought centre (*manas*) and a storehouse-consciousness (*ālaya*). This latter stores and co-ordinates all the ideas reflected in the mind, and is the source from which arise all the phenomena of the universe. But the storehouse-consciousness has no active energy. It is disturbed by the thought-centre (*manas*) which is always active and works in conjunction with the senses to bring forth perception, cognition and judgment. *Manas* is thus the connecting link between the storehouse-consciousness and the six sense consciousnesses. It is intelligent and capable of enlightenment. The aim of Buddhist discipline is, therefore, to get *manas* to function so as to feed only good seeds into the storehouse-consciousness. This is achieved only through the attainment of wisdom, of truth beyond all duality.

The school made a serious attempt to provide a sound psychological and metaphysical basis for the pure idealism of the Mahāyāna. Though its teachings, developed as they were by the great T'ang Master and translator, Hsüan-tsang (596–664), were beyond the grasp of most of the Buddhist monks and laymen, they had a great influence on the philosophically-minded. They contributed greatly to the development of neo-Confucianism in the Sung dynasty, and to the development of Chinese Buddhist thought down to our own time.

Lü or the School of Discipline. The *Lü*, or School of Discipline, derived its main inspiration from the Hīnayāna, laying great emphasis on monastic discipline. Its founder, Tao-hsüan (595–667) used as a basic scripture the *Sūtra of Brahma's Net (Fan Wang Ching)* which contained rules for the organisation of the monastic life and the ordering of the daily life of monks and nuns. In the famous monastery of Pao-hua-shan near Nanking the sect gained a wide reputation for the severity and purity of the ascetic life. Its high standards for ordination, the devotion of its monks to the study of the scriptures, and the austerity of their lives provided an example to monks of other sects. The School of Discipline has maintained its influence to the present day, especially in the coastal provinces of China.

Chên Yen or Mi Tsung. Tantric Buddhism. Early in the eighth century three Buddhist missionaries arrived in China from India, bringing with them the esoteric teachings of Tantric Buddhism. Subhākarasimha (Shan-wu-wei) (637–735) translated the basic scripture of the school, the *Mahāvairocana Sūtra* and he was followed by two monks, Vajrabodhi (Chin-kang-chih) (663–723) and Amoghavajra (Pu-k'ung) (705–74). These missionaries taught that, though man is sunk in ignorance, he has the Buddha-nature within him. But that Buddha-nature can only be realised and full salvation attained by carrying into practice certain esoteric teachings which have made considerable borrowings from Hindu mythology. The cosmos is conceived of as a great being, the manifest expression of the great Vairocana Buddha; gods and goddesses being symbols of its function, energy and will. Magic formulae are used to invoke the gods, and much use is made of *mantras* (mystic symbols), *mudras* (signs made by positioning hands and fingers) and *mandala* (cosmograms). Tantra taught that *mantras* contain all the secrets of sound, and *mudras* the secrets of touch. Entry into the *mandala* is called *abhisheka* or 'initiation into the secrets of the school'. Tantra made use of complicated rituals, sprinkling with holy water, wearing a crown, a sacred band over the shoulders, the touching of a bell or a representation of the thunderbolt. It included the taking of vows and being given a secret name. Tantra also taught an extreme form of idealism. It argued that no action is in itself moral or immoral, but intention or motive is the basis of moral judgment.

The aim of Tantra was to win full enlightenment in this life, and also to gain health, wealth and power. It thus had a popular appeal, especially as it taught that magical rituals, the use of charms and the pronouncement of the sacred Buddha-name were the surest means of attaining salvation.

It was chiefly the Right-handed Tantra, developed by Amoghavajra, which interested the Chinese. Amoghavajra served under three T'ang emperors, who held him in high esteem. His teaching, derived from the *Mahāvairocana Sūtra (P'i-lu-chên-na Ching),* represented Ultimate Reality as the universe, his body being divided into two complementary constituents, an active, material 'diamond-element' and a passive, mental 'womb-element.' This had affinities with the Taoist concept of the *yang* and the *yin*. The *mantra* was for Tantric Buddhism the chief vehicle of salvation, the means of direct communication with the unseen forces of the universe through their personifications. A miraculous force was deemed to reside in the *mantras* so that by pronouncing them unlimited merit is acquired.

This Tantric form of Buddhism, known in China as the *Chên Yen* or *Mi Tsung,* entered China about the same time as Nestorian Christianity. Reichelt is of the opinion that it was largely due to Nestorian influence that Amoghavajra, who lived side by side with the Nestorians in Sian, introduced masses for the dead into Chinese Buddhism.[50] The festival known as the 'Feast of wandering spirits' or *Yü-lan-p'en Hui* (Sanscrit: *Ullambana*) became one of the most popular festivals in Chinese Buddhism. Its object was to conduct the souls of the departed as rapidly as possible over the sea of troubles which resulted from their sins.

Though the *Chên Yen* school merged with other Buddhist schools in China, Tantric Buddhism received fresh inspiration from Tibet, from which country it was carried into Mongolia to become the religion of the Mongol founders of the Yüan dynasty. It flourished up to modern times as the Tibetan Esoteric Sect (*Tsang Mi Tsung*).

The Chinese Buddhist Canon

Extant Chinese Buddhist scriptures are known as the *San Tsang* or the Chinese Tripitaka. This is a misnomer, as Chinese Buddhist scriptures differ from the Pali canon in having four and not three divisions. In addition to the *Sūtras (Ching)*, the *Vinaya (Lü)* and the *Abhidharma (Lun)* it contains numerous important works by Chinese Buddhist scholars which are catalogued as 'Miscellaneous Works' (*tsa*).

The Chinese Tripitaka is a massive work consisting, in the modern editions, of some fifty-five volumes.[51] K. L. Reichelt estimates that it is seven hundred times larger than the Christian Bible.[52]

By the end of the first millennium AD when the first printed edition of it appeared, the Tripitaka was virtually completed. It contains both Mahāyānist and Hīnayānist texts, though the latter are only a small portion of the whole. The Sūtra section is by far the largest, containing 1,081 works. Among them are some very ancient texts common to the various Hīnayānist schools, but the works which became most authoritative for Chinese Buddhism were the great Mahāyānist sūtras translated from the Sanscrit.

The great work of translating the Indian Buddhist scriptures was, from the time of Kumārajiva, carried on by teams of Chinese scholars under the guidance of Buddhist missionaries and 'Masters of the Dharma'. As early as the time of Tao-an (AD 374) the need arose for the compilation of catalogues giving the titles and the names of principal translators. The oldest extant catalogue is that by Sêng-yu (*c.* 518) and since his day a succession of catalogues of Buddhist scriptures have been compiled, the most important of which is the K'ai-yüan which was completed in AD 730. The oldest extant Buddhist work in Chinese is a book, now in the British Museum, containing excerpts from the *Diamond Sūtra,* and produced by block printing in 868. It was discovered at the famous monastery at Tun-huang. By the year 983 the whole of the Chinese Tripitaka, apart from later additions to the 'Miscellaneous Works' under the Yüan and Ming dynasties, was printed.

The deep philosophical penetration of many of these works, the beauty of their style in the Chinese classical tradition, the intensity of their religious feeling and the scope of their imaginative constructions have made a perennial appeal to the educated Chinese people. The setting of the sūtras is usually a great gathering to which the Buddha calls myriads of Buddhas, bodhisattvas, disciples, gods and demons, to listen in breathless adoration and expectancy as he expounds some aspect of his teaching.

The care and reverence with which the sacred scriptures were kept in the monasteries witness to that reverence for the written word which has characterised the Chinese scholar throughout history. Each monastery had its own library, usually on the second floor in order the better to preserve the books from danger and mildew. The library was 'generally a very dignified room with special altars and statues usually to Vairocana, Kuan-yin, Amitābha or Śākyamuni Buddha'.[53]

Up to the present time only a few of the major works in the Chinese Tripitaka have been translated into English. Though there are many works of major importance which are still untranslated, the abnormal length and repetitiousness of several of the sūtras makes them tedious in the extreme to the Western reader.

Buddhism in Decline.

After the fall of the great T'ang dynasty the hard lines of division between the various schools tended to be obliterated. Most Buddhists came to accept as their own the salient features which had in the past distinguished the various schools from each other. Only Pure Land and *Ch'an* remained active throughout the Sung dynasty, and neither of these schools laid much emphasis on Buddhist scholarship. No new schools of Buddhist thought developed, and Buddhism no longer produced outstanding masters. The Buddhist community continued to build monasteries and temples, to ordain monks and to carry on religious activities. But there was a sad moral decline. This was evidenced by the growth of a spirit of worldliness among the higher clergy, many of whom lived in conditions of pomp and magnificence, and sought power through association with the Confucian hierarchy.

The rise of neo-Confucianism during the Sung dynasty, and the expansion of the civil service examinations by which scholars were forced to seek office through a study of the Confucian classics, contributed to the decline of Buddhism. Any ambitious scholar who wished to rise to a position of responsibility and power found that he could only do so by years of intensive application to Confucian studies or by seeking the patronage and assistance of some great Confucian official.

Furthermore, Buddhism was in decline in the country of its origin. Indian Buddhism was rapidly losing ground before a resurgent Hinduism and an aggressive Islam. Many of the great monastic foundations in northern India lay in ruins, with the monks and nuns dispersed. Thus what had been a perennial source of inspiration to Chinese Buddhism dried up.

With the overthrow of the Sung dynasty by the Mongols in 1280, and the establishment of the Yüan dynasty in China, Tibetan Buddhism, or Lamaism became prominent in China under the protection and patronage of Mongol emperors. When, however, the Ming established a purely Chinese dynasty in 1368, the neo-Confucian philosophy again became the official doctrine of the state,[54] and opposition to Buddhism increased. This state of affairs continued, in general, throughout the Ch'ing (Manchu) dynasty down to modern times, although some of the Ch'ing emperors professed themselves to be devout Buddhists. 'With the Buddhist religion forbidden to officials and declared undesirable even for common folk, and the monks confined to an ascetic life within the temples and cut off from secular society, the effectiveness of Buddhism as a popular religion could only wane.'[55] The secular, this-worldly attitude of the literate classes, concerned only for the promotion of human happiness in a well organised state, was inimical to Buddhism and Taoist alike. In general, Buddhism was tolerated but despised as a mass of crude superstitions fit only to provide some measure of comfort and escape for the illiterate masses of the people.

If Buddhism was to continue as an effective religious force in China there was need for drastic reform and an intellectual awakening. Towards the end of the Ch'ing dynasty this began to take place, and gathered momentum during the early decades of the twentieth century. This was in large measure the result of the stimulus of Christianity and Western influences. The account of the reforms instituted by T'ai-hsü (1890–1947) and the intellectual awakening which goes back to Yang Wen-liu (1837–1911), together with the set-back to Buddhism, and indeed to all religions through the rise of a militant Communism, will be dealt with in the chapter on the religious situation in modern China.

CHAPTER ELEVEN

THE STATE CULT OF CONFUCIANISM

It was not until the early days of the Han dynasty that the elaborate state cult was firmly grounded in the doctrines of Confucianism and that Confucius and his most prominent disciples were deemed worthy of sacrificial honours paid to them, not simply by their own descendants, but by the emperor and his officials. With Han Wu Ti (141–87 BC) the ritual and sacrificial system was elaborated. Confucius himself came to be honoured and worshipped and Confucian principles were adopted in government. Thus was established what might be called a Confucian state cult which was to continue till the early decades of the twentieth century.

However, as we have seen in the previous two chapters, the influence of Buddhism and Taoism was so pervasive that many of the emperors and leading scholars were ardent adherents of these faiths. It was not until the rise of the Sung dynasty (960–1279) that there arose such a resurgence of the Confucian culture that there was a reassertion of the classical Confucian religion centring in the supremacy of heaven and the place of the emperor as True Son of heaven. This state cult, based upon a reinterpretation of the Confucian classics by neo-Confucian scholars, who had been greatly influenced by the philosophy of Buddhism, continued as the official state religion for the next thousand years, except for a brief Mongol period when Buddhist influence dominated the court.

Though the state rituals were performed for the benefit of the people as a whole, they had no part in them. The emperor, assisted by his nobles and great officers, performed the state sacrifices, whilst his appointees and representatives functioned at the lesser sacrifices performed at prefectural and county levels. What Gibbon wrote concerning the policy of the state to religion in the Roman empire at the time of the Antonines might well apply, in general, to the official attitude to religion in China from the Sung dynasty down to the twentieth century.

> The policy of the emperors and the senate, as far as it concerned religion, was happily seconded by the reflections of the enlightened, and by the habits of the superstitious, part of their subjects. The various modes of worship, which prevailed in the Roman world, were all considered by the people, as equally true; by the philosophers, as equally false; and by the magistrate, as equally useful. And thus toleration not only produced mutual indulgence, but even religious concord . . . As soon as it was allowed that sages and heroes, who had lived, or who had died for the benefit of their country, were exalted to a state of power and immortality, it was universally confessed that they deserved, if not the adoration, at least the reverence of all mankind . . . The pontiffs were chosen among the most illustrious of the senators; and the office of supreme pontiff was constantly exercised by the emperors themselves. They knew and valued the advantages of religion, as it was connected with civil government. They encouraged the public festivals which humanise the manners of the people. They managed the arts of divination, as a convenient instrument of policy.[1]

It was part of state policy to give recognition to Confucianism, Taoism and Buddhism, but to keep a strict control over all public religious activities. Emperors and officials contributed to the erection and maintenance of their temples, and made acts of worship before their deities. It was an important part of official duty to assist in maintaining the religious life of the nation.

From the Sung dynasty onwards, whatever the personal predilections of the emperor might be – he was often predisposed to Taoism or Buddhism – it was considered indispensable to the well-being of the empire, conceived of as the entire civilised world, that a harmonious relationship should be maintained between heaven, earth and man. This relationship could only continue unimpaired if the emperor performed, with deep reverence and with a careful attention to the minutest detail, as Son of Heaven, the sacred and sacrificial ritual which was believed to have originated in hoary antiquity. Yet it must be emphasised that it was as a 'man', in sight of heaven, a very humble and abject man, that the emperor performed those high-priestly functions which only he, as unique man, could perform.[2] The ceremonies of the state cult were so numerous and elaborate that they not only demanded much of the emperor's time and attention, but the establishment of one of the most important of the departments of state, the Board of Rites (*Li Pu*). No god or spirit or deified hero, from the supreme God of heaven down to His lowest spiritual minion, could be neglected if the spiritual influences upon the nation as a whole were to remain favourable.

The Imperial ceremonies

These consisted of three classes:

1. First there were the great ceremonies, performed by the emperor himself, for the worship of heaven, earth, the imperial ancestors, and the gods of land and grain.
2. Second, there were the medium sacrifices for the worship of sun and moon, the rulers and great men of former dynasties, the patron of agriculture and the patroness of silkworms, and the numerous spirits of earth and sky.
3. Finally there were the lesser sacrifices, which consisted of some thirty 'small' sacrifices, in very few of which the emperor took part personally. These were sacrifices to minor gods, such as the patron of medicine, the god of fire, the god of literature, the gods of mountains, lakes, rivers and springs, the polar star and the city gods. 'Most of the spirits represented in the imperial sacrifices were worshipped also on a minor scale on the monarch's behalf by officials in special temples throughout the provinces, prefectures and districts of the realm.'[3]

The highest act of national worship, and central to the imperial cult, was the great annual sacrifice to *Shang Ti* which took place at the altar of heaven at the winter solstice. 'Only the emperor, the high priest of "the world", the Son of Heaven, might perform this great sacrifice.'[4] It was performed in the early hours before dawn to the light of flaming torches. It took place on an open altar, made of glistening white marble, rising in three circular terraces of impressive simplicity, situated in parkland to the south of the ancient city walls. 'The total area of this parkland is a little over seven hundred English acres.'[5] Near to the altar is the magnificent 'Temple of the Prosperous Year', with its triple roof of azure tiles, the Hall of Abstinence where the emperor reverently prepared himself for his supreme religious task, and a complex of other buildings. 'Without exaggeration', writes J. Bredon, 'we may say that no other sanctuary on earth has a more profound or grandiose conception, or more adequately expresses the instinctive desire of humanity to show reverence for a Power above and beyond its puny self . . . One man, and only one, the emperor, the Son of Heaven, was thought fit to ascend this worshipping place and, under the dome of the sky which covers it like a hollow turquoise, to make obeisance to the Supreme Being.'[6]

Everything was first prepared with meticulous care under the guidance of the Board of Rites, and the programme and prayers were submitted to the emperor for his approval several days before the event. A three-days' fast and vigil was obligatory for the emperor, the princes and the officials who took part. The third day of the vigil was observed by the emperor in the 'Hall of Abstinence' situated near to the great altar. After the emperor had visited the altar, the sacred tablets in the adjacent temples, and inspected the sacrifices to see that they were without blemish, he purified himself, and then proceeded to the great altar. Meanwhile the tablets of the Supreme God and all his satellites were set up with the utmost care and reverence on marble pedestals and under tents of blue silk on the topmost tier of the altar, whilst beneath were the bullocks on wooden tables and the viands spread before their shrines. When everyone had taken up his appropriate station, the Son of Heaven mounted the altar, and proceeded by sacrifice and prayer to worship the Supreme Deity, thus ensuring for himself and his people every spiritual blessing. 'The whole service was a thanksgiving to *Shang Ti* and to the great dynastic ancestors, and to the host of heaven for the blessings bestowed from above during the year, as the sacrifice to earth was a similar thanksgiving for the favours it had bestowed.'[7]

The sacrifice to *Shang Ti* distinguished him above all other spiritual beings, and signified that all power and authority belonged to him. In token of this a sceptre of blue jade was reverently placed before his shrine, and a whole burnt offering of a bullock of one colour and without blemish was made.

As part of the ceremony an invocation was read, whilst all were reverently kneeling. This was then placed before the shrine of *Shang Ti,* and afterwards burnt along with the other offerings. J. Legge gives *in extenso* a translation of the prayer offered on the occasion of a special solstitial sacrifice made in the year AD 1538 by the then emperor of the Ming dynasty.[8] We give below a few brief extracts from this prayer, which reveal the profound religious character of the ceremony. After precious silks and stones have been presented, the emperor prays:

Thou hast vouchsafed, O *Ti,* to hear us, for Thou regardest us as our Father. I, Thy child, dull and unenlightened, am unable to show forth my feelings. I thank Thee that Thou hast accepted the intimation. Honourable is Thy great name. With reverence we spread out these precious stones and silk, and, as swallows rejoicing in the spring, praise Thy abundant love.

Later on, at the second drink offering, the prayer continues:

All the numerous tribes of animated beings are indebted to Thy favour from the beginning. Men and creatures are emparadised, O *Ti,* in Thy love. All living things are indebted to Thy goodness, but who knows whence his blessings come to him? It is Thou alone, O Lord, who art the true parent of all things.

When the various offerings have been removed, the emperor continues:

The service of song is completed, but our poor sincerity cannot be fully expressed. Thy sovereign goodness is infinite. As a potter Thou hast made all living things. Great and small are curtained round [by Thee from harm]. As engraven on the heart of Thy poor servant is the sense of Thy goodness, but my feelings cannot be fully displayed. With great kindness Thou dost bear with us, and, notwithstanding our demerits, dost grant us life and prosperity.

Making all due allowances for the hyperbolical nature of such utterances, they remain a heart-felt expression of gratitude towards a Supreme Deity who transcended the material order. The whole ceremony was conducted throughout with the utmost reverence. The magnificent ritual, the solemn music, the oblations and invocations all witness to the fact that this and kindred ceremonies for the honouring of earth and the various celestial and terrestrial deities were religious in character, and their performance was considered essential for the prosperity of the state. This ceremony differed only from all the other sacrifices in that it was more magnificent and considered 'more complete', for this ritual alone consisted of nine parts, three times three, the heavenly number.[9]

On a lower level, the religious duties of a city magistrate were neither few nor easy. At certain times of the year he had to visit the temples of various public deities and there perform solemn acts of worship. In times of calamity through drought, famine or pestilence, he had the responsibility of finding wherein the local gods had been offended, and of instituting the appropriate ceremonies for their placation. Knowledge of the rituals and sacrifices was part of the intellectual equipment of an official. Chinese law in the nineteenth century stipulated that the duty of the chief official in any district included officiating at the sacrifices to gods of earth and grain, mountains, rivers, clouds, winds, thunder and rain, and also to the spirits of sage emperors, brilliant princes, loyal officials and heroic martyrs whose temples lay within his district. Severe punishment was ordained for any official who neglected these tasks. About twenty-five per cent of the temples belonged to the official cult.[10]

In all kinds of ways religion played an important role in justifying political power, in establishing administrative authority, in maintaining peace and order, in upholding civic values, inspiring faith in the government and raising public morale in times of crisis. The cults connected with the state religion cannot be explained, as some Chinese scholars have sought to do, as mere formalities. As the *Li Chi* says, 'Of all the ways of keeping men in good order, there are none more important than the *li*. The *li* are of five kinds, and none of these is more important than sacrifice.[11] The ethico-political cults with their temples, sacrifices and mythological lore were an integral part of the political life right down to the institution of the communist régime.[12]

The worship of Confucius

Confucius has, in the main, been worshipped by the scholar-class only, and that worship seems to have developed in the schools.[13] The worship seems to have developed on the principle that, just as a family sacrifices and prays to the spirits of its ancestors, and just as each trade or guild pays annual reverence to its patron god, so the scholar-class deemed it fitting to make regular acts of worship in the temples erected to the memory of Confucius, who was deemed to be the fountain-head of all Chinese learning and wisdom. As reverence was paid to Confucius as the great master, so too reverence was paid to his disciples and to all the great scholars of the past whose teachings had made a notable contribution to learning and morality.

There was no cult of Confucius outside his own family before the time of the Han emperor Kao-tzŭ (195 BC),[14] and the first clear instance of a regular cult of Confucius in the schools is a decree made by emperor Ming (AD 59) by which Confucius became the deified patron of the scholars. Sacrifices were ordered to be offered to him. Wu Ti of the Liang dynasty (502–50) was the first emperor to have erected public temples to Confucius in which sacrifices were offered every year to the memory of the sage. From the time of the northern Ch'i dynasty

(550–77) Confucius received sacrifices twice a year, in the spring and autumn, whilst in the schools small shrines were erected to Confucius and Yen Hui, his favourite disciple. Libations of wine were offered on the first day of the new moon, when students made obeisance to the master.[15]

In the year 630, the T'ang emperor T'ai Tsung issued a decree that temples to Confucius should be erected in all districts, and sacrifices were offered by scholars in their capacity of government officials. Later in his reign (AD 647) T'ai Tsung placed tablets of twenty-two worthies in the Confucian temples for the first time, and thus made these temples into 'Halls of Fame'.[16]

> It soon became the proper thing in practice for every district to have its own temple to the great master . . . The chief sacrifices to the master took place twice a year. Cattle were slain, and the blood sprinkled before the altar. The president of the temple's board of control, one of the oldest and most regarded scholars of the place, officiated at the ceremony, and all the literati of the region participated with reverential attitude.[17]

The fact that in these temples Confucius was represented, in these early days, by actual images is attested by the petition of Li Yüan-kuan to the emperor in AD 720 to have ten other seated images placed in the main hall of the Confucian temples along with those of Confucius and Yen Hui, whilst pictures of the seventy disciples and the twenty-two worthies were painted on the walls. 'From this time until 1530 the whole cult of Confucius was so similar to those of unquestioned divinities such as the city-gods that he can be regarded only as a god himself.'[18] This tendency to deify Confucius was in constant conflict with the tendency of more rationalistic scholars to consider him as no more than a human being, howbeit the greatest of all human sages. But it was not until the reign of the Ming emperor Chia Ch'ing that this more rationalistic attitude triumphed. In the year 1530 images were forbidden in Confucius' temples and replaced by tablets. At the same time the term *tien* (hall) was substituted for that of *miao* (temple). Thus, by the time the Jesuit mission became established in Peking, Matteo Ricci could believe and argue that the veneration paid to Confucius was not different from that paid to ancestors, and in his *Commentari* he asserts that here there was no whiff of idolatry and no superstition. The reverence paid to Confucius was no more than a recognition of him as a great man.[19] This, however, was not the opinion of Pope Clement XI and the Roman Congregation of Rites, who forbade ritual acts in honour of Confucius to Chinese Christian officials.[20]

The cult of Confucius was encouraged by the state as a buttress to public morality, and in order to sustain the power and authority of the scholar-class, which remained throughout Chinese history as the chief instrument of government administration. 'It is doubtful,' writes Shryock, 'whether he [Confucius] ever received worship from large numbers of people at any time. He was the patron of scholars, and came to receive worship from the state because the state was interested in the creation and maintenance of the scholar class.'[21] There was never any need to develop a professional priesthood, the scholars themselves performing all the necessary rites. Nor did the cult develop anything in the nature of a creed, but always allowed the greatest liberty of individual belief. It was firmly based in a belief in the moral nature of the universe and in the perfectibility of man. It was agnostic as regards life after death, and saw no need for any saviour-god to whom the individual might turn in his sin and misery.

Until the year 1906, the sacrifices to Confucius were not included among the 'Great Sacrifices' of the imperial cult. In that year, the 'medium sacrifice' which had been offered to the sage was changed to a 'great sacrifice' at which the emperor should personally attend. With the birth of the republic of China, though the age-old sacrifices to heaven and earth and all the other 'great sacrifices' were abandoned, the worship of Confucius was continued. Indeed, a serious attempt was made to elevate the cult of Confucius to be the official state religion of China, but it failed completely in face of the mounting opposition of prominent Confucian scholars, together with Christian, Buddhist and Muslim leaders.[22]

CHAPTER TWELVE

ISLAM, CHRISTIANITY AND OTHER WESTERN FAITHS IN CHINA

Although, according to the Han dynasty history, the imperial policies of the Han emperors had opened up the long central Asian trade routes to Parthia and Bactria, and many other kingdoms of western Asia, and even brought to the Chinese some knowledge of the Roman empire,[1] internal dissension within China and constant warfare among the tribes inhabiting central Asia made cultural contacts extremely hazardous. Such contacts, however, continued, and Buddhism, as we have seen, made its influence increasingly felt in China. It may well be that travellers of Zoroastrian, Manichaean and Nestorian faiths occasionally penetrated to the Chinese capital. We know that during the sixth century AD relations between China and Persia were frequent, and a Zoroastrian temple was established at Ch'ang-an, to be rebuilt in AD 631 by order of the emperor, when a *Mu-lu* or Zoroastrian priest was received at the court.[2]

But it was during the T'ang dynasty that these Western religions found a footing in China, as also did Islam in the seventh century.

> The T'ang emperors did not fear foreign intercourse as a menace to the state, whilst the spirit of intellectual curiosity and tolerance which marked the age encouraged a sympathetic attitude to religious and artistic ideas of foreign origin . . . The T'ang court welcomed foreigners, took a keen interest in alien customs and religions, and extended a friendly welcome to priests and travellers from Western regions.[3]

The temples which were permitted to be built in the capital and in some of the larger cities were, in the first place, for the use of foreigners, but Chinese converts were numerous.

Zoroastrianism existed in the T'ang dynasty mainly to meet the needs of Persian refugees who had fled to China on the fall of the Sassanian dynasty, and the conquest of Persia by the Muslims (AD

637–42). The last Sassanian emperor, Yesdegerd, had appealed to the Chinese for help against the Muslims, and though direct military help was not forthcoming, the son of Yesdegerd, by name Firuz, made his way to Ch'ang-an where he was given an appointment as a general of the imperial guard. He died at Ch'ang-an and left behind him a son who is known only by his Chinese name, Ni-ni-shih. The Persian refugees were permitted to build temples and to practise the Zoroastrian faith, but they do not seem to have made converts among the Chinese themselves. With the great persecution of all foreign religions in AD 843–5 Zoroastrianism in China died out.

The story of Manichaeism in China is more interesting, and the spread of its influence far more extensive. Mani, a Persian prophet who had been put to death in AD 274, had combined elements drawn from Zoroastrianism, Christianity and Buddhism to create an eclectic 'gnostic' religion based on a dualism which had as its aim the freeing of the principle of light from the captivity of matter. The new faith seems to have been highly successful and spread across Asia, winning the allegiance of several nomadic peoples. There is evidence of Manichaean influence upon Taoism as early as the end of the fourth century AD.[4] According to Chinese sources[5] Manichaeism entered China in AD 694, but it was in the early decades of the eighth century that the Uighurs were converted to Manichaeism, and with this strong and virile people the Chinese were in constant diplomatic contact. During the rebellion of An-lu-shan in the middle of the eighth century, the Uighurs gave to the emperor invaluable military assistance. Many of them were permitted to settle in China, and this led to the toleration and spread of Manichaeism and to the building of several temples. Archaeological discoveries in central Asia reveal that Manichaeism was strong in Turfan and other places. Rare Manichaean texts have been recovered from the Buddhist monastery at Tun-huang.[6] Between the years 766 and 779 Manichaean temples were constructed at Ching-chou in Hupeh, at Yang-chou, Nanking and even as far south as Shao-hsing in Chekiang province. The communities which they served included large numbers of Chinese converts.

When the Uighurs were decisively beaten by the Khirgiz in 840, the Manichaeans in China could no longer rely on Uighur protection, and in AD 843 an imperial decree ordered the confiscation of their properties, the burning of Manichaean books and the destruction of their temples and images. Over seventy Manichaean nuns were put to death in the capital, Ch'ang-an, and everywhere throughout the empire the priests of this religion had to abandon their distinctive dress and accept lay status. Manichaeism in China never recovered from this blow, though the teachings of Mani seem to have exerted considerable influence right down to the Sung and Yüan dynasties. It is probable that the sect visited by Marco Polo and his uncle when they visited the city of Fu-chou, and whom Marco believed to be Christians, were in reality crypto-Manichaeans. No doubt the estimate of Marco Polo that in these southern regions of China there were seven hundred thousand families who adhered to this 'unknown' faith is highly exaggerated, but that there were large numbers who were neither Taoist, Buddhist nor Muslim is beyond doubt.[7] Trade relations by the sea route with the Persian Gulf during the Sung and Yüan dynasties led to the establishment of temples to serve the needs of the foreign communities who resided in the great trading ports. Recent researches at Ch'üan-chou, near the coast of Fukien province, by Wu-wen-liang[8] have proved that there was a small Manichaean temple in the hills outside the city (familiarly known as Zaiton) in the Yüan dynasty. An image of Mani in the central hall of the temple is very different in style from any Buddhist image. A great halo of light surrounds the head, whilst two long plaits of hair descend from the head and shoulders. Nearby a stone inscription, most of which is now indecipherable, indicates that the image was erected in AD 1340 by a disciple, Ch'ên-ch'i-tzŭ, whilst a further inscription of the year AD 1426 exhorts men to meditate on the pure radiance, the omnipotent wisdom and the peerless purity of the illustrious Mani.

The adherents of Manichaeism were gradually absorbed into Buddhist or Taoist sects until practically no trace of them remained.

Christianity in China

In the course of some thirteen centuries Christian missionaries from the West have entered China to preach and propagate their faith in four distinct and separate movements. In each case they have built their churches, made converts among the Chinese and gradually increased their influence, only to be finally driven out as a result of changes in the political situation, and because of the hostility and fear aroused by a religion which could never accommodate itself to certain fundamental Chinese beliefs and practices. The Chinese in general have always looked upon Christianity as 'foreign', and though its indirect influence in China has been considerable, it has never at any time won the allegiance of more than a tiny fraction of the population. In this respect both Buddhism and Islam have won far greater success.

The four great periods of Christian missionary enterprise in China are as follows:

1. The Nestorian mission from the seventh to the ninth centuries.
2. The Franciscan mission, which began its work about the middle of the thirteenth century and continued throughout the Yüan (Mongol) dynasty until its complete obliteration about the middle of the fourteenth century.
3. The Jesuit mission which began in the latter decades of the sixteenth century. Through the learning and zeal of Jesuit missionaries the Christian Church was firmly established during the seventeenth century. Their success led to a large influx of Dominicans, Franciscans and Lazarists, and Christian missions spread into nearly all the provinces. But in the persecution of AD 1724, apart from the capital Peking, where a few missionaries were allowed to reside, the Christian Church was again virtually destroyed. Thereafter only sporadic attempts were made to propagate the faith by a few heroic missionaries until the breaking of the barriers to Chinese isolation by the British in AD 1839.
4. The era of modern Protestant and Roman Catholic missions which continued throughout the nineteenth and twentieth centuries until the expulsion of foreign missionaries by the Communists in the years following their rise to power in 1949.

The Nestorian Church in China. It was not until the discovery of the famous Nestorian stele[9] near to Hsian-fu, the former capital of China, in the year 1625 that the existence of a strong and flourishing Nestorian Church in T'ang dynasty China became known. Since that time the discovery of Nestorian texts at Tun-huang,[10] and archaeological finds at Ch'üan-chou and various other cities have added to our knowledge.

The inscription on the stele, part in Chinese and part in Syriac, reveals that the stele was erected in the year 781. A brief account is given of the progress of Nestorianism from its introduction into China by A-lo-pên, a monk from Ta-chin (probably Syria). A-lo-pên was welcomed by the T'ang emperor, T'ai-tsung, and commanded to build a church and monastery in the capital. Orders were also given to translate his religious books into Chinese, and he and his followers were given the right to propagate their faith. By the time the stele was erected Nestorianism had won numerous adherents and the support of some of the most influential people. These latter included Kuo-tzŭ-i, supreme commander of the army and chief minister of state. He spent large sums of money on the restoration of churches and for the support of monks and clergy. The name given to the Nestorian faith was *Ching-chiao* or 'Luminous Religion'. The inscription on the stele states that under Kao-tsung, the son and successor of T'ai-tsung, churches were built in every prefectural city, so that for a while Christianity seems to have flourished throughout the empire.

We have already indicated that in the early days there was considerable collaboration between Buddhists and Nestorians, and that the introduction of masses for the dead into Buddhism is probably due to Nestorian influence.[11] There is also evidence that the Nestorians suffered a good deal of obstruction and persecution from their Buddhist rivals.

The Nestorian Church suffered severely along with other 'foreign' religions in the great persecution of AD 845, and it was not until the thirteenth century that groups of Christians were again permitted openly to engage in the practice of their religion. Nestorian missionaries had had considerable success among several of the tribes inhabiting central Asia. Many Uighurs, Kirghiz, Kitans, Keraits, Naimans and Alans had been converted to the faith. When the Mongol armies finally conquered China, and Kublai Khan became emperor, great movements of population throughout the vast Mongol empire led to the settlement of many Christians in China. William of Rubruck (*c.* 1254), who visited the court of the great Mangu Khan at Karakorum, reported that there were Nestorians in fifteen cities of China, with a bishop residing at Hsian-fu.[12] When John of Montecorvino reached Peking, as the first Franciscan missionary, in 1294, the Nestorians in that city sought to hinder his work; according to the Dominican John di Cora, archbishop of Soltanta (*c.* 1300) there were thirty thousand Nestorians in China at that time.[13] With the collapse of the Mongol dynasty in 1368 toleration of Christians in China ceased, and the Nestorian Church died out.

Several factors, besides the xenophobia of the Ming emperors, contributed to the total destruction of the Nestorian Church in China. Nestorianism in west and central Asia virtually collapsed before the expansion of Islam and the slow penetration of Tantric Buddhism.

The preference of the Nestorian clergy for the cenobitic life militated against zealous missionary activity within the community. There is no evidence of the Nestorians training an indigenous clergy able to carry on when they themselves were expelled. Finally, the Chinese could see little difference between Nestorian and Buddhist rites and ceremonies, and when leadership was withdrawn, they found little difficulty in becoming absorbed into Buddhist and Taoist sects.

The Franciscan mission. The activities of the early Franciscan mission to China were of comparatively short duration. The great Mongol empire, which spread over the whole of central Asia in the thirteenth century, was tolerant of religion, eager to absorb foreign ideas, and desirous of using distinguished and learned men of whatever faith.

John of Montecorvino (1247–1328) was the first Roman Catholic priest to set foot on Chinese soil. He established himself in Peking, where he was allowed to build a church, probably completed in 1300.[14] He began to make converts and by 1305 he had baptised some six thousand persons. He took under his protection about one hundred and fifty boys, children of pagan parents, to train them in the Christian faith, teaching them Greek and Latin and employing them to write out psalters and other Christian literature. Some of them he trained as a choir. Early in the fourteenth century three other friars arrived in Peking to assist him, and the work began to expand. John himself was elevated by the pope to be archbishop and patriarch of the whole East. In 1313 a rich Armenian lady gave money to build a church in the great port of Zaiton (Ch'üan-chou) which had extensive trade with the Persian Gulf. This was made into a cathedral, and later a friary was attached and other churches built in the city. No doubt these churches were used in the main to serve the needs of Christians who formed part of a large foreign trading community in that port. The missionary force in China was pitiably small, and again and again reduced by death. Although several attempts were made to send groups of missionaries from Europe, few of them were ever able to complete the long and hazardous journey to China. Contacts between the missionaries and the Holy See were almost impossible to maintain in spite of heroic attempts to reinforce the China mission. As Cary-Elwes writes, 'Not only were bishops appointed by the Holy See, but groups of missionary friars were sent out from time to time, to be swallowed up by the vastness of the East, and not to be heard of again.'[15] Few native Chinese were converted to Christianity, and the Church consisted in the main of foreign traders, Alan Christian residents in China and some Nestorians who were won over to the Catholic faith; so that when virulent persecution again broke out and the missionaries were expelled, there was no indigenous leadership to hold together the scattered groups of Christians until more peaceable times ensued.

The Jesuit mission. With the rise of the Ming dynasty China closed its doors to foreigners, and for a century and a half there was virtually no contact between China and the West. At the beginning of the sixteenth century, Portuguese traders appeared at the mouth of the Hsi-chiang in south China, and though not permitted to live on the mainland they were allowed to build for themselves temporary quarters on an island at the mouth of the river, living there each year through a few months of summer and carrying on a lucrative trade with the local Chinese. They proved useful in clearing out pirates who infested the area, and were finally given permission to establish for themselves a more permanent city at Macao. Missionaries followed in the wake of the traders, and though it was the Jesuits who were to become a dominant influence in the establishment of a Christian Church in China from the closing decades of the sixteenth century, it was Dominicans, Franciscans and Augustinians mainly from the Spanish-held Philippines, who made the first attempts to break open the closed door to Christian influence which it was the policy of the Ming emperors to keep firmly shut. It was by the sea-route to south China, and not along the central Asian trade routes, that missionaries now came to China, establishing themselves in Macao, which had by now become a large and prosperous trading post. Great rivalry and considerable hostility grew up between the Spanish and Portuguese missionaries. The Spaniards had had great success in planting the Christian religion in the Philippines, where large colonies of Chinese resided. With the help of Chinese converts they made several attempts to enter China. Rivalry between the Portuguese and Spaniards, and the hostility of the merchant community who feared that missionary activity might bring about the revocation of their hard-won trade concessions, made abortive the first missionary efforts.

It was the zeal, perseverance and scholarship of Matteo Ricci (1552–1610) which finally opened the way for the establishment of a Christian mission on the mainland. With great tact and persistence he slowly won the friendship of scholars and magistrates. Here was a 'scholar' like themselves, and one from whom they had much to learn. Through their assistance, first at Chao-ch'ing (1583), then at Shao-chou (1589) and later at Nanking, Ricci managed to obtain permission for himself and his colleagues to reside. He made friends with the literati and gradually extended Christian influence. But he knew that unless he could obtain recognition from the emperor, there could be no hope of establishing a permanent mission. He finally entered Peking on 4 January 1601 and, in spite of opposition, managed to get verbal permission to reside in the capital. Slowly he and his companions gained a reputation for scholarship, won over several of the literati, gained a number of converts and established a Christian Church.

The Jesuits in Peking made themselves so useful to the emperor that, in spite of fierce opposition and brief periods of persecution, they managed to consolidate their mission. Permission was given to build churches in several cities, and the work was gradually extended through the provinces. A more conciliatory attitude on the part of the Chinese authorities in the early decades of the seventeenth century made possible the establishment of Dominican and Franciscan missions in several cities in south China, but their missionary methods often proved of great embarrassment to their Jesuit co-religionists. The uncouth manners, the alien customs, and the intolerant attitude to native beliefs of many of these missionaries roused the suspicion, hatred and contempt of the majority of the Chinese, so that the period which marked the fall of the great Ming dynasty was one in which many priests and Chinese converts perished.

In Peking itself it was the scientific knowledge of the Jesuits which won their acceptance at court. In 1629 one of Ricci's successors, Adam Schall, was appointed a member of the Bureau of Astronomy which had the special task of reforming the calendar. In 1645 he was elevated to be president of the Bureau. For a while the Jesuits basked in the patronage of the first Manchu emperor, Shun-chih, but their enemies were ever on the alert to bring about their disgrace and ruin. On Shun-chih's death in 1662 the attack began. The 'Christian law' was condemned as immoral, favouring rebellion and foreign invasion. European science was condemned as bad and Schall, together with five others, was condemned to a horrible death. The sentence on Schall was never carried out, but as the result of close imprisonment he died in 1666. A decree was issued proscribing the Christian religion in China. Apart from four Jesuits who remained in Peking, all the foreign priests, including eleven Dominicans and one Franciscan, were rounded up and conveyed to prison in Canton.

In 1669 the young emperor, Kang-hsi, reached his majority, and largely through the influence of Verbiest, who had served as tutor to the young prince, the Jesuit mission now entered on its most glorious period of expansion. In 1671 an edict granted the re-entry of the Catholic fathers at Canton. At the court in Peking Fathers Verbiest, Grimaldi, Pereira and Thomas exerted themselves making scientific instruments and writing works of science, philosophy and religion. In 1692 the emperor signed a decree of the Board of Rites granting protection to Catholic missions and missionaries. Part of the decree runs as follows:

> We decide that all temples dedicated to the Lord of heaven, in whatever place they may be found, ought to be preserved, and that it may be permitted to all who wish to worship this God to enter these temples, offer Him incense, and perform the ceremonies practised according to ancient customs by Christians. Therefore let no one henceforth offer them any opposition.[16]

The Christian Church in China at the beginning of the eighteenth century seemed far more likely to succeed than had the two previous missions of the Nestorians and the Franciscans. In the first place the Jesuits had won a reputation for learning and scholarship so dear to the Chinese. They were in the main men of broad tolerance and were prepared to accept the rites connected with the ancestor cult and the cult of Confucius as in no wise inimical to the practice of the Christian faith. The missionaries also set about the systematic training of Chinese in the faith, and ordained several Chinese as priests, and consecrated one as bishop. The Catholic Church allowed the Chinese clergy to use Chinese as their liturgical language. The Bible, the Missal, the Breviary, books for the instruction of catechumens in Christian doctrine, and even the *Summa Theologica* of St Thomas Aquinas were translated. Whilst many of the illiterate masses were attracted by the assurance of eternal salvation, the sacrifice of Christ on the cross, and the veneration of the Virgin Mary, the scholars, who found the concept of a suffering and dying God repellent, were nevertheless attracted to the Christian belief in an eternal, omnipotent and righteous God. Contacts with Europe were now far easier than they had been in the previous centuries, and the flow of recruits to the mission field could be easily maintained.

Yet with the dawn of the eighteenth century the situation of the Christian Church in China began perceptibly to change.

Ever since the first arrival in China of Friar Juan Bautista de Morales in the year 1633 the Dominican and Franciscan friars had grown suspicious that the excessive caution of the Jesuits was in fact compromising the purity of the Christian faith. The Rites which Ricci had pronounced as not being idolatrous and probably not superstitious seemed to the friars to be totally incompatible with the Christian religion and they forbade them to their converts. Sharp controversy arose within the Christian missionary body, both sides appealing to Rome. National jealousies and ecclesiastical differences led to bitter reproaches on both sides. Matters came to a head in 1704, when the pope and the Congregation of Rites issued the now famous decree by which they authorised 'one name and one only for God in Chinese, *T'ien-chu,* or Lord of heaven . . . Ritual acts in honour of Confucius had also to stop, not even on the occasion of the graduation of the literati were they allowed. Veneration of ancestors and even of their tablets were prohibited by the decree.'[17] De Tournon was sent to Peking as a papal legate, but 'his behaviour, once he had set foot on Chinese soil, could scarcely have been more calculated to embitter the quarrel and alienate the emperor'.[18] In the summer of 1706 an imperial decree was issued expelling from China all missionaries who refused to swear to keep the rules formerly laid down by Matteo Ricci concerning the Chinese Rites. Though sincere attempts at reconciliation were made, the situation went from bad to worse. A year after the death of K'ang-hsi, in 1724, all Christian missionaries in China, apart from those who continued to serve the government in Peking, were expelled to Canton, and later to Macao. Churches all over the provinces were desecrated or destroyed. Only the churches in Peking remained open. In spite of the repression, numerous priests at the risk of their lives continued the work of evangelisation, circulating secretly from place to place, and hiding usually in barges. In 1746 the persecution was intensified, until in 1773, on the suppression of the Jesuit order, the Christian mission in China sank almost to extinction. The Jesuit work in Peking was mainly taken over by Lazarists, and though a number of foreign priests remained in various parts of China, they had to remain in hiding, risking death or expulsion.

In the closing decades of the eighteenth century the power of Spain and Portugal had sadly declined, and Catholic missions throughout the world were suffering from lack of support. The Protestant Dutch and English were rapidly extending their trade in the far east. Though there were thousands of Christians and a few Chinese priests scattered throughout the vast Chinese empire only sporadic missionary activity was possible until the opening up of China began with the Opium Wars of 1839–40.

The modern era. 1839–1949. Until the beginning of the nineteenth century the Protestant countries of Europe and America had made no attempt at the Christian evangelisation of the Chinese. From the middle of the seventeenth century English and Dutch traders had sailed their ships in far eastern waters and carried on a lucrative trade. But 'their activities in those parts consisted often enough, from the religious point of view, only in spreading untrue and dangerous rumours about the Catholic missionaries, or in behaving in such an unruly way as to jeopardise the whole missionary work of the Catholic Europeans'.[19] As Spanish and Portuguese power declined, the trade with China came more and more into the hands of the English and the Dutch. It was from the shelter of foreign trading ports and under the protection of well-armed ships that the first Protestant missionaries were able to get a first foothold in China. Although to penetrate on to the mainland of China was extremely dangerous, Dr Robert Morrison (1782–1834), the pioneer among Protestant missionaries to China, arrived in Canton in 1807, and divided his time between Canton and Macao as an employee of the East India Company. By 1824 he had translated and printed the whole Bible in Chinese, but could only claim ten converts to Christianity. It was not until 1839–40, when the defeat of the Chinese by the English in the so-called Opium War led to the opening up of five 'treaty ports' to foreign trade and the ceding of Hongkong to Britain, that the modern missionary movement got under way. By 1845 thirty-one male Protestant missionaries had established missions in the treaty ports, the majority being from America. At the same time, Catholic missionaries under the protection of the French government re-entered China. In spite of hostility, suspicion and hatred, converts to Christianity rapidly increased. Local persecutions of Christians were liable to break out at any time, but as these invariably resulted in the punishment of the offenders and the exaction of still more concessions to the Western powers, it is no wonder that many Chinese came to view the missionaries as agents of Western imperialism and promoters of a cultural aggression which had as its aim the destruction of the Chinese way of life.

Constant friction led to a second war, in 1856–60, in which the British and French joined to defeat the Chinese. More ports were opened to foreign residence and trade, foreigners were allowed to travel in the interior of China, and the Chinese government was forced to allow missionaries freely to teach religion, to erect churches and make converts. From this time onwards both Protestant and Roman Catholic missions grew rapidly, until by the closing decades of the nineteenth century there were some two thousand Christian missionaries residing in China, and Christian churches had been established throughout the whole vast Chinese empire.

During the years 1850–65 the T'ai P'ing rebellion swept over the country like a forest fire, and almost brought down the crumbling Manchu dynasty. It was only suppressed after the loss of some twenty million lives, and with the aid of the foreign powers. Its leader, Hung Hsiu-ch'üan had come under the influence of Christian missionaries, and though fundamentally the rebellion was a rising of land-hungry peasants smarting under burdensome taxation and cruel oppression, it possessed a marked religious character. Hung sought to establish a purely Chinese dynasty under the title *T'ai P'ing* or 'Great Peace' and derived much of the idealism of his movement from Christian sources.

Most of the missionaries were men and women of simple piety, zealous only for the conversion of the Chinese from what they deemed to be idolatrous superstitions to the true faith through which alone all men might attain salvation. By their zeal and self-sacrificing love they made a remarkable impact upon the cultural and social life of the Chinese, bringing to them what they believed to be a far superior way of life. But the movement was vitiated by several factors. It was regarded as a 'foreign' religion, dominated by missionaries whose presence in the country was only tolerated because of the superior military strength of the West, and because many Chinese were attracted by the advantages of Western education, medicine, technical and scientific knowledge, and by the wealth and prestige of the great Western democracies. The educated Chinese were quick to note that though Protestants and Roman Catholics both claimed to be Christian, their attitude to one another was often marked by hostility, hatred and contempt. The Roman Catholics believed that the Protestants were dangerous heretics, hindering the work of Christ. Most of the Protestants had been taught to believe that the pope was anti-Christ, and that Roman Catholicism was a corrupt form of Christianity. Furthermore, the Protestants were divided into a great number of sects, each believing that they alone preached the Gospel in all its purity. As for the long-established religions of China, the missionaries believed and taught their converts to believe that they were idolatrous superstitions which merited condemnation and destruction.

In the Boxer uprising at the turn of the century all the pent-up hatred, suspicion and fear of the foreigners blazed forth in an abortive attempt to rid China once and for all of their influence. The national humiliation that resulted from the suppression of the Boxers awakened the Chinese to the realisation of their own weakness and backwardness in face of the power, wealth and scientific achievements of the Western world. They looked across the sea to Japan, rapidly gaining recognition as a world power. A movement for reform and revolution gained momentum, together with a burning desire to learn what the West could teach. The opportunity was avidly seized by the Christian churches, particularly those from England and America. Men and money were poured into the China missions in the belief that the time was now ripe for the evangelisation of the whole of China. How could the Chinese fail to see that the Christian Gospel was the greatest treasure that the West had to offer? Mission schools and hospitals were multiplied, and intelligent Chinese students were encouraged to study abroad. Increasing emphasis was placed upon the training of the Chinese clergy, and the training of evangelists, teachers, nurses and doctors to staff the Christian missions. By the year 1920 the Protestant Christian community was numbered at more than eight hundred thousand.

At the same time a much more tolerant, enlightened and co-operative spirit was developing among the missionaries, together with an increasing emphasis on the building up of an indigenous Chinese Church in which the control should be more and more placed in Chinese hands. By the year 1922 the National Christian Council came into being, whilst several Christian universities, run on a co-operative basis, were training a new Chinese intelligentsia.

But the Chinese renaissance which had led to the establishment of a Chinese republic, so largely aided by the Christian enterprise, became more and more pervaded by a spirit of religious scepticism. This, combined with a rabid nationalism, led to anti-Christian and anti-missionary activity. The foreigners in China were seen as imperialist aggressors who had gained a strangle-hold upon the economy. The missionaries with their mission stations in every province, with their western-type schools, colleges and hospitals, were objects of the greatest opprobrium. They were denounced as 'cultural aggressors', destroying by their subtle propaganda the very foundations of Chinese civilisation. The more radical element denounced the missionaries as 'imperialists' and 'capitalists', sheltering behind gunboats and unequal treaties, and the Chinese Christians were 'running dogs of the imperialists'. Thus, though the Christian Church in China grew in strength and numbers and gradually turned from a foreign mission into a Chinese Church in which Chinese leadership slowly began to predominate, the forces of rabid nationalism, anti-Christian agitation, religious scepticism and Communism on the one hand, and the growing feeling in the West that every country had the right of self-determination on the other hand, finally led to the great débâcle which followed on the seizure of power by the Communists in 1949. Once more all missionaries, Roman Catholic and Protestant, were ejected from China.

They had left behind them, however, a small but vigorous Christian community. It consisted of not more than half of one per cent of the population, but it possessed a trained leadership and many outstanding personalities. All ties between the Christian Churches in China and the West were cut. Though the Communists insisted that freedom of religious belief was granted to all people, and overt persecution on religious grounds was no part of their policy, the Christian Church was once more subjected to rigorous control. The Christians found themselves faced with such serious restrictions that the proper functioning of the Christian Church in China became once more impossible. Many Christians fled to Hongkong and Taiwan to swell the ranks of the Chinese Christians in those places. In Hongkong about one in twelve of the population are regarded as Christian, and in 1959 an estimate of the Christians in Taiwan, Roman Catholic and Protestant, gives four hundred thousand members and adherents.[20]

Islam in China

From its earliest beginnings in China, Islam followed a different path from that taken by Christianity. Christian missionaries had come to

China, as we have seen, to attempt the conversion of the Chinese to Christianity. The Muslims came as immigrants or traders, who married Chinese wives and were content so long as they were allowed to follow their own distinctive customs and religion and bring up their children in the Muslim faith. They had apparently no 'urge to extend their faith and political influence by the warlike methods usually associated with their creed'.[21] They soon became completely naturalised, and apart from individuals who served the government with distinction they made little impact on Chinese culture in general.

The Chinese government has, on the whole, been tolerant of religious beliefs and practices which did not threaten either the supreme authority of the state over the lives of its subjects, or the established patterns of public morality. Throughout the centuries, and indeed until modern times, Islam in China was practically isolated from the rest of the Islamic world, and thus interference from outside on behalf of the Muslims in China never constituted a threat to the government. The Muslims were, on the whole, industrious and law-abiding, they took good care of their own poor and indigent, and their code of behaviour was at least as high as that of their Chinese neighbours.

In the year AD 651 an embassy from the Caliph Othman arrived at the T'ang capital, Ch'ang-an, and was received with every mark of distinction by the emperor. This date is usually accepted for the entrance of Islam into China. Apart, however, from a few Arab traders there is no evidence of any considerable settlement of Muslims in China before the middle of the eighth century. Though Zoroastrian temples and Nestorian churches were built in China in the seventh century, there is no record of a Muslim mosque.

Between the years 705 and 713, Kutaiba, the general for Caliph Walid, set about the conquest of central Asia. This greatly perturbed the Chinese emperor, who had dependencies in that area. A Chinese army sent to oppose him was decisively beaten. There followed a further embassy to the T'ang court in AD 713, and though they refused as Muslims to perform the customary prostration before the emperor, they were courteously received. Fortunately for China internal dissensions within the Muslim world removed all danger of Arab attack.

It was Arab mercenaries, sent by the Caliph Abu Jafar al Mansur, who in AD 756 assisted in the defeat of the Tartar rebel, An Lu-shan, and in gratitude for their services some four thousand Muslims were allowed to settle in China. They married Chinese women and soon became naturalised. They strictly observed the tenets of their own religion, but there is no authentic record of their building permanent religious edifices until the Sung dynasty (960–1275).

During the T'ang dynasty, Canton in south China was the centre of a flourishing sea-borne trade with the Persian Gulf, a trade largely carried on by Arab sailors. In the large foreign community established in that city the Muslims had a Kadi, elected by themselves, and were subject to Koranic law. Ch'üan-chou also seems to have had a considerable Muslim community, for according to the *Records of Fukien (Min Shu Chi Tsai)* a cemetery for Muslims was established as early as the T'ang dynasty.

It was during the Yüan dynasty that there was a large Muslim infiltration. Muslim scholars, traders and craftsmen were encouraged to make their home in China. Several distinguished officials of the dynasty were Muslims. They introduced Muslim science and proved particularly useful in astronomy and the preparation of the calendar. It is probably at this time that they got their distinctive Chinese name *Hui-hui*. They spread into every province, but especially into the western provinces of Kansu, Szechuan and Yunnan. In most areas they lived in their separate communities, often called *ying* or barracks, revealing their military origin. They were distinguished by their dress, food and customs. They greeted each other in Persian or Arabic and many wore a white turban. They practised circumcision and had distinctive marriage and funeral customs. They shunned usury, divination, geomancy and stage-acting. They built their own mosques and schools where Arabic was taught and the Qur'an was the basis of instruction. Many rose to distinction within the imperial service. Perhaps the most famous Muslim of the time was the grand eunuch Chêng-ho, imperial envoy and commander-in-chief of a great expedition to Hormuz on the Persian Gulf. A stele on a hill outside the city of Ch'üan-chou marks the spot where he sought divine protection for his perilous enterprise.[22] The muslims developed a special interest in such trades as transport, horse-dealing, inn-keeping, metal-work and butchery.

Throughout the Ming and Ch'ing dynasties the Muslim population in China continued to increase. Intermarriage with non-Muslim Chinese was frowned upon, though in times of famine girls from pagan homes were sometimes bought and later married within the Muslim community. Throughout the nineteenth century the Muslims in Yunnan and north-west China, smarting under the cruel exactions of Chinese officials, rebelled on several occasions (in 1818, 1826, 1834, and finally in the great rebellion of 1855–78). These rebellions were fostered not so much by religious as racial feeling. They were cruelly suppressed. Whole districts were devastated, Muslim cities sacked, men, women and children massacred, and harsh restrictions placed upon the Muslim population. A legacy of race hatred continued till the fall of the Manchu dynasty, and the recognition of the Muslims as an integral part of the new republic, symbolised by the white stripe in the five-barred flag.

Various estimates have been made of the Muslim population of China, varying from three to eighty million. A government estimate of 1924 gave the figure as between fifteen and twenty million. Mosques are to be found in many of the larger cities of China. In Canton there are five, and the city is a place of Muslim pilgrimage because of the legend that Mohammed's maternal uncle was buried there. A splendid mosque was built in Peking by Ch'ien-lung, the Manchu emperor. In Nanking, besides the mosques, there is a theological seminary for the training of the ahongs or teachers. Except in Turkestan, where mosques are of Arabic design with minaret and towers, the mosques conform to a Chinese style of architecture, and outwardly differ little from the temples of other faiths. Usually they display over the front entrance the three Chinese characters *ching chên ssŭ* meaning 'the pure and true religion'. Within the mosques are Arabic inscriptions, and a cleanliness and austerity foreign to Buddhist and Taoist temples. The services are conducted by the ahong, and follow the usual Muslim form, with emphasis on previous lustration, the removal of shoes, prayers recited with the face turned towards Mecca, and the usual prostrations before Allah.

In general, the Chinese followers of Islam observe the five pillars of the faith, but with the exception of the mullahs and ahongs who recite their daily prayers within the mosques, few Muslims keep strictly to the rules concerning the daily prayers. Ramadan is strictly observed, and in some places the rite of circumcision. The ahongs are in charge of the Muslim schools, in which a smattering of Arabic is taught, but the average Muslim in China cannot read the Qur'an in Arabic.

Islam in China has produced no distinctive sect or prophet. Most follow the Sunnite tradition, and a distinction is made between the very conservative 'Old Sect' and the more liberal 'New Sect'. During the past century great, and indeed revolutionary, changes have taken place. The mosque has ceased to be the sole centre of Muslim activity. The result has been a movement towards liberalism, the translation of the Qur'an into Chinese, an intellectual awakening and a closer identification with the national life.

Traditionally each mosque is independent, being governed by a group of elders who elect their own 'Iman', chosen for his experience, character and scholarship. He has general oversight of the mosque and is leader in prayer. Whenever the community feels strong and wealthy enough the Iman and elders invite an ahong whose duty is to preach the doctrines, explain the laws, officiate in name-giving, circumcision, weddings and funerals. He is expected to settle disputes within the community. He is not a priest but a teacher and adviser. The Muslim women have considerable freedom. They dress like their Chinese neighbours. There are no harems in Chinese Islam, no purdah or veil. A Muslim is usually monogamous, but will take a second wife if the first wife is childless. It is unusual for Muslim women to attend the mosque services, but women have been known to become ahongs. The organisation of the community is essentially democratic. Islam is held together, not by ecclesiastic authority but by community feeling.

The need to be represented nationally and have a voice in public affairs led to the formation of a Chinese Islamic Society (1912) which by 1923 claimed to have some three thousand branches throughout China. Its avowed purposes were mutual aid, social reform and national salvation. Thus was formed a new centre outside the mosque for Islamic activities. Within the mosques themselves there has been considerable revival, resulting in the formation of 'Young Muslims' associations and 'Knowing Allah' associations.

Owing to China's isolation, Muslim customs in China deviated in many respects from the prescriptions of the Qur'an. During the seventeenth century Chinese pilgrims to Mecca became increasingly aware of these diversities, and on their return started a movement for a more literal observance of the teachings of the Qur'an. This led to considerable heart-searchings within the Muslim community in China and even to bitter dispute.

With the founding of the Chinese Republic in 1911, the Muslims in China were recognised as an integral part of the Chinese nation. In 1948 they had eighteen members in the National Assembly. Under the Communists they have been given representation as a minority group, and certain areas, predominantly Muslim, have been recognised as 'autonomous' legislative areas.

In the eleven years prior to 1934 only 834 Chinese Muslims went on pilgrimage to Mecca, but by 1937 there were more than 170 each year. During the period of the republic more and more went abroad for study, and good-will missions were sent to Egypt, Syria, Iraq, Iran and Turkey. These wider contacts have helped the Chinese Muslims to realise their solidarity with the Islamic world, and brought a further realisation of the dominant place of the Qur'an in Muslim life. The present strength and cohesion of the Muslim community in China makes it unlikely that their religious influence can be entirely obliterated by the Communists.

The Jews of K'ai-feng-fu

In the year 1912, the site of what had been the Jewish synagogue of K'ai-feng-fu, in the province of Honan, was sold to the Canadian Episcopal Church. Thus was finally closed one of the most fascinating chapters of Jewish history. For almost eight hundred years the Jews of K'ai-feng-fu had worshipped in their synagogue, which, through fire, flood and rebellion had been destroyed and rebuilt many times. Cut off from their co-religionists in other lands, these Jews had maintained their distinctive witness, customs and law. They had become known to their neighbours as the *T'iao-chin-chiao,* the religion of those who pick out the nerves and sinews from their meat. Only the remnants of seven clans remained of what had once been a wealthy and flourishing community. They were leaderless. Their last Rabbi had long since died and their synagogue had crumbled to ruin. Their treasured rolls of the Law had been destroyed. Their Sabbath worship was ended. Little distinguished them from their neighbours save the fact that they would eat no pork, refused to worship idols and to burn incense to their ancestors.[23]

The evidence is too scanty to say with any certainty when the first Jews settled in China. According to their own traditions, their ancestors had entered China during the Han dynasty, 206 BC–AD 225. It may well be that Jewish merchants and traders did penetrate as far as China in this early period, but if so they left behind no record. Jews are mentioned in an account of the sack of Canton by the rebel general Huang Ch'ao in the year AD 879.[24]

It was in the Sung dynasty, in the year 1163, that the emperor, Hsiao Tsung, gave permission to the Jews to build a synagogue at K'ai-feng. In AD 1446, when the synagogue had been in existence almost three hundred years, it was destroyed by flood, and the precious rolls of their Sacred Scriptures perished. At that time a Jewish colony at Ningpo in the province of Chekiang also had their synagogue, and in AD 1462 a Jew from that city brought a complete copy of the Law to K'ai-feng. In AD 1490 the synagogue was rebuilt. In the opening decades of the seventeenth century, the synagogue at K'ai-feng was again destroyed, this time by fire, and all the books were burned. A generation later, in AD 1642, the synagogue was again destroyed in a terrible siege of the city. Twenty-six of the precious synagogue books were destroyed, but by AD 1654 the synagogue was again rebuilt, and the rolls of the Law and other books were transcribed.[25]

It was the famous Jesuit missionary, Matteo Ricci, who at the beginning of the seventeenth century first revealed to the West the existence of a Jewish colony at K'ai-feng. On hearing of foreigners who worshipped the True God, and were not Muslims, one of their number journeyed to Peking and called on Ricci. He revealed that there were ten or twelve clans of Jews living at K'ai-feng, and that they had recently restored their synagogue at a cost of ten thousand crowns. He also informed Ricci that several Jewish families lived at Hangchow, the former capital of the Sung dynasty, and they too had their synagogue. Shown a Hebrew Bible, he recognised the script but could not read it. He claimed that his brother was proficient in Hebrew. Some attempts were made, without success, to convert these Jews to Christianity. Between the years 1712 and 1723 two Jesuit scholars versed in Hebrew paid frequent visits to the synagogue at K'ai-feng, making a sketch-plan of the synagogue and copying the inscriptions on the walls. With the expulsion of missionaries from the interior of China all contact ceased until Dr W. A. P. Martin visited them in 1866.[26] Dr Martin first sought information at one of the six mosques of the city. The mufti denounced the Jews as unbelievers and informed Martin that their synagogue had been utterly demolished. A stele survived with an inscription commemorating the erection of the synagogue in 1183, and its subsequent rebuilding. Dr Martin contacted six representatives of the remaining Jewish families, who confessed that their holy and beautiful synagogue had reached such a state of ruin that they had with their own hands demolished it. They were impoverished. They had lost all knowledge of Hebrew, had ceased their ritual worship, and no longer handed down the traditions of their fathers. One had become a Buddhist priest; others had embraced Islam.

In its hey-day, the synagogue, as described in the letters of the Jesuit fathers Domenge and Gaubil was a magnificent complex of courts and buildings. The synagogue itself was sixty by forty feet, covered with a handsome roof. In the centre was 'Moses' Seat' a magnificent and elevated chair with an embroidered cushion on which the book of the Law was placed. Nearby was the emperor's name in golden letters, surmounted by the Shema in Hebrew letters of gold and beyond this a triple arch bore the Hebrew inscription: 'Blessed be the Lord for ever. The Lord is God of gods and the Lord, a great God, strong and terrible.' A large table bore six candlesticks in line and nearby stood a laver. Finally there was the Beth-El, the *T'ien T'ang,* or House of Heaven. Into this place none but the Rabbi entered during the time of prayer. On separate tables stood thirteen rolls of the Law each enclosed in a tent of silken curtains. On the extreme western wall were the ten commandments in gold lettering, and besides each a closet containing books and manuscripts. The congregation was separated from the Beth-El by a balustrade.

Shoes were discarded on entering the synagogue. A blue headdress was worn, which distinguished them from the Muslims who wore white. When reading the Law, the minister covered his face with a transparent gauze veil, and wore a red scarf hanging from his right shoulder and tied under his left arm. The prayers were chanted. There were no musical instruments. The congregation wore no talith during the service.

The Jews of K'ai-feng observed circumcision, the Passover, the Feast of Tabernacles, the Rejoicing for the Law, and, perhaps, the Day of Atonement, for it was said that on one day they fasted and wept together in the synagogue. They kept the Sabbath strictly, never attempted to make proselytes, and refused to marry with gentiles. They used their sacred books for casting lots. They never pronounced the name of God, but used the word 'Adonai', and in writing Chinese rendered the word God by *T'ien.* They believed in the unity of God, heaven and hell, the resurrection of the dead, a day of judgment, and in a hierarchy of angels. They were adamant against idolatry. They prayed facing westward, towards Jerusalem.

That a small colony of Jews in the heart of China, isolated from the rest of the Jewish world, should thus persist in their religion, through wars, calamities, changes of dynasties, for almost eight hundred years is one of the most remarkable facts in the history of religion in China. It witnesses alike to the strong hold of religious beliefs and traditions, and to the tolerance of the Chinese in respect of religion so long as religion threatens neither the authority of the state nor the well-ordering of society.

CHAPTER THIRTEEN

THE RELIGIOUS SITUATION IN MODERN CHINA

In the previous chapters we have endeavoured to trace the development of religion in China from the earliest historical times in the Shang dynasty of the second millennium BC. We have seen that though foreign religions introduced into China from outside made a considerable impact, and Buddhism in particular gained the adherence of the majority of the population throughout many centuries, it was the Confucian tradition which, from the neo-Confucian revival of the Sung dynasty, reasserted itself as the predominant influence in the cultural life of the Chinese people. It did so largely because it kept firm control over the educational system, and also provided an ideological framework for the government of the country. But the religious expression of Confucianism in the elaborate state cult was the concern only of the enlightened and educated scholar-class. Though performed on behalf of the whole country, it scarcely touched the masses who had no part in it. Their religious urge had to find expression in the worship of the numerous divinities of Taoism and Buddhism, the manes of their family ancestors, and the countless spirits which were believed to reside in or control natural phenomena.

Early in the twentieth century, with the fall of the Manchu dynasty, the state cult fell into disuse. Buddhism and Taoism were both in sad decline. They were both organisationally weak, and failed to provide a trained and educated leadership adequate for the religious needs of the populace. Hence the popular religion had become a strange amalgam of beliefs drawn from Taoist, Buddhist and other sources. From time to time some outstanding religious figure, often of peasant origin, would draw round him a considerable following. At times there would be sporadic but localised outbursts of intense religious fervour. But in general the masses of the people visited their temples and shrines in search of temporal blessings, had a fatalistic attitude to life, and put their faith in astrology, geomancy, witchcraft, fortune-telling, charms, magic and spiritualism. There were, as W. T. Chan has pointed out,[1] two levels of Chinese religion: the religion of the enlightened, and the religion of the masses. It is our aim, in this concluding chapter, briefly to examine religion at these two levels in the closing years of the Manchu dynasty and up to the establishment of the Communist régime.

The popular religion

A visitor to China during the closing years of the Manchu dynasty would have been forcibly impressed by the strength and pervasive influence of religion in the lives of the masses. In every city were several large temples, among which was the temple dedicated to *Ch'êng Huang*, the protective deity of the walls and moats whose office was to look after the welfare of the inhabitants. Nearly every street, village and hamlet had its small shrine to *T'u Ti,* the local tutulary deity. Wealthy families possessed their own ancestral temples, but almost every family had its little shrine, *Chia-t'ang,* in which were placed images or tablets of certain family divinities. Scarcely a home was without its protective door-gods, the hearth-god, and pictures of the god of wealth, the goddess of mercy, etc. The landscape was dotted with Buddhist temples and pagodas or Taoist temples, often sited in beautiful surroundings and of great architectural beauty. Along the roads were innumerable wayside shrines dedicated to the spirit of some great hero or for the worship of various nature divinities. Many mountains were venerated as sacred and to their temples endless streams of peasants made their pilgrimages. Each trade guild had its appropriate god with his annual festival, and his image presided over the affairs of the guild. The annual country fairs in north China, usually lasting from three to five days, were usually organised round some temple, and opened with appropriate sacrifices and ceremonies before the image of the protective god. Most of the festivals throughout the year were of a semi-religious character and closely bound up with religious practices. The great events of family life, birth, marriage, sickness and death, were marked by religious observance and demanded the services of Taoist or Buddhist priests. The souls of the dead had to be sent off to their judgment by the gods of the underworld to the accompaniment of masses for the dead intoned by the Buddhist clergy, whilst the almost universal belief in *Fêng-shui* (geomancy), exorcism, necromancy, prognostication and the like demanded the constant service of Taoist masters.

Although there were several great temples and monasteries where Buddhism and Taoism were practised by trained and disciplined monks in comparative purity, and although there were societies of laymen who banded together for the study and practice of these faiths, the popular religion of China could be described as neither Confucian, Buddhist nor Taoist. As H. Maspero wrote:

> The three religions, as definite systems, have now for centuries had only historical interest: the people neither practise all three together, nor each of the three separately. Little by little throughout the ages a popular religion has taken shape, which borrowed various features from all three, but which is definitely distinct from them all, and must be regarded as a system apart. [2]

This popular religion was served partly by state functionaries who, as we have seen in the chapter on state religion, had prescribed religious obligations to the community and district which they administered, and partly by specialist priests. It was Buddhist priests, who had had some training and ordination in the large temples and monasteries, who administered most of the local temples, living mainly on revenues derived from temple property. They were recognised by their shaven heads and distinctive dress. The Taoist monks usually lived in monasteries and were subjected to rules and discipline very similar to those which governed the Buddhist clergy, but there were large numbers of Taoist lay-masters, who lived in the world and were married, and who acted as mediums, exorcists and healers, passing on their arts from father to son. Great variety of religious expression was evident in different parts of China. 'The popular religion is far from being one and the same; if certain fundamental ideas are found from one end of China to the other, the details vary infinitely from one place to another.'[3] In some areas Buddhist influence predominated; in others, Taoist ideas were particularly strong.

The pantheon of the popular religion was of the utmost diversity. The Buddhas, bodhisattvas and arhats of Buddhism, the Immortals and Heaven-honoured Ones of Taoism, the deified emperors, empresses, scholars and heroes of Confucianism, the nature-spirits and household gods of a primitive animism were all accepted. Most of the innumerable gods worshipped had once been human beings who, for various reasons, had been promoted after death to some important function or office in the spiritual world. It would need a large volume even to enumerate and characterise the gods and goddesses of popular religion in China. All we can do here is to refer briefly to a few of the most important divinities whom the Chinese elevated to positions of special influence and power in the spiritual world.[4]

Throughout China a supreme deity was recognised as sovereign ruler over the whole universe and over the hierarchy of spiritual beings. He was known by the title of *Yü-huang-Shang-ti*, or the Supreme August Jade Emperor, or more familiarly by the peasants as *Lao-T'ien-Yeh*, the Ancient-Ancestor-Heaven. He had been incorporated into the popular religion from Taoism, being the second of a supreme Triad that dwelt in the highest of the thirty-six heavens, and to whom the first of the Triad, the Primordial Heaven-honoured One, had long since resigned the government of the world. He is represented as a celestial emperor, surrounded by his court and a whole army of ministers, officials and generals who are always ready to do his bidding.

The temples devoted to the worship of the Dragon-King *(Lung Wang)* are particularly numerous in north China. His primary function is to control the rain, and associated with his worship are many rain-making ceremonies.

Another important deity of Taoist origin is *T'ai-shan*, the god of the great and holy *T'ai* mountain in Shantung, whose function, under the supreme authority of the Jade Emperor, is to preside over human life, appointing to each his destiny, the times of his birth and death. One can see the powerful influence of the Buddhist doctrines of karma and rebirth in the concept of this god keeping strict account of all men's good and evil deeds, and apportioning their place in the next life accordingly.

Of the innumerable Buddhas and bodhisattvas of Buddhism, the ones which have most universal appeal in the popular religion of China are the Buddha Amitābha, *(O-mi-t'o fo)*, and his great assistants, the budhisattvas *Kuan-yin* and *Ti-ts'ang*. As regards the latter, all that need be said here is that he is the great lord of the underworld, and as such is thought of as the great mediator and protector of the unfortunate souls suffering torment for their evil deeds. He is ever seeking to implant in their breasts the holy longings which will initiate the process which will lead to their ultimate salvation.

It is Amitābha, the Buddha of infinite light, the personification of compassion in its ultimate form,[5] the ruler of the Western Paradise, the

'Land of the Blessed' who, more than any other deity, has captured the hearts of millions of Chinese. 'In times of sickness and loss, in calamity by fire and water, when attacked by robbers, or in the anguish of death, he is the refuge sought in prayer. And this prayer is very brief. It consists simply in naming his name.'[6] His name, *O-mi-t'o Fo*, is found everywhere. To pronounce it in true faith is to assure salvation. He is the Buddha who has made an eternal vow to save all living creatures.

Along with the worship of Amitābha is the cult of *Kuan-yin*, more properly *Kuan-shih-yin*. This great bodhisattva, whose name in Chinese is due to a misinterpretation of the Sanscrit name, Avalokitésvara, appears to have been introduced into China about the fifth century AD. Represented in early iconography in male form, it was as a great female divinity that she gained a supreme place in popular religion. As the protectress of women and children, the giver of children, the guardian of sailors and the great compassionate saviour, it is practically impossible to distinguish her from the Taoist inspired *T'ien Hou* (Empress of Heaven), the Holy Mother *(T'ien Shang Shêng-mu)*, or the Princess of the Variegated Clouds *(Pi-hsia Yüan-chün)*. Temples in her honour are to be found all over China and she unquestionably occupies a supreme place in the affection of the masses as one whose tender heart of compassion is always ready to hear the cry of the afflicted and to hasten to act on their behalf. As Doré writes, 'In northern Buddhism, no divinity holds so large a place in popular worship as *Kuan-yin*. It may even be said that she has eclipsed Buddha himself and the other great Bodhisattvas. This is due to the mysterious and merciful function which she fulfils in the Buddhist world.'[7]

In the popular religion the chief concern was salvation; not only salvation from the ills of this life, but salvation from the retribution that inevitably awaits the soul in the world beyond on account of the accumulation of evil deeds performed in this life. The Buddhist doctrines of karma and rebirth had profoundly influenced the masses. Through popular books, stories and pictures, and in the iconography of the temples, the people were ever reminded of the wheel of transmigration on which all sentient life was bound, until its final release. In numerous temples the ten hells of Buddhism were depicted in all their gruesome detail, and were a constant reminder of that judgment from which no soul could escape. Over the fifth of these hells Yama, the king of the dead according to Hindu mythology, presided, a position to which he had been demoted because he had proved too lenient in his judgments.

The Buddhist priests were not only prominent in the official festivals and fasts, but were felt to be indispensable for the performance of the elaborate funeral ceremonies and for chanting the masses for the dead. 'It is the conviction of the ordinary Chinese that he must have Buddhist monks if his affairs after death are to be taken care of. He may add that they are a "necessary evil", and he may use the opportunity to pour out the vials of his satire and contempt upon the whole business of monkhood. But the result is nevertheless a qualified acknowledgment.'[8]

Undoubtedly the popular religion has suffered a serious decline during the course of the twentieth century. The preaching of the Christian missionaries, the growth of a modern western-type education, the strong anti-religious movements, the sequestration of temples, the weakening of family ties, and the growth of materialism and secularism have all tended to break the hold of traditional religious practices. The Communist régime, whilst proclaiming freedom of personal belief, has been unremitting in an attempt to eradicate what it deems to be useless, harmful and wealth-consuming superstitions.

It is, however, quite possible to underestimate the diffused influence of popular religion in Communist China. It has, throughout many centuries, so permeated the life and thought of the Chinese people that one is inclined to believe that it only awaits a more favourable political climate to blossom forth in renewed activity. Its influence on literature, art, folk-lore and common customs has been immense. Only a small percentage of the population of China has accepted, or even understands, the Marxist ideology. Though that small percentage is a governing élite wielding immense power, the vast majority, whilst grateful for stable government and the economic advantages of the Communist system, repudiates the militant atheism which has no place for a spiritual interpretation of man's life and destiny.

Wherever the Chinese live outside the control of the Communists and are allowed freedom of religious expression the popular religion flourishes. The vitality of religion in Taiwan is reflected in the fact that, apart from the growing strength of the Christian Churches, for a population estimated at some thirteen millions there are about four thousand temples, divided about evenly between Taoism and Buddhism.[9] The Chinese quarters in such places as Singapore give the impression that the traditional beliefs and practices of the folk-religion are very much alive. Chinese temples and shrines are everywhere in evidence, served by priests who pursue a lucrative trade in the sale of charms and magical prescriptions for the cure of sickness, and engage in communications with the dead, fortune-telling and such-like practices.

The religion of the enlightened

At the end of the nineteenth century the great Sung dynasty philosopher, Chu Hsi (1130–1200) was still regarded as the most orthodox interpreter of Confucian thought. His rationalistic interpretation of Confucianism was authoritative for most of the Confucian scholars. The emperor, Kuang Hsü, even issued a decree in the year 1894 proscribing under the most severe penalties the sale of any books attacking his doctrines.[10] Yet there were many important scholars who had been profoundly influenced by the more idealistic interpretation of Wang Yang-ming (1472–1529). They saw in his moral teachings, which gave primacy to the life of the mind, justification for asserting the superiority of Confucianism over the scientific materialism of the West. They felt that in Confucianism could be found the most satisfying and rational 'spiritual' interpretation of man's place and function in the universe. As a consequence, a serious attempt was made to elevate Confucianism into a state religion, as had been done in the case of Shinto in Japan. In 1906 an edict was issued to place sacrifices to Confucius on equality with those made to heaven. The famous scholar-statesman, K'ang Yu-wei (1858–1927) had a considerable following in regarding Confucius as the founder of a religion, and in vigorously advocating Confucianism as the state religion of China. He was strongly opposed, not only by leaders of other faiths, but by several of the most prominent Confucians of his time, men like Chang T'ai-yen (1868–1936) and Ts'ai Yüan-p'ei (1867–1940), who refused to acknowledge that Confucianism was a religion at all. They argued that Confucianism lacked practically all the essentials of a religion, and was simply an ethical and political philosophy. The movement to make Confucianism into a state religion failed completely, and with the birth of the republic of China the state sacrifices to heaven and Confucius soon fell into disuse.

Increasing contacts with the scientific, sociological and philosophical thought of Europe and America produced a ferment of new ideas. Western books on science and philosophy were eagerly translated and read. A growing number of Western-trained intellectuals came to accept Comte's axiom of the three ages of mankind, culminating in the scientific age in which all religion has become an anachronism, a relict from man's growing-up stage which must inevitably fade away as men became more enlightened. A few voices were raised to insist that only a religious interpretation of reality could form an adequate basis for morality and decent human relationships. Others contrasted the 'spirituality' of the East, as represented by the religions of China and India, with the gross materialism of the West.

In the period immediately following on the First World War a strong anti-religious movement grew up among the young intellectuals, stimulated by the teachings of scientific humanism, neo-realism and dialectic materialism. All religions came under sharp criticism. In the name of science and democracy Confucianism came under bitterest attack. It was regarded as the enemy of progress, the emblem of obscurantism and despotism, the main bulwark in China of conservative, backward and stereotyped thought.[11] Its emphasis on *li* (porpriety) was incompatible with modern ideas of progress and equality. Its doctrine of filial piety, the subordination of women, its archaic customs and elaborate funeral ceremonies were all unsuited to modern life and thought.

With the establishment of the Chinese Republic the religious aspects of Confucianism virtually died out. It was growingly felt, however, that there was a moral and spiritual vacuum, and under Chiang K'ai-shek a serious attempt was made to restore the ancient ideals of the Confucian ethic. The New Life Movement, using methods derived from Christianity, sought to revive the great Confucian virtues in an attempt to provide an ideology to combat materialism and class strife. But the New Life Movement, however good its intention, only touched the fringe of the deep-seated problem of moral and spiritual renewal. After years of civil strife followed by a devastating war with Japan the Chinese intellectuals faced spiritual bankruptcy. A few found what they were seeking in Christianity. Others sought a revival and reform of Buddhism. Still others turned to the teachings of Lao-tzŭ and Chuang-tzŭ. But more and more of the young intellectuals of China sought for national salvation and personal fulfilment in Communism. To many of them Communism became a substitute for religion, indeed a new religion, a religion whose Bible was Marxism and Leninism as interpreted by Mao Tse-tung, whose god-image was found in the father-figure and national saviour, Mao Tse-tung, a religion which demanded the utmost surrender of the individual in service to and sacrifice for the state. It was a militant and missionary religion which sought to expunge heterodoxy and establish communist orthodoxy by disciplined training and thought-control. Every religion, every ideology which did not conform to the pattern officially laid down was branded as 'bourgeois' or 'feudalistic' or 'superstition' and therefore inimical to the best interests of the Chinese people.

The attempt at Buddhist revival

To a superficial observer, Buddhism in China at the end of the nineteenth century presented an unattractive picture of superstition, magic and idolatry. The main occupation of the monks and nuns in the monasteries was the performance of rituals and the endless repetition of sūtras which were little understood. The *Sangha* consisted largely of illiterate or semi-illiterate monks. For several hundred years Chinese Buddhism had been practically reduced to the Pure Land School. The time was ripe for an intellectual awakening and for drastic reform. Many notable scholars contributed to this awakening, and modern reform was chiefly brought about by the exertions and under the leadership of the celebrated monk, T'ai Hsü (1889–1947).

In the intellectual awakening laymen played a prominent part. Attempts were made to form a national organisation which laid stress on education and sought to protect temple properties from sequestration. In 1929 a Chinese Buddhist society was formed but its organisation was never very strong. There was a revival in the study of Buddhist literature, and lost or forgotten texts were brought over from Japan. The publication of the Buddhist Tripitaka was undertaken, and Buddhist research institutes were established in many cities. Owing largely to Yin Kuang (1861–1940) new meaning was given to traditional practices and new life infused into the daily observances. But Yin Kuang, learned in the sūtras, was only concerned for the revival of Pure Land Doctrine and for preaching salvation by faith in Amitābha. He refused to adapt Buddhist doctrine to modern conditions, and was one of the chief opponents of T'ai Hsü's reforms. Believing that Buddhism held the absolute truth, he considered it to be impiety to try to harmonise it with modern philosophy and scientific theories.

Laymen organised themselves into some four hundred societies to encourage the Buddhist way of life and to study such texts as the Heart Sūtra *(Hsin Ching)*, to engage in meditation, join in retreats, and seek merit by acts of charity. Buddhist scholars revived their interest in the great idealistic schools of the Mahāyāna, and made their teachings the basis for a new Buddhist philosophy. The initiator of this movement was a layman, Ou-yang Ching-wu (1871–1943) who founded at Nanking the Chinese Academy for the study of Buddhism.

It was, however, the monk, T'ai Hsü, who became the dominant figure in the moral and intellectual awakening.

> Entering very young into the monastic life, he felt keenly the decadence of his religion and the contempt which surrounded the bonzes . . . He was convinced that it was necessary to effect a revolution within Buddhism by modernising it, by breaking with tradition in many points. The bonzes had no idea of social service, did not seek in any way to adapt their doctrine to the exigencies of the times, knew nothing of the sciences or occidental philosophy, and lived in ramshackle monasteries falling to ruins, where life was encrusted with archaic practices. Conscious of all these deficiencies and all this wretchedness, he intrepidly undertook to remedy the state of affairs.[12]

T'ai Hsü sought reform along three lines 1. a regeneration of the clergy, 2. the rededication of Buddhist properties for the benefit and use of the people, and 3. a reconstruction of Buddhist doctrine. He had a great intellectual influence through his writings, and especially through the review which he edited, called the *Hai-ch'ao-yin* or *The Sound of the Tide*. He sought to synthesise Buddhism with Western thought and modern science. He proclaimed that Buddhism is atheistic, and that the Buddha is leader and master only because he leads towards the enlightenment inherent in our own nature. Such an interpretation could easily come to terms with the rationalistic philosophy of the modern Confucians and even with Communism.

Under Communism whatever strength remains in Chinese Buddhism resides in the laymen. The Communist system had little use for people who made practically no economic contribution to the nation's life. Consequently those monks who felt that they could not revert to the lay status in the community tended to migrate to Taiwan, Malaya and other Eastern countries where they could continue their monastic life and spread the teachings of Buddhism among the Chinese dispersion.

Taoism in the twentieth century

There has been no significant revival of Taoism in the twentieth century, yet, as Professor T'ang Chun-i writes, 'The religion that is most deeply rooted in the lower class Chinese remains Taoism.'[13] Before the great advances in education, industrialisation and science, Taoism had little to offer. Its priests were more and more regarded as the agents for the perpetuation of gross superstitions, and the charlatan purveyors of earthly blessings which could be far better provided by modern medicine and hygiene and by scientific methods of raising the standard of living.

Several religious societies owed their inception to Taoism. These societies are often secret and are semi-religious, semi-political in nature. Several of these societies have lived on in secret, breaking out in sporadic revivals from time to time and causing considerable anxiety to government officials. Such societies are The Way of Pervading Unity; the Big Swords; the Little Swords; the Heavenly Gate; the Yellow Sect; the Eight Trigrams; the Society of Filial Sons; the White Robe Society, etc., and it is even reported that the Communist government has had considerable trouble in suppressing some of them. New societies which gained a considerable following during the twentieth century were more religious in character: the Society of World Religions; the *Tao Yüan* and the *T'ung Shan Hui*. These societies have drawn their membership largely from the peasants, but in the cities groups of more educated people have often banded together to study the Taoist classics, to practise mild forms of abstinence and to engage in good works.

It seems that Taoism as a religion, however much it may flourish among the Chinese outside China, has little hope of regaining renewed vitality under Communism. As a philosophy, the great writings of Chuang-tzŭ and Lao-tzŭ will remain a perennial source of inspiration. They will help to keep alive a sense of wonder before the illimitable mystery of the universe, recalling men to a reverent acknowledgment of that eternal principle from which all creation derives its origin and life.

Conclusion

China, like the rest of the civilised world, has been caught up in the process of secularisation in which all the religious interpretations of man and the universe have been seriously undermined. It might seem, as indeed many prominent Chinese have argued, that religion has no place or function in modern China. The traditional religious sytems of

China have put up little overt opposition to the materialism and atheism of militant Communism. They possess nothing analogous to the Christian Church, especially in its Roman Catholic form, with its highly centralised authority, its well-trained priesthood, its Holy Bible whose teachings are definitive for faith, its creeds and dogmas, its regular weekly services for the faithful. They have practically no missionary zeal, nor any well developed system of education and discipline for the instruction of the faithful in the rudiments of their faiths.

To many Chinese it is just these seeming weaknesses which are the strength of religion in China. True religion, they affirm, needs none of these things. It diffuses itself and permeates deep into the life of society and the individual, influencing the lives of men and women of every social stratum and meeting their spiritual needs at every level. 'The fragrance of holiness travels even against the wind.' Throughout Chinese history it is what is called 'diffused' religion rather than 'organised' religion that has been strong, deriving and renewing its inspiration from many sources, not concerned so much as to whether some religious teaching should be labelled Confucian, Buddhist or Taoist, but concerned as to whether or not it helps to satisfy the desire for the good life and for a meaningful interpretation of existence.

It would be wrong to conclude that because of the Communist occupation of the mainland of China the Chinese people are irreligious, materialistic by nature or generally intolerant towards religions. It is hard to believe that a whole body of ancient religious teaching which has dominated Chinese thought for twenty centuries can be completely obliterated. It is true that, in general, religion in China has emphasised the ethical and social and tended to be humanistic and this-worldly. But most Chinese cling to the belief that the nature of man is in essence one with the true nature of the entire universe: the *Tao* of Taoism, the *Chên Ju* or 'Thusness' of Buddhism, and the *Li* (Reason, law, principle) of Confucianism. To fulfil and to seek to perfect that human nature is to serve heaven. This the 'perfect sages' of Confucianism, the 'immortals' of Taoism and the 'bodhisattvas' of Buddhism have done, and because of their superhuman achievements they are honoured, worshipped and glorified.

NOTES

INTRODUCTION

1. Shih Ching-ch'êng, 'Art: Notes on a phrase in the *Tso Chuan*', *Chinese Culture*, vol. 2, no. 3, Dec. 1957.
2. A. F. Wright, *Buddhism in Chinese History*, Stamford, 1959, p. 81.
3. *Chinese Culture*, vol. 3, no. 1, Oct. 1960, p. 17.
4. C. K. Yang, *Religion in Chinese Society*, California, 1960, p. 20.
5. *Ibid.*, Chapter IV.

CHAPTER I: CHINESE RELIGION IN THE SHANG DYNASTY

1. Chêng Tê-k'un, *Archaeology in China*, vol. 1, Cambridge, 1959, p. 69.
2. In recent years Chinese, Japanese and Western scholars have made intensive studies of these 'oracle bone inscriptions'. These were, in the main, the scapula bones of sheep and oxen, which were extensively used in divination, and on which the earliest known specimens of Chinese writing are found. A good account of the discovery and interpretation of these oracle bones is to be found in H. G. Creel, *Studies in Early Chinese Culture*, London, 1938.
3. For accounts in English of the excavations of the Shang dynasty capital city see: H. G. Creel, *The Birth of China*, London, 1936; *Studies in Early Chinese Culture*, London, 1938; Li Chi, *The Beginnings of Chinese Civilisation*, Seattle, 1957; Chêng Tê-k'un, Cf., *Archaeology in China*, vol. 2, Cambridge, 1959.
4. Jao Tsung-i, article in Chinese in the *Ta Lu Tsa Chih*, Taiwan, Feb. 1954, on prehistoric remains in south China and the Yin Hsü culture. Also Creel, *Studies*, p. 168. 'According to the opinion of scholars, many of the fundamental elements of Chinese culture of the Bronze Age were imported into China from outside . . . the potter's wheel, the horse-drawn chariot, and the casting of bronze.'
5. Li Chi, *The Beginnings of Chinese Civilisation*, Seattle, 1957, p. 20.
6. *Ibid.*, p. 25.
7. *Cf. Shu Ching*, Section Chun Shih 8–9, *Sacred Books of the East*, vol. 3, pp. 206–7.
8. Prêta. Sanscrit term, lit.–'the departed'. It was popularly believed in ancient China that some souls did not enter at once on death into the spirit world, but wandered for a while on earth, congregating at cross-roads or outside the homes of relatives, seeking sustenance. Their maleficent influence was greatly feared.
9. *Cf.* Hou Wai-lu, *Chung Kuo Ssû-hsiang T'ung-shih*, vol. 1, Peking, 1957, p. 63.
10. *Ibid.*, p. 61.
11. Fu Ssû-nien, *Hsing-ming Ku-hsün Pien chang*, vol. 2, Shanghai, 1947, pp. 4 ff.

12. Lo Chen-ju, *Yin-hsü Shu-chi Chien pien*, 1913, chuan 4, p. 8b; *Hsü P'ien*, 1933, chuan 1, p. 10b.
13. Kuo Mo-jo, *Nu-li chih Shih-tai*, 1952, pp. 68–9, 73–4.
14. 'Le dieu du sol est la personnification des energies qui résident dans le sol. Chaque parcelle de sol a son dieu qui lui appartient en propre; mais la division du sol, étant déterminée par les groupements humains qui l'occupe, varie suivant l'extension de ces groupements; à ces répartitions diverses du territoire correspond toute une hiérarchie de dieux du sol.' E. Chavannes, *Le T'ai Chan*, Paris, 1910, p. 437.
15. 'Dans la haute antiquité, l'arbre est chose essentielle sur l'autel du dieu du sol; bien plus, rien ne le distingue du dieu du sol lui-même; il est le dieu du sol. N'est-ce pas en effet dans l'endroit ou s'élève un arbre de belle venue que sont concentrées toutes les vertus créatrices et nourricières du sol? Cet arbre ne jaillit-il pas du sein de la terre comme la vivante expression de sa fécondité?' *Ibid.*, p. 471.
16. *Mo-tzû*, Chinese text, Sun I-Jang's ed. in the *Wan Yu Wen Ku*, vol. 2, p. 151.
17. Quaritch Wales, *The Mountain of God*, London, 1936, p. 47.
18. H. G. Creel, *Studies*, p. 237.
19. Andersson, *Children of the Yellow Earth*, London, 1934, ch. 5.
20. C. Hentze, *Tod, Auferstehung, Weltordnung: Das Mystiche Bild in Altesten China*, Zurich, 1955.
21. C. A. S. Williams, *Outlines of Chinese Symbolism*, Peking, 1931, p. 62; Laufer, *Jade*, Passadena, new ed. 1946, p. 299.
22. *Cf.* Marcel Granet, *Chinese Civilisation*, London, 1930, pp. 155 ff.
23. James Legge, *The Chinese Classics*, vol. 3, pt. 1, Hongkong, 1865, pp. 24–5.

CHAPTER 2: RELIGIOUS DEVELOPMENTS FROM THE ESTABLISHMENT OF THE CHOU DYNASTY TO THE BIRTH OF CONFUCIUS

1. See Chêng Tê-k'un, *Archaeology in China: Chou China*, Cambridge, 1964, p. 282.
2. A standard English translation of the *Shu Ching* is J. Legge, *The Chinese Classics*, vol. 3, Oxford, 1865. For a discussion of the authenticity of the *Shu Ching*, *cf.* H. G. Creel, in the *Yen ching Journal of Chinese Studies*, no. 18, Dec. 1937; B. Karlgren, *Book of Documents*; H. G. Creel, *Studies in Early Chinese Culture*, 1937, pp. 55 ff.
3. For translations of the *Shih Ching*, see J. Legge, *The Chinese Classics*, vol. 4; B. Karlgren, *The Book of Odes*, Stockholm, 1950; A. Waley, *The Book of Songs*, London, 1937. It is generally accepted by Chinese and Western scholars that the *Shih Ching* was used by Confucius and his followers for moral instruction, though some doubt has been expressed as to whether Confucius had a hand in forming the collection. *Cf.* A. Waley, *The Book of Songs*, p. 18.
4. M. Granet, *Chinese Civilisation.* English trans., London, 1930, p. 2.
5. The evidence for this rebellion is to be found in several of the authentic chapters of the *Shu Ching;* The Tai Kao, To Shih, To Fang and Lo Kao.

See Couvreur, *Chou King*, Hsien Hsien, 1927, pp. 220 ff.

6. For the duke of Chou, see A. Waley, *The Analects of Confucius*, London, 1938, p. 47: 'To Confucius, however, it was neither Wên nor Wu, but Wu's brother Tan, duke of Chou, who was the real hero of the Chou conquest.' Shigeki Kaizuka, *Confucius*, London, 1956, p. 24: 'The general belief, firmly held by the people of the Chou dynasty, and especially by those of Lu, the state of Confucius, was that the duke of Chou created the system of ritual and music of the dynasty, and that he founded the whole of the Chou civilisation–with its individual administrative organisation, its social system, its code of morality and its arts.'
7. For a discussion of the significance of *T'ien*, see A. Waley, *The Analects of Confucius*, pp. 41 ff.
8. In this connection, *cf. Chinese Culture*, vol. 3, no. 1, Oct. 1960, a manifesto on the reappraisal of Chinese culture. 'China's ancient classics emit a profound sense of reverence towards God and true faith in heaven . . . Jesuit missionaries, who visited China three hundred years ago, noticed this in the solemn rites paying tribute to heaven and earth held to be of ultimate significance by later Chinese scholars. Rituals such as these were reverently observed by all Chinese rulers throughout various dynasties, even to the early years of the new republic.'
9. See chapter 1, pp. 6 ff.
10. J. Legge, *The Chinese Classics*, vol. 5, p. 109.
11. *Ibid.*, pp. 291–2.
12. *Ibid.*, pp. 47–8.
13. *Ibid.*, p. 607.
14. *Ibid.*, p. 607.

CHAPTER 3: THE SIGNIFICANCE OF CONFUCIUS FOR RELIGION

1. The origin and significance of the *Ju* have been much debated, notably by Hu Shih in his *Lun Hsüeh Chin Chu*, Shanghai 1935, pp. 3–81; by Fung Yu Lan in *Chung-kuo Chê-hsüeh Shih Pu*, Shanghai 1934, pp. 28, 59; by Kuo Mo-jo in *Ch'ing T'ung Shih Tai*, Peking N.D., pp. 134–6; and by H. G. Creel in *Confucius, the Man and the Myth*, London, 1951, pp. 313–14.
2. *Analects* 7:1. In this and subsequent quotations I have often availed myself of the excellent translation made by A. Waley, *The Analects of Confucius*, London, 1938.
3. *Cf.* Fung Yu-lan, *A Short History of Chinese Philosophy*, p. 207; and W. T. Chan, *Religious Trends in Modern China*, p. 5.
4. See, for example, K. L. Reichelt, *Religion in Chinese Garment*, London, 1951, pp. 45 ff., for a description of the rituals performed at the Altar of Heaven in Peking, and a translation of a prayer made to the Supreme Deity by the emperor on the Altar of Heaven at the winter solstice, 22 Dec. 1539.
5. Ssu-ma Ch'ien, *Shih Chi*, chapter 47.
6. Pronouncements concerning Confucius are to be found in the *Tso Chuan*; *Kung-yang Chuan*; *Ku-liang Chuan;* the *Kuo Yü*; *Mo-tzu*; *Mêng-tzu*; *Hsün-tzu*; the *Li Chi*; the *Ta Tai Li Chi*;

the *Lü Shih Ch'un Ch'iu*; the *Huai Nan Tzu*; and also the later *Han Shih Wai Chuan*; *Shang Shu Ta Chuan* and the *Shuo Yüan*. Sayings hostile to Confucius are found in several of the Taoist writings, where again he is often referred to as making typical Taoist pronouncements. Much of the Confucian lore not found in the *Analects* is gathered together in the *K'ung Tzu Chia Yü*.

7. Several translations of the *Analects* have been made into English. Those by J. Legge (1861), Ku Hung-ming (1898) and W. Soothill (1910) may be mentioned. The more recent scholarly translation by A. Waley (1938) can be heartily recommended, not only because of the author's felicity as a translator, but because of the invaluable introduction and notes which greatly assist the English reader.
8. See W. T. Chan, *Religious Trends in Modern China*, pp. 12 ff. For accounts of Confucius' life and times see J. Legge, *The Life and Teaching of Confucius*, London, 1875; R. Wilhelm, *Confucius and Confucianism*, tr. G. H. and A. P. Danton, London, 1931; Shigeki Kaizuka, *Confucius*, London, 1956; H. G. Creel, *Confucius, the Man and the Myth*, London, 1951.
9. *Analects* 7: 20.
10. *Analects* 5: 12.
11. There is considerable evidence that Confucius did for a time occupy the position of prime minister of the state of Lu. It was a small and, from a political point of view, comparatively insignificant state. Confucius' thirteen years of exile from Lu and his wanderings from court to court suggest that his talents were never adequately recognised during his lifetime, except by a few intimate disciples.
12. *Cf.* Fu Ssu-nien, *Hsin Ming Ku Hsün Pien Chêng*, vol. 2, p. 38a. Also H. G. Creel, *Confucius, the Man and the Myth*, pp. 129–30.
13. *Cf.* Essay by Ch'ên Ta-chin in *K'ung Hsüeh Lun Chi*, Taiwan, 1957, pp. 1–33.
14. *Tao Tê Ching*, ch. 5.
15. See Dobson, *Mencius*, Oxford, 1963, p. 194, note 37: 'The word *li* which I have translated variously as "rites, propriety, courtesy, protocol, or good manners" as occasion demands, strictly denotes a rite, a form of procedure proper to the solemn ceremonies of sacrifice, of the burial of the dead, of the attainment of puberty, and of marriage. But it also denotes the rules that decorum and seemliness suggest in social intercourse, or what we should call etiquette . . . *Li* is also concerned with the formal aspects of ceremonial at court and in diplomatic interchange, which we in recent years have come to call protocol.'
16. *Cf.* A. Waley, *The Analects*, London, 1938, pp. 54 ff.

CHAPTER 4: CONFUCIAN INTERPRETERS: THE CHUNG YUNG; MENCIUS; HSŬN-TSŬ

1. In this book our concern is with the growth and development of distinctively religious ideas and expressions. In the nature of the case it has been

necessary to be selective. It is not possible to deal with all the various schools of thought which proliferated in China in the closing centuries of the Chou dynasty, most of which would be classified as philosophy rather than religion. Introductions to the development of Chinese philosophical thought in this period are to be found in E. R. Hughes, *Chinese Philosophy in Classical Times* London, 1942; Fung Yu-lan, *History of Chinese Philosophy*, vol. 1, Peking, 1937; and W. T. Chan, *A Source Book of Chinese Philosophy*, London, 1963.

2. W. T. Chan, *Source Book of Chinese Philosophy*, p. 95.
3. For a translation of the *Chung Yung* and a discussion of its significance, see E. R. Hughes, *The Great Learning and the Mean in Action*, London, 1942.
4. W. T. Chan, *Source Book of Chinese Philosophy*, p. 95.
5. A definitive translation of Mencius is by J. Legge in *The Chinese Classics*, vol. 1, Oxford, 1893 and reprinted by Hongkong Univ. Press in 1960. A recent translation by W. A. C. H. Dobson, *Mencius*, Oxford, 1963, has rearranged the order of the original paragraphs, and annotated them for the use of the general reader.
6. Ssŭ-ma Ch'ien, *Shih Chi*, chapter 74.
7. *Chuang-tzu*, chapter 33.
8. W. T. Chan, *Source Book of Chinese Philosophy*, p. 50.
9. *Ibid.*, p. 82.
10. A translation of Hsün-tzu into English is H. H. Dubs, *The Works of Hsün-tzŭ*, London, 1928.
11. I am indebted to H. H. Dubs' translation for several of the quotations in this section.

CHAPTER 5: THE RELIGION OF MO-TZŬ

1. There is some doubt as to the birthplace of Mo-tzŭ and no conclusive evidence as to the dates of his birth and death. The *Lü-shih-ch'un-ch'iu* states that he was born in Lu, but the *Wên-hsüan*, *Hsün-tzŭ* and the *Ho-kung, Shên Hsien Chuan* say that he was born in Sung. The commentator, Pi-yüan, says that he was born in Ch'u about or soon after the death of Confucius. W. T. Chan in his *Source Book in Chinese Philosophy*, p. 212, says that 'probably he was born before Confucius died and died before Mencius was born'.
2. Hu-shih, *The Development of the Logical Method in Ancient China*, Shanghai, 1922, p. 57.
3. Y. P. Mei, *The Ethical and Political Works of Mo-tzŭ*, and *Mo-tzŭ: Rival of Confucius*, London, 1929.
4. Originally the *Works* of Mo-tzŭ comprised fifteen books in seventy-one chapters, but ten of these chapters were lost before the end of the twelfth century AD, and another eight were lost subsequently.
5. *Huai-nan-tzŭ*, chapter 20.
6. *Chung-yung*, chapter 1. 1.
7. *Mo-tzŭ*, 2, 'Anti-Confucianism'. See Y. P. Mei, *The Works of Mo-tzŭ*, p. 212, and '*Kêng-chu*', *Ibid.*, 215. Y. P. Mei misses the significance of this juxtaposition of *Tao* and *Chiao* in his translation.
8. Y. P. Mei, *Mo-tzŭ, Rival of Confucius*, p. 160.
9. In the quotations from the works of

Mo-tzu I have made extensive use of Y. P. Mei's excellent translation.

10. Y. P. Mei, *Mo-tzŭ, Rival of Confucius*, p. 160.
11. *Ibid.*, p. 160.
12. *Mencius*, Book 3b, 9:9.
13. *Han-fei-tzu*, chapter 1.
14. Y. P. Mei, *Mo-tzŭ, Rival of Confucius*, p. 173.
15. Y. P. Mei, *Mo-tzŭ, Rival of Confucius*, p. 173.
16. See H. A. Giles, *Chuang-tzŭ*, 2nd ed., London, 1961, p. 315.
17. W. T. Chan, *Source Book in Chinese Philosophy*, p. 123.
18. Y. P. Mei, *Mo-tzŭ, Rival of Confucius*, p. 82.

CHAPTER 6: THE CONTRIBUTION OF EARLY TAOISTS TO RELIGION

1. According to Holmes Welch, *The Parting of the Way*, Boston, 1957, pp. 4–5, the *Tao Tê Ching* has been translated into English thirty-six times. He claims that 'no translation can be satisfactory in itself because no translation can be as ambiguous as the Chinese original'.
   A most useful translation by Arthur Waley, *The Way and its Power*, London, 1934, contains an excellent introduction and helpful notes.
   There is need for a new and up-to-date translation of the *Book of Chuang-tzu*. The translation by H. A. Giles, *Chuang-tzŭ: Taoist Philosopher and Chinese Mystic*, London, 1889, was reprinted in 1961. The translation by J. Legge, *Texts of Taoism*, vol. 1, London, 1891, is still of great value to the student.
2. For a discussion of the provenance and date of the *Tao Tê Ching* see A. Waley, *The Way and its Power*, pp. 86 ff.; W. T. Chan, *A Source Book in Chinese Philosophy*, London, 1963, pp. 136 ff.; C. Burton Day, *The Philosophers of China*, London, 1962, pp. 16–18; Fung Yu-lan, *History of Chinese Philosophy*, vol. 1, Princeton, 1951, p. 172.
3. See W. T. Chan, *A Source Book in Chinese Philosophy*, p. 179, note.
4. See H. A. Giles, *Chuang-tzŭ*, pp. 11–12.
5. The *Lü-shih-ch'un-ch'iu* (third cent. BC?) was undoubtedly greatly influenced by Taoist thought. The quotation is taken from the chapter on 'The Importance of Living'.
6. W. T. Chan, *A Source Book in Chinese Philosophy*, p. 181.
7. H. A. Giles, *Chuang-tzŭ: Taoist Philosopher and Chinese Mystic*, p. 36.

CHAPTER 7: FURTHER RELIGIOUS DEVELOPMENTS IN PRE-HAN CHINA

1. See Y. P. Mei, *The Ethical and Political Works of Mo-tzŭ*, London, 1929, p. 151, note 1; *cf.* also p. 132, note 1, where 'Chung Kuo' is contrasted with the neighbouring barbarian states and the semi-barbarian states of Ch'u and Yüeh.
2. *Ibid.*, p. 133, where Mo-tzŭ refers to tribes to the east of Yüeh and to the south of Ch'u which practised cannibalism, and to tribes to the west of Ch'in which cremated their dead, both customs abhorrent to the Chinese.
3. *Mencius*, 3a, 4: 14.

4. *Cf.* Mircea Eliade, *Shamanism*, London, 1964, pp. 147 ff.
5. De Groot, *The Religious System of China*, vol. 6, Leiden, 1892 ff., pp. 1205 ff.
6. An excellent edition of the *Ch'u Tz'ŭ* in Chinese was published in Peking in 1953. A useful translation of the *Li Sao* by Lim Boon Keng with Chinese text, introduction and notes was published in Shanghai in 1929. A. Waley translated some of the poems of the *Ch'u Tz'ŭ* in his *Chinese Poems*, London, 1949, and in *The Nine Songs*, London, 1955. D. Hawkes, *The Ch'u Tz'ŭ*, Oxford, 1959, is our best guide in English to these poems.
7. See J. Legge's translation in *Sacred Books of the East*, vols. 27 and 28, Oxford, 1885. Also the *I Li* translated by J. Steele, 2 vols., London, 1917, with its detailed account of the rites of the Chou dynasty. This book was probably compiled earlier than the *Li Chi*.
8. J. Legge's translation of the *I Ching*, *Sacred Books of the East*, vol. 16, Oxford, 1899, has recently been edited with an introduction and study guide by Ch'u Chai and Winberg Chai, New York, 1964. Of value to the student is R. Wilhelm, *The I Ching*, 2 vols., translated into English by Cary F. Baynes, London, 1951; and Hellmut Wilhelm, *Eight Lectures on the I Ching*, London, 1960.
9. R. Wilhelm, *A short History of Chinese Civilisation*, London, 1929, p. 171.
10. D. Hawkes, *The Ch'u Tz'ŭ*, Oxford, 1959.
11. *Ibid.*, p. 8.
12. A. Waley, *The Nine Songs*, London, 1955, p. 15.
13. An excellent translation of this poem is found in A. Waley's *Chinese Poems*, under the title, 'The Great Summons'.
14. Wu Yang was one of ten shamans believed to live on a holy mountain in the west.
15. D. Hawkes, *The Ch'u Tz'ŭ*, p. 103.
16. *Li Chi*, Book 7: 1; 7, and Book 19:3.
17. Y. P. Mei, *The Ethical and Political Works of Mo-tzu*, pp. 200–1
18. D. Hawkes, *The Ch'u Tz'ŭ*, p. 45.
19. See Lim Boon Keng, *The Li Sao*, Shanghai, 1929.
20. A. Waley, *The Nine Songs*, p. 10.
21. W. T. Chan, *A Source Book in Chinese Philosophy*, Princeton, 1963, pp. 279 ff.
22. *The Kuo Yü*, 'Chin Yü', 4:9.
23. See *The Ch'un Ch'iu, Tso Chuan* under the years 672–537 BC.
24. Fung Yu-lan, *A History of Chinese Philosophy*, vol. 1, Peking, 1937, p. 383.
25. See the *Chung Yung*, 31: 4.
26. *I Ching*, third appendix, Section 1: 34.

CHAPTER 8: RELIGIOUS ECLECTICISM IN THE HAN DYNASTY

1. See above, pp. 85–86.
2. W. T. Chan, *A Source Book in Chinese Philosophy*, Princeton, 1963, p. 271.
3. The *Ch'un Ch'iu Fan Lu* (tr. *Luxuriant Dew of the Spring and Autumn Annals*), consists of eighty-two short essays on philosophical and political subjects. There is no complete translation in English. See Yao Shan-yu, 'The Cosmological and Anthropological Philosophy of Tung Chung-shu' in the *Journal of the North China Branch of the Royal Asiatic Society*, vol. 73, Shanghai, 1948. Also Otto Franke,

Studien zur Geschichte des konfuzianischen Dogmas und der chinesischen Staatsreligion: das problem des Tsch'un-Ts'iu und Tung Tschung-schu's Fan Lu, Hamburg, 1920.

4. The *Po Hu T'ung*, in forty-four chapters, is based on the discussion of the Classics held by scholars in AD 79. See *Po Hu T'ung: the Comprehensive Discussions in the White Tiger Hall*, 2 vols., Leiden, 1949 and 1952.
5. Wang Ch'ung, *Lun Heng* in eighty-five chapters, translated into English by Alfred Forke, 2 vols., London, 1907.

CHAPTER 9: THE RISE AND DEVELOPMENT OF RELIGIOUS TAOISM

1. Holmes Welch, *The Parting of the Way*, Boston, 1957, p. 88.
2. See L. Wieger, *Le Taoisme*, Hsien-hsien, 1911, for a full discussion of the Taoist Canon.
3. H. Maspero, *Mélanges Posthumes sur les religions et l'histoire de la Chine*, vol. 2, Paris, 1950, p. 76.
4. *Ibid.*, p. 77.
5. Ships were sent out on these maritime expeditions as early as the duke Wei of Ch'i (357–320 BC). See Holmes Welch, *The Parting of the Way*, p. 97.
6. L. Wieger, *Textes Historiques*, Hsien-hsien, 1929, vol. 1, pp. 212 ff.
7. L. Wieger, *Textes Historiques*, pp. 443 ff.; Holmes Welch, *The Parting of the Way*, pp. 99 ff.
8. Ssŭ-ma Ch'ien, *Shih Chi*, tr. E. Chavannes, vol. 3, pp. 463–4.
9. Holmes Welch, *The Parting of the Way*, p. 100.
10. L. Wieger, *Textes Historiques*, pp. 328 ff. Holmes Welch, *The Parting of the Way*, p. 104.
11. See H. Maspero, *Mélanges Posthumes*, vol. 2, pp. 85–147, for a more de, tailed account of this school.
12. The *Pao P'u Tzŭ* was a fundamental treatise on alchemistic Taoism, dietetics and magic. It was attributed to Ho Kung, *c.* AD 326; *cf.* L. Wieger, *China Throughout the Ages*, Hsien-hsien, 1928, p. 483.
13. H. Maspero, *Mélanges, Posthumes*, vol. 2, p. 87.
14. Quoted by H. Maspero, *Melanges Posthumes*, vol. 2, p. 100.
15. Holmes Welch, *The Parting of the Way*, pp. 133 ff.
16. *Ibid.*, p. 117.
17. H. Maspero, *Mélanges Posthumes*, vol. 2, p. 155.
18. W. T. Chan, *A Source Book in Chinese Philosophy*, Princeton, 1963, p. 333.
19. J. Dyer Ball, *Things Chinese*, 5th ed., Shanghai, 1925, p. 635.
20. Holmes Welch, *The Parting of the Way*, p. 152.
21. Holmes Welch, *The Parting of the Way*, p. 144. Maspero, *Mélanges Posthumes*, vol. 2, pp. 179 ff.
22. W. T. Chan, *Religious Trends in Modern China*, New York, 1953, p. 153.

CHAPTER 10 : BUDDHISM IN CHINA

1. E. Zürcher, *The Buddhist Conquest of China*, Leiden, 1959, pp. 19–22.
2. H. Maspero, 'Le songe et l'ambassade de l'empereur Ming, étude critique

des sources', *BEFEO* X, 1910, pp. 95–130.

3. T'ang Yung-t'ung, *Han Wei liang-Chin Nan-pei-ch'ao fo-chia Shih*, 2 vols., Shanghai, 1938, chapter 2.
4. E. Zürcher, *The Buddhist Conquest of China*, pp. 26 ff.
5. *Ibid.*, pp. 36 ff.
6. *Ibid.*, p. 32.
7. *Hou Han Shu*, 72, 4b; 103, 11a (see *Ssu-pu Pei-yao* edition).
8. *Hou Han Chi*, 10, 5a (*Ssu-pu ts'ung-k'an* edition).
9. E. Zürcher, *The Buddhist Conquest of China*, p. 28.
10. *Ibid.*, p. 61.
11. Demieville, 'La Pénétration du Buddhisme dans la Tradition Philosophique Chinoise, *Cahiers d'histoire mondiale*, III, 1956, pp. 19–38.
12. E. Zürcher, *The Buddhist Conquest of China*, p. 61.
13. *Ibid.*, p. 63.
14. For an English appraisement and abbreviated translation see W. E. Soothill, *The Lotus of the Wonderful Law*, Oxford, 1930.
15. The five sūtras are: Prajnāpāramitā; Sūryamgamasamādhi; Vimalakīrti-nirdesa; Saddharmapundarīka; Sukhāvatīvyūha.
16. E. Zürcher, *The Buddhist Conquest of China*, pp. 181–3
17. E. R. and K. Hughes, *Religion in China*, London, 1950, p. 69.
18. See H. A. Giles, *The Travels of Fa Hsien*, Cambridge, 1923.
19. E. Zürcher, *The Buddhist Conquest of China*, pp. 184 ff.
20. *Ibid.*, p. 190.
21. K. S. Chen, *Buddhism in China: a historical survey*, Princeton, 1964, pp. 142–4.
22. *Ibid.*, p. 144.
23. K. W. Morgan (ed.), *The Path of the Buddha*, New York, 1956, chapter by Zenryu Tsukamoto, p. 198.
24. *Ibid.*
25. K. L. Reichelt, *Truth and Tradition in Chinese Buddhism*, Shanghai, 1927, p. 307.
26. W. T. Chan, 'Pure Land Schools', in Ferm (ed.), *Encyclopedia of Religion*, p. 106.
27. Translations of the *Ch'i Hsin Lun* were made into English by D. T. Suzuki in 1900 and by T. Richard in 1907 and 1910, the latter being republished in 1961, edited by A. H. Walton. Both translators attribute the work to Ashvagosha, an attribution which is now unacceptable. Of the translations that by Suzuki is much to be preferred. A full critical discussion of the *Ch'i Hsin Lun* is to be found, in Chinese, in the *Ta Ch'êng Ch'i Hsin Lun Chên Wei Pien*, Peking, 1956.
28. K. L. Reichelt, *Truth and Tradition in Chinese Buddhism*, p. 226.
29. C. Burton Day, *The Philosophers of China*, London, 1962, p. 115.
30. For a detailed account of the life and work of Hui-Yüan see E. Zürcher, *The Buddhist Conquest of China*, pp. 204–53.
31. *Ibid.*, p. 208.
32. K. L. Reichelt, *Truth and Tradition in Chinese Buddhism*, p. 132.
33. *Ch'i Hsin Lun*, my translation.
34. W. T. Chan, *A Source Book in Chinese Philosophy*, London, 1963, p. 357.
35. C. Humphreys, *Zen Buddhism*, London, 1949, p. 26.
36. Hu Shih, 'Ch'an (Zen) Buddhism in China: its History and Method', *Philosophy East and West*, 3, 1953, p. 12.
37. C. Humphreys, *Zen Buddhism*, p. 1.
38. See W. T. Chan, *A Source Book in Chinese Philosophy*, p. 425, note. Hu Shih rejects the traditional date and

believes that Bodhidharma came to China between 470 and 475.

39. C. Burton Day, *The Philosophers of China*, p. 130.

40. W. T. Chan, *A Source Book in Chinese Philosophy*, p. 428.

41. Alan Watts, *The Spirit of Zen*, London, 1936, pp. 11–12.

42. C. Humphreys, *Zen Buddhism*, p. 81.

43. *Cf.* W. E. Soothill, *The Lotus of the Wonderful Law*, Oxford, 1930.

44. K. S. Chen, *Buddhism in China*, p. 310.

45. K. W. Morgan, *The Path of the Buddha*, p. 202.

46. K. L. Reichelt, *Truth and Tradition in Chinese Buddhism*, p. 53.

47. W. E. Soothill, *The Lotus of the Wonderful Law*, p. 13.

48. W. T. Chan, *A Source Book in Chinese Philosophy*, p. 406.

49. K. W. Morgan (ed.), *The Path of the Buddha*, p. 209.

50. K. L. Reichelt, *Truth and Tradition in Chinese Buddhism*, p. 89 ff.

51. The Taisho edition of the Chinese Tripitaka was published in Tokyo, 1922–33.

52. K. L. Reichelt, *Truth and Tradition in Chinese Buddhism*, p. 203.

53. *Ibid.*, p. 213.

54. K. W. Morgan, *The Path of the Buddha*, p. 222.

55. *Ibid.*, pp. 222–3.

CHAPTER II: THE STATE CULT OF CONFUCIANISM

1. E. Gibbon, *Decline and Fall of the Roman Empire* (abridged ed.), London, 1966, pp. 55–8.

2. See D. H. Smith, 'Divine Kingship in Ancient China', *Numen*, vol. 4, Fas. 3, 1957, p. 200.

3. Bredon and Mitrophanow, *The Moon Year*, Shanghai, 1927, p. 68.

4. W. E. Soothill, *The Three Religions of China*, Oxford, 1923, p. 229.

5. J. Bredon, *Peking*, Shanghai, 1931, p. 156.

6. *Ibid.*, p. 157.

7. Soothill, *The Three Religions of China*, p. 232.

8. J. Legge, *The Religions of China*, London, 1880, pp. 43 ff.

9. Bredon and Mitrophanow, *The Moon Year*, p. 58.

10. C. K. Yang, *Religion in Chinese Society*, California, 1961, p. 147.

11. *Li Chi*, chapter 21. See Fung Yu-lan, *Hist. of Chinese Philosophy*, tr. Derk Bodde, Peking, 1937, vol. 1, p. 350.

12. C. K. Yang, *Religion in Chinese Society*, p. 179.

13. J. K. Shryock, *Origin and Development of the State Cult of Confucianism*, New York, 1932, p. 75.

14. *Ibid.*, p. 97.

15. *Ibid.*, pp. 120–1.

16. *Ibid.*, pp. 134–5.

17. K. L. Reichelt, *Religion in Chinese Garment*, London. 1951, p. 55.

18. J. K. Shryock, *Origin and Development of the State Cult of Confucianism*, p. 139.

19. Matteo Ricci, *Commentari*, I, pp. 91 ff. See C. Cary-Elwes, *China and the Cross*, London, 1957, pp. 99 and 147.

20. *Ibid.*, p. 152.

21. J. K. Shryock, *Origin and Development of the State Cult of Confucianism*, p. 224.

22. For a full account of the twentieth-century debate on the place and position of Confucianism, see W. T. Chan, *Religious Trends in Modern China*, New York, 1953, chapter 1.

NOTES

CHAPTER 12: ISLAM, CHRISTIANITY AND OTHER WESTERN FAITHS IN CHINA

1. *Hou Han Shu*, chapter 118; *cf.* C. P. Fitzgerald, *China*, London, 1935, revised edition, 1950, ch. 8.
2. L. Wieger, *A History of the Religious Beliefs and Philosophical Opinions in China*, tr. E. C. Werner, Hsien-Hsien, 1927, p. 533; E. H. Parker, *China and Religion*, London, 1905, p. 110.
3. C. P. Fitzgerald, *China*, p. 325.
4. Werner Eichhorn, chapter 10 on Taoism in *Concise Encyclopedia of Living Faiths*, ed. R. C. Zaehner, London, 1959, pp. 387, 394–6.
5. Tung Hêng, 'Mo-na Chiao ju Chung-kuo K'ao', in *Kuo Hsüeh Chi K'an*, vol. 1. No. 2.
6. P. Pelliot, 'Two new Manichaean manuscripts from Tun-huang', *J.R.A.S.*, 1925, p. 113.
7. *Travels of Marco Polo*, tr. R. E. Lathom, London, 1958, pp. 207–8.
8. Wu Wen-liang, *Ch'üan-chou Tsung-chiao Shih-k'o*, Peking, 1957, pp. 44–7.
9. H. Havret, 'La stèle chrétienne de Si-ngan-fou', *Variétés Sinologiques*, Nos. 7, 12 and 20, pts. 1, 2 and 3, Shanghai, 1895, 1897 and 1902; P. Y. Saeki, *The Nestorian Monument in China*, London, 1916; A. C. Moule, *Christians in China before the Year 1550*, London, 1930.
10. P. Pelliot, 'Chrétiens d'Asia Centrale et d'Extrême Orient', *Toung Pao*, Leiden, 1914, p. 628.
11. See chapter 10, p. 136.
12. C. Cary-Elwes, *China and the Cross*, London, 1957, p. 46.
13. H. Yule, *Cathay and the Way Thither*, new ed., by Cordier, 4 vols., London, 1913–16, vol. 3, pp. 89 ff.
14. C. Cary-Elwes, *China and the Cross*, p. 58.
15. *Ibid.*, p. 69.
16. Quoted from C. Cary-Elwes, *China and the Cross*, p. 122; Huc, *Christianity in China, Tartary and Thibet*, 3 vols., London, 1858, vol. 3, pp. 202–3.
17. C. Cary-Elwes, *China and the Cross*, p. 152.
18. *Ibid.*, p. 155.
19. *Ibid.*, p. 209.
20. K. S. Latourette, *Christianity in a Revolutionary Age*, vol. 5, London, 1963, pp. 407–8.
21. E. R. and K. Hughes, *Religion in China*, London, 1950, p. 98.
22. Pelliot, *Toung Pao*, no. 31 (1935), pp. 274–9, 314, no. 32 (1936), pp. 211–12. Duyvendak, *Toung Pao*, no. 34 (1939), p. 381.
23. See *China: Provincial Atlas and Geography*, Shanghai, 1934, p. 20; E. W. Geil, *Eighteen Capitals of China*, London, 1911, pp. 356–7.
24. C. P. Fitzgerald, *China*, revised ed., 1950, p. 306; R. Grousset, *Rise and Splendour of the Chinese Empire*, London, 1952, p. 173.
25. James Finn, *The Jews in China*, London, 1843, p. 57.
26. The account of Dr Martin's visit to K'ai Feng was read to the North China Branch of the Royal Asiatic Society on 29 March 1866 and was subsequently published in the *J.R.A.S.* Dr Martin later included the account in his *Hanlin Papers*, London, 1880.

CHAPTER XIII: THE RELIGIOUS SITUATION IN MODERN CHINA

1. W. T. Chan, *Religious Trends in Modern China*, New York, 1953, ch. 4.
2. H. Maspero, 'The Mythology of Modern China', *Asiatic Mythology*, J. Hackin, London, 1932 and 1963, p. 252.
3. *Ibid.*, p. 262.
4. For more detailed accounts see: J. J. M. de Groot, *The Religious System of China*, 6 vols., Leiden, 1892; H. Doré, *Recherches sur les Superstitions en Chine*, 15 vols., Shanghai, 1914–29; H. Maspero, 'The Mythology of Modern China', *Asiatic Mythology;* C. B. Day, *Chinese Peasant Cults*, Shanghai, 1940.
5. See *A Buddhist Student's Manual*, ed. C. Humphreys, London, 1956, p. 121.
6. K. L. Reichelt, *Religion in Chinese Garment*, London, 1951, p. 144.
7. H. Doré, *Chinese Superstitions*, Eng. tr., Shanghai, 1914, vol. 6, p. 205.
8. K. L. Reichelt, *Religion in Chinese Garment*, p. 149.
9. *New York Times*, June 1966, Section 11, p. 15.
10. O. Briere, *Fifty Years of Chinese Philosophy*, 1898–1950, London, 1956, p. 13.
11. *Ibid.*, p. 23.
12. *Ibid.*, p. 40.
13. *Relations among Religions To-day*, ed. M. Jung *et al.*, Leiden, 1963. p. 41.

SELECTED BIBLIOGRAPHY

GENERAL

W. T. Chan, *A Source Book in Chinese Philosophy*, London, 1963.

E. Chavannes, *Les Mémoires Historiques de Sê-Ma Ts'ien*, 5 vols., Paris, 1895–1905.

S. Couling, *Encyclopaedia Sinica*, Shanghai, 1917.

S. Couvreur, *Les Quatre Livres*, Hsien-hsien, 1930;
Cheu King, Hsien-hsien, 1926;
Chou King, Hsien-hsien, 1927;
(ed.) *Li Ki*, 2 vols., Paris, 1950;
Tch'ouen Ts'iou et Tso Tchuan, 3 vols., Paris, 1951.

H. Doré, *Recherches sur les Superstitions en Chine*, 15 vols., Shanghai, 1914–29.

A. Forke, *Geschichte der alten chinesischen Philosophie*, Berlin, 1927;
Geschichte der mittelalterlichen chinesischen Philosophie, Hamburg, 1934;
Geschichte der neueren chinesischen Philosophie, Hamburg, 1938.

Fung Yu-lan, *History of Chinese Philosophy*, tr. Derk Bodde, vol. 1, Peking, 1937; vol. 2, London, 1953.

H. A. Giles, *Chinese and English Dictionary*, 2nd. ed., Shanghai, 1912.

J. J. de Groot, *The Religious System of China*, 6 vols., Leiden, 1892.

J. Legge, *The Chinese Classics*, tr. into Engl. with Chinese text, 5 vols., Oxford, 1861–72;
The Texts of Confucianism, Engl. tr., in *Sacred Books of the East*, ed. Max Muller, nos. 3, 16, 27, 28, Oxford, 1879, 1888, 1899;
The Texts of Taoism, Engl. tr., *S. B. E.*, nos. 39, 40, Oxford, 1891.

R. H. Mathews, *Chinese-English Dictionary*, Cambridge, Mass., 1947.

J. Needham, *Science and Civilization in China*, vols. 1 and 2, Cambridge, 1954 and 1956.

E. T. C. Werner, *Dictionary of Chinese Mythology*, Shanghai, 1932.

L. Wieger, *History of Religious Beliefs and Philosophical Opinions in China*, Engl. tr. E. T. C. Werner, Hsien-hsien, 1927.

C. A. S. Williams, *Outlines of Chinese Symbolism*, Peking, 1931.

Works in Chinese

There are several good standard editions containing the works of all the great Classical writers. I have preferred to use the *Ssu Pu Pei Yao* and the *Wan Yu Wen K'u*, both published in Shanghai. The twenty-four Dynastic Histories are invaluable for source material. A modern edition, published in Shanghai, is not dated. For the *Buddhist Tripitaka in Chinese*, the Taisho edition, published in Tokyo, 1922–33, is a standard work. The *Tao Tsang* was published in Shanghai in 1924–6.

Modern Authors

Chang Chia *et al.*, *Chung-kuo Fo-chiao Shih Lun-chi*, 3 vols., Taiwan, 1956.
Ch'ên Ta-chi *et al.*, *K'ung-hsüeh Lun Chi*, 2 vols, Taiwan, 1957.
Ch'ien Mu, 'Po Hu-shih chih Shuo Ju', *Journal of Oriental Studies*, Hongkong, 1954.
Ch'u Tz'ŭ Chin Chu, Peking, 1953 (The Poems of Ch'u).
Fu Ssŭ–nien, *Hsing-ming Ku-hsün Pien-chêng*, 2 vols., Shanghai, 1947.
Fung Yu-lan, *Chung-kuo Chê-hsüeh Shih*, Shanghai, 1934.
Hou Wai-lu *et al.*, *Chung-kuo Ssŭ-hsiang T'ung Shih*, 3 vols., Peking, 1957.
Hu Shih, *Lun Hsüeh Chin-chi*, vol. 1, Shanghai, 1935;
Chung-kuo Chê-hsüeh Shih Ta-kang, Shanghai, 1919;
Hu Shih Wên-ts'un, 3 series, Shanghai, 1921, 1924, 1930.
Huang Chien-chung *et al.*, *Chung-kuo Chê-hsüeh Shih*, 3 vols., Taiwan, 1958.
Jao Tsung-i 1954 'Shih Ju', *Journal of Oriental Studies*, Hongkong, 1954.
Kuo Mo-jo, *Chia-ku Wên-tzŭ Yen-chiu, Peking*, 1952;
Nu-li chih Shih-tai, Peking, 1952.
P'ei Wên-chung, *Chung-kuo Shih-ch'i Shih-tai ti Wên-hua*, Peking, 1954.
Shih Chün *et al.*, *Chung-kuo Chin-tai Ssŭ-hsiang Shih*, Peking, 1955.
T'ang Ching-kao, *Mo-tzŭ*, Shanghai, 1930.
Tu Kuo-hsiang, *Hsien-Ch'in Chu Tzŭ Ssŭ-hsiang Kai-yao*, Peking, 1955.
Wei Yüan, *Lao-tzŭ Pen I*, Peking, 1955.

CHAPTER I

J. J. Andersson, *Children of the Yellow Earth*, London, 1934;
Archaeological Research in Kansu. Chinese Geological Survey, Series A, Peking, 1925.
A. Bulling, *The Meaning of China's Most Ancient Art*, Leiden, 1952.
E. Chavannes, *Le Tai Chan*, Paris, 1910.
Chêng Tê-k'un, *Archaeology in China*, 2 vols., Cambridge, 1959.
H. G. Creel, *The Birth of China*, London, 1936;
Studies in Early Chinese Culture, 1st. series, London, 1938.
M. Granet, *Chinese Civilisation*, Engl. tr., London, 1930.
C. Hentze, *Tod, Auferstehung, Weltordnung: Das Mystiche Bild in altesten China*, Zürich, 1955.
Li Chi, *The Beginnings of Chinese Civilisation*, Seattle, 1957.

B. Laufer, *Jade: A Study in Chinese Archaeology and Religion*, Pasadena, U.S.A., new ed., 1946.
D. H. Smith, 'Religion in the Shang Dynasty', *Numen*, vol. 8, fasc. 2, Leiden, 1961;
'Chinese Concepts of the Soul', *Numen*, vol. 5, fasc. 3, 1958.
Quaritch Wales, *The Mountains of God*, London, 1936.
W. Watson, *China before the Han Dynasty*, London, 1961.

CHAPTER 2

Chêng Tê-k'un, *Archaeology in China*, vol. 2, Cambridge, 1959.
H. H. Dubs, 'The Archaic Royal Jou Religion', *T'oung Pao*, vol. 46, Libr. 3–5, Leiden, 1959.
M. Granet, *Chinese Civilisation*, Engl. tr., London, 1930;
Fêtes et Chansons Anciennes de la Chine, Paris, 1926, Engl. tr., London, 1932;
La Féodalité Chinoise, Oslo, 1952;
La Pensée Chinoise, Paris, 1934;
La Religion des Chinois, Paris, 1951.
R. Grousset, *Histoire de la Chine*, Paris, 1942.
B. Karlgren, *The Book of Odes*, Stockholm, 1950.
K. S. Latourette, *The Chinese: their History and Culture*, London, 1934.
H. Maspero, *Mélanges Posthumes*, vol. 1. *Les Religions Chinoises*, Paris, 1950.
D. H. Smith, 'Religious Developments in Ancient China prior to Confucius', *Bulletin of John Ryland's Library*, vol. 44, no. 2, Manchester, 1962.
A. Waley, *The Book of Songs*, London, 1937.
W. Watson, *China before the Han Dynasty*, London, 1961.

CHAPTER 3

The following translations of the *Analects of Confucius* may be recommended:

J. Legge, *Chinese Classics*, vol. 1, 2nd ed., Oxford, 1893.
W. E. Soothill, *The Analects of Confucius* (Engl. tr. with Chinese text), Tokyo, 1910.
L. A. Lyall, *The Sayings of Confucius*, 3rd. ed., London, 1935.
A. Waley, *The Analects of Confucius*, London, 1938.
S. Couvreur, *Les Quatre Livres*, Hsien-hsien, 1930.
R. Wilhelm, *Kung Futze Gespräche*, Berlin, 1923.
H. O. H. Stange, *Gedanken und Gesprache des Kongfuzius*, Berlin, 1953.
Ch'ên Ta-chin, *K'ung Hsüeh Lun-chi*, Taiwan, 1957, pp. 1–33.

Chêng T'ien-hsi, *China Moulded by Confucius*, London, 1946.
H. G. Creel, *Confucius: The Man and the Myth*, London, 1951; *Chinese Thought from Confucius to Mao tsê-tung*, London, 1954.
C. Crow, *Master Kung*, London, 1937.
C. B. Day, *The Philosophers of China*, London, 1962.
Fung Yu-lan, *A Short History of Chinese Philosophy*, New York, 1948.
H. A. Giles, *Confucianism and its Rivals*, London, 1915.
E. R. Hughes, *Chinese Philosophy in Classical Times*, London, 1942.
E. R. and K. Hughes, *Religion in China*, London, 1948.
R. P. Kramers, *K'ung Tzŭ Chia Yü*. (tr.), Leiden, 1930.
J. Legge, *The Life and Teaching of Confucius*, London, 1875.
Lin Yutang, *The Wisdom of China and India*, New York, 1942.
Liu Wu-ch'i, *A Short History of Confucian Philosophy*, London, 1955.
K. L. Reichelt, *Religion in Chinese Garment*, London, 1951.
Shigeki Kaizuka, *Confucius*, London, 1956.
D. H. Smith, 'The Significance of Confucius for Religion', *History of Religions*, vol. 2, no. 2, Chicago, 1963.
W. E. Soothill, *The Three Religions of China*, 2nd. ed., Oxford, 1923.
A. Waley, *Three Ways of Thought in Ancient China*, London, 1939.

CHAPTER 4

W. T. Chan, 'Mencius', *Encyclopaedia Britannica*, vol. 15, 1960.
H. G. Creel, *Chinese Thought*, London, 1954.
C. B. Day, *The Philosophers of China*, London, 1962.
W. A. C. H. Dobson, *Mencius*, Oxford, 1963.
H. H. Dubs, *Hsün Tzŭ: The Moulder of Ancient Confucianism*, London, 1928; *The Works of Hsün Tzŭ* (tr.), London, 1928.
Fung Yu-lan, *History of Chinese Philosophy*, vol. 1, Peking, 1937, pp. 106–31, 279–311.
H. A. Giles, *Confucianism and its Rivals*, London, 1915.
E. R. Hughes, *Chinese Philosophy in Classical Times*, London, 1942; *The Great Learning and The Mean in Action*, London, 1942.
J. Legge, *The Life and Works of Mencius*, London, 1875.
Lin Yutang, *The Wisdom of China*, London, 1949.

CHAPTEB 5

W. T. Chan, *A Source Book in Chinese Philosophy*, London, 1963, pp. 211–31.

H. G. Creel, *Chinese Thought*, London, 1954.

A. Forke, *Mê Ti, des Socialethikers und seiner Schüler philosophische Werke*, Berlin, 1922.

Fung Yu-lan, *History of Chinese Philosophy*, vol. 1, Peking, 1937, pp. 76–105.

Hu Shih, *The Development of the Logical Method in Ancient China*, Shanghai, 1922.

Y. P. Mei, *The Ethical and Political Works of Mo-Tzŭ*, London, 1929;
Mo-Tzŭ: Rival of Confucius, London, 1929.

H. H. Rowley, *Prophecy and Religion in Ancient China and Israel*, London, 1956.

L. Tomkinson, 'The Social Teachings of Meh Tse', *Transactions of the Asiatic Society of Japan*, 2nd. series III., 1927.

H. R. Williamson, *Mo Ti: a Chinese Heretic*, London, 1942.

CHAPTER 6

The following translations of the *Tao Tê Ching* will be found useful:

R. B. Blakney, *The Way of Life: Lao tzŭ*, New York, 1955.

J. J. L. Duyvendak, *Tao To King: Lé Livre de la Voie et de la Vertu*, Paris, 1953, Engl. tr., London, 1954.

Ch'u Ta-kao, *Tao Tê Ching*, London, 1937.

J. Legge, *Sacred Books of the East*, vol. 39, London, 1891.

Lin Yutang, *The Wisdom of Lao Tzŭ*, New York, 1948.

A. Waley, *The Way and Its Power*, London, 1934.

C. Burton Day, *The Philosophers of China*, London, 1962.

W. T. Chan, *A Source Book in Chinese Philosophy*, London, 1963, pp. 136–210.

W. Eichhorn, 'Taoism', *Concise Encyclopaedia of Living Faiths*, ed. R. C. Zaehner, London, 1959, ch. 10.

Fung Yu-lan, *The Spirit of Chinese Philosophy*, Engl. tr. E. R. Hughes, London, 1947;
History of Chinese Philosophy, vol. 1, Peking, 1937, pp. 170–91, 221–45.

H. A. Giles, *Chuang Tzŭ: Taoist Philosopher and Chinese Mystic*, London, 1889; new ed., 1961.

A. C. Graham, *The Book of Lieh Tzŭ*, London, 1960.

E. Herbert, *A Taoist Notebook*, London, 1955.

Lin Yutang, *The Wisdom of China*, London, 1949.

A. Waley, *Three Ways of Thought in Ancient China*, London, 1939.

Holmes Welch, *The Parting of the Way*, Boston, 1957.

CHAPTER 7

For translations of the *Li Chi* see J. Legge, *Sacred Books of the East*, vols. 27–8, London, 1885; S. Couvreur. *Li Ki*, 2 vols., Paris, 1950. For the *Ch'u Tz'ŭ*, see D. Hawkes' translation, Oxford, 1959. For the *I Ching*, J. Legge's translation in *S.B.E.*, vol. 16, London, 1899. A new edition of this work, recently edited by Ch'u Chai and Winberg Chai, New York, 1964.

E. Biot, *Le Tcheou Li ou Rites de Tcheou*, 3 vols., Paris, 1851.
Lim Boon-keng, *The Li Sao*, Shanghai, 1929.
J. Steele, The *I Li*, 2 vols., London, 1917.
A. Waley, *The Nine Songs*, London, 1955;
Chinese Poems, London, 1949.
Hellmut Wilhelm, *Change: Eight Lectures on the I Ching*, London, 1960.
R. Wilhelm, *The I Ching*, 2 vols., Engl. tr., Cary F. Baynes, London, 1951.
Yang Hsien-i and Gladys Yang, *Li Sao, and other poems of Ch'u Yüan*, Peking, 1953.

CHAPTER 8

W. T. Chan, *A Source Book in Chinese Philosophy*, London, 1963, pp. 271–304.
C. B. Day, *The Philosophers of China*, London, 1962.
A. Forke, *Wang Ch'ung: Lun Hêng*, Engl. tr., 2 vols., London, 1907 and 1911.
O. Franke, *Studien zur Gechichte des Konfuzianischen Dogmas und der chinesischen Staatsreligion: des Problem des Tsch'un Ts'iu und Tung Tschung-schu's Fan Lu*, Hamburg, 1920.
Fung Yu-lan, *History of Chinese Philosophy*, vol. 2, London, 1953, pp. 7–167.
Liu Wu-chi, *A Short History of Chinese Philosophy*, London, 1955.
Tjan Tjoe-som, *Po Hu T'ung: the Comprehensive Discussions in the White Tiger Hall*, 2 vols., Leiden, 1949 and 1952.
Yao Shan-yu, 'The Cosmological and Anthropological Philosophy of Tung Chung Shu', *Journal of the Royal Asiatic Society* (North China Branch), vol. 73, Shanghai, 1948.

CHAPTER 9

W. Eichorn, 'Taoism', *Concise Encyclopaedia of Living Faiths*, ed. R. C. Zaehner, London, 1959, chapter 10.
C. P. Fitzgerald, *China*, rev. ed., London, 1950, chapter 12.

H. Maspero, *Mélanges Posthumes*, vol. 2, *Le Taoïsme*, Paris, 1950.
K. L. Reichelt, *Religion in Chinese Garment*, London, 1951.
W. E. Soothill, *The Three Religions of China*, Oxford, 1923.
L. Wieger, *Le Taoïsme*, Hsien-hsien, 1911;
History of Religious Beliefs and Philosophical Opinions in China, Engl. tr. E. C. Werner, Hsien-hsien, 1927.
R. Wilhelm, *A Short History of Chinese Civilisation*, London, 1929.
Holmes Welch, *The Parting of the Way*, Boston, 1957.

CHAPTER 10

K. S. Chên, *Buddhism in China: A Historical Survey*, Princeton, 1964.
W. T. Chan, 'Pure Land Schools', *Encyclopaedia of Religion*, ed. Ferm.
E. Conze, *Buddhism: its Essence and Development*, London, 1953.
P. Demieville, 'La Pénétration du Buddhisme dans la Tradition Philosophique Chinoise', *Cahiers d'Histoire mondiale*, iii, Paris, 1956.
J. Edkins, *Chinese Buddhism*, London, 1879.
E. J. Eitel, *Handbook of Chinese Buddhism*, London, 1870.
H. A. Giles, *The Travels of Fa Hsien*, London, 1923.
R. F. Johnston, *Buddhist China*, London, 1913.
C. Humphreys (ed.), *A Buddhist Student's Manual*, London, 1955.
Hu Shih, 'Ch'an (Zen) Buddhism in China: its History and Method', *Philosophy East and West*, no. 3, 1953.
H. Maspero, 'Le Songe et l'ambassade de l'empereur Ming: étude critique des sources', *Bulletin de l'école française d'Extrême-Orient*, 1910.
K. W. Morgan, *The Path of the Buddha*, New York, 1956.
K. L. Reichelt, *Truth and Tradition in Chinese Buddhism*, Shanghai, 1927; *Religion in Chinese Garment*, London, 1951.
T. Richard, *The Awakening of Faith*, new ed. by A. H. Walton, London, 1961.
D. H. Smith, 'Saviour Gods in Chinese Religion', *The Saviour God*, Manchester, 1963.
W. E. Soothill, *The Lotus of the Wonderful Law*, Oxford, 1930.
D. T. Suzuki, *The Awakening of Faith in the Mahāyāna*, London, 1900.
Alan Watts, *The Spirit of Zen*, London, 1936.
A. F. Wright, *Buddhism in Chinese History*, London, 1959.
E. Zürcher, *The Buddhist Conquest of China*, 2 vols., Leiden, 1959.

CHAPTER 11

J. Bredon, *Peking*, Shanghai, 1931.

J. Bredon and Mitrophanow, *The Moon Year*, Shanghai, 1927.
W. T. Chan, *Religious Trends in Modern China*, New York, 1953.
C. Cary-Elwes, *China and the Cross*, London, 1957.
J. Legge, *The Religions of China*, London, 1880.
K. L. Reichelt, *Religion in Chinese Garment*, London, 1951.
J. K. Shryock, *Origin and Development of the State Cult of Confucianism*, New York, 1932;
The Temples of Anking, Paris, 1931.
D. H. Smith, 'Divine Kingship in Ancient China', *Numen*, vol. 4, fasc. 3., 1957.
W. E. Soothill, *The Three Religions of China*, Oxford, 1923.
C. K. Yang, *Religion in Chinese Society*, California, 1961.

CHAPTER 12

C. Cary-Elwes, *China and the Cross*, London, 1957.
J. Finn, *The Jews in China*, London, 1843.
C. P. Fitzgerald, *China*, revised ed., London, 1950.
H. Havret, 'La stèle crétienne de Si-ngan-fou', *Variétés Sinologiques*, Nos. 7, 12, 20, Shanghai, 1895, 1897 and 1902.
L'Abbé Huc, *Christianity in China, Tartary and Thibet*, 3 vols., London, 1858.
K. S. Latourette, *Christianity in a Revolutionary Age*, vol. 5, London, 1963.
W. P. Martin, *Hanlin Papers*, Shanghai, 1880.
A. C. Moule, *Christians in China before the Year 1550*, London, 1930.
E. H. Parker, *China and Religion*, London, 1905.
P. Pelliot, 'Two New Manichaean Manuscripts from Tun-Huang', *Journal of the Royal Asiatic Society*, 1925.
P. Y. Saeki, *The Nestorian Monument in China*, London, 1916.
P. A. Varg, *Missionaries, Chinese and Diplomats*, Princeton, 1958.
H. Yule, *Cathay and the Way Thither*, new ed., by Cordier, 4 vols., London, 1913–16.

CHAPTER 13

C. B. Day, *Chinese Peasant Cults*, Shanghai, 1940.
W. T. Chan, *Religious Trends in Modern China*, New York, 1953.
J. G. Cormack, *Chinese birthdays, weddings and funerals*, Shanghai, 1923.
H. Doré, *Recherches sur les superstitions en Chine*, 15 vols., Shanghai, 1914–29.
A. J. A. Elliott, *Chinese Spirit Medium Cults in Singapore*, London, 1955.

W. Eichhorn, 'Taoism', *Concise Encyclopaedia of Living Faiths*, ed. R. C. Zaehner, London, 1959.

B. Favre, *Les Sociétés Secrètes en Chine*, Paris, 1933.

J. J. M. de Groot, *The Religious System of China*, 6 vols., Leiden, 1892.

L. Hodous, *Folkways in China*, London, 1929.

C. Humphreys (ed.), *A Buddhist Student's Manual*, London, 1956.

R. F. Johnston, *Confucianism in Modern China*, London, 1934.

M. Jung *et al.* (eds.), *Relations among Religions to-day*, Leiden, 1963.

H. Maspero 'The Mythology of Modern China', *Asiatic Mythology*, J. Hachin, London, 1933.

O. Brière, *Fifty Years of Chinese Philosophy: 1898–1950*, London, 1956.

A. H. Smith, *Village Life in China*, London, 1900.

Tun Li-chan, *Annual Customs and Festivals in Peking*, tr. D. Bodde, Peking, 1936.

GLOSSARY OF CHINESE TERMS USED IN THE TEXT

The names of Chinese persons, books and places are not included.

ch'an	dhyāna, to sit in contemplation, to meditate. Buddhist school
chao hun	calling back the soul
chên ju	thusness, Reality, Buddha
chên yen	true word, Buddhist school
ch'êng	sincerity
ch'êng huang	guardian god of city walls and moats
ch'i	breath, air, life principle
chia t'ang	household shrine
ching	classic, sacred book, sūtra
ch'ing	emotions, feelings
ch'ing miao	temple
ch'ing t'an	pure conversations
ching t'u	Pure Land
chih	wisdom
chün-tzu	princely or noble man
chung	loyalty
chên jen	perfected man, a spiritual man who has attained Tao
chu	to bless, hence, invoker, sacrificer
fa hsiang	Buddhist sect
hsiao	filial piety
hsiao t'i	the less essential parts of human nature
ho	harmony
hsien	immortal, spiritual being
hsin mao	28th day of sexagenary cycle
hsin wei	8th day of sexagenary cycle
hsüan hsüeh	mysterious or dark learning
hui hui	name for Muslims
hun	the spiritual part of man that ascends to Heaven
i	justice, righteousness
i	change, easy, name for Book of Changes
ju	learned scholar, Confucian
ju chiao	Confucianism

jên	love, goodness, kindness, benevolence
Ju Lai	name for Buddha
kuan	to observe, insight
Kuan Yin	name of the great bodhisattva
kuei	disembodied spirit,
kuei min	demon people (Taoist)
kuei tsu	demon soldiers (Taoist)
kung an	koan, a problem or exercise which cannot be intellectually solved
Lao-T'ien-Yeh	popular name for God
li	propriety, rite, ceremonial
li	principle
liang hsin	conscience
lun	discuss, reason, essay
lung	dragon
lung wang	dragon king
lü	law, rule, name for Buddhist School
Mi-lo-fo	name for Maitreya
mi tsung	name for Tantric Buddhism
miao	temple
ming	mandate, decree, destiny
O-mi-t'o-fo	Name for Amitābha
pa	tyrant
pên wu	original negation
p'o	the animal or inferior soul
pu	to divine, foretell
san lun	Three treatises (Buddhist) sch.
Shang Ti	Supreme Deity
shên	spirit, god, divine, soul
shê chi	altars of earth and grain
shên chu	spirit tablet
shêng jen	sage
shih	to divine by stalks
Shih-chia-mo-ni fo	The Buddha Sakyamuni
shou	to receive
Ssŭming	arbiter of destinies, Taoist god
shu	reciprocity
ta t'i	the essential part of human nature
T'ai I	The Grand Unity (Taoist deity)
T'ai P'ing	Great Peace
tao t'ieh	a fabulous monster, gluttonous ogre

tao	way, The Way, Eternal Principle
tao shih	Taoist master
tê	virtue, power
Ti	God, deified being, emperor
Ti Ts'ang	god of the underworld
T'ien	Heaven, name for supreme God
T'ien Chu	Heavenly Lord (R.C. name for God)
T'ien hou	Queen of Heaven (Taoist)
T'ien-shang Shêng-mu	Holy Heavenly Mother (Taoist)
T'ien shih	heavenly instructor
T'ien T'ang	temple, holy place in synagogue
T'ien T'ai	name for Buddhist school
T'ien Tzŭ	Son of Heaven, name given to emperor
tsa	miscellaneous, section of Chinese Tripitaka
tsu	ancestor
t'u ti	tutelary deity, earth god
wang	king
wên	literature, elegant, refined, culture
wei shih	consciousness only, name of Buddhist school
wu chia	shaman family
wu erh	shaman child
wu jên	shaman, magician, sorcerer
wu hsing	five elements, or movers
wu wei	non-activity, inaction
yang	light, bright, positive principle of Chinese dualism; see 'yin'
yin	dark, negative principle
yin chê	hermit, recluse
ying	barracks, designation of many Muslim villages
Yü-huang-shang-ti	Jade emperor

LIST OF QUOTATIONS FROM CHINESE CLASSICAL WORKS

From the *Shih Ching (Book of Poetry)*

From the *Shu Ching (Book of History)*

From the *Li Chi (Book of Rites)*

The Analects of Confucius

LIST OF QUOTATIONS

The Chung Yung (Doctrine of the Mean)

Mencius

Hsün-tzŭ

Mo-tzŭ

LIST OF QUOTATIONS

Tao Tê Ching

Chuang-tzŭ

Ch'un Ch'iu Fan Lu

INDEX